MW01130555

Learning the Bible with Martin Luther
The Workbook for Luther's Small Catechism

By,

Peter Kucenski

_____'s

(Your name here)

Guide to the Bible

INRI

© Peter Kucenski 2017. All rights reserved.
Illustrations by, Peter Kucenski and Larry Ruppert
Cover art illustrated by, Jay Montgomery

Edition	ISBN-13	ISBN-10
Color interior	978-0-9993567-0-8	0-9993567-0-4
Black and white interior	978-0-9993567-1-5	0-9993567-1-2
eBook	978-0-9993567-2-2	0-9993567-2-0

Scripture taken from the New King James Version.
Copyright © 1979, 1980, 1982 by Thomas Nelson, Inc.
Used by permission. All rights reserved

PREFACE

Those who have read or studied Luther's Small Catechism with Explanation know that without the explanation the catechism is very short and easily summarizes Christian doctrine. However, once it is unpacked in the explanation, it becomes a behemoth of various Christian doctrines jumping from one topic to the next. While this might flow eloquently through the book, it can become very difficult to focus on individual topics. It can also make it difficult to follow the breadcrumbs back to individual topics at a later date (if you do not study the catechism often).

My father once told me that his catechism was his guide to the Bible. It is with that core idea and foundation that I wrote this workbook. *Learning the Bible with Martin Luther* is your guide that clearly and concisely outlines the base Christian doctrines as written in the Bible and explained through Luther's Small Catechism. That is why it is organized very differently than most workbooks and even the order of Luther's Small Catechism with Explanation. By using this workbook, you will be able to quickly find information on the variety of Christian doctrines taught in the catechism. Plus, each lesson is complete with memorization, questions that build on each other, additional Bible passages, and finally resources that will help you understand the topic at hand and remember it later.

This is a workbook for adults and for youth for independent study or in a confirmation class setting. For confirmation class, this book can be used in a classroom setting, independently, or a combination thereof. It can be completed by people with little or no understanding of the Bible or by people looking for a deeper understanding. *Learning the Bible with Martin Luther* begins with "Does God Exist?" This first question is indeed the most important "why" of why we should study the Bible and also the catechism. After all, there simply is no reason to study either if God does not exist unless we just want to understand Christians. After that, we need to know "what is the catechism?" And "why this catechism?" Indeed, there are many catechisms and many explanations of the Bible. This section demonstrates who wrote this catechism and why. After that, we look at understanding the Bible and how to read and interpret it. That lays the foundation for how we are going to study the Bible and glean the truths from it. These three sections lay the foundation for the why and how we are going to study the Bible and Christian doctrine. After that, it flows topically through the catechism identifying who God is, what He has done, the gifts He has given, and finally how we should live in the position and in the occupations we have.

With that in mind, the memorization is not just for those going through confirmation class. The memorization added into the workbook at the beginning of most lessons is an important aspect. Each was picked to highlight the key points of that particular lesson or summarize it. If you are doing this on your own outside of confirmation class, I would still highly recommend you learn the memorization.

It is my prayer that this workbook would be utilized by you not just once, but many times to refresh and maintain your understanding of basic Christian doctrine, so that through this you can defend yourself against false doctrine and hold fast to the truth.

– Peter Kucenski

TABLE OF CONTENTS

WORKBOOK INSTRUCTIONS

Materials:

Required Resources:

1. A Bible
2. Luther's Small Catechism with Explanation, 2005 NIV edition published by Concordia Publishing House (ISBN 978–0–7586–1121–5) (Note: CPH's 1991 edition as well as their 2008 ESV edition of the Small Catechism will also work, but the page numbers for questions and answers may vary.)

Optional Resources:

1. The movie "Luther" (2003) by director Eric Till. It is used to give a person a visual understanding of Luther and his life and help you complete Lesson 10.
2. The internet – There are several websites and resources referenced in the workbook. Also, free online lectures are available for each lesson at www.LearningTheBibleWithMartinLuther.com.

Answering the questions:

Every answer is found in the Bible, Luther's Small Catechism or this workbook. Therefore, read each Lesson/ Section introduction and the listed questions/answers in their entirety. Depending on your learning style it may be easier to read the questions in the workbook first. Doing that may help you get an idea of what you are learning before you begin to read the learning material. (Note: the official answers to each question are available in the Facilitator's Edition. The Facilitator's Edition also includes exams for either individual or classroom use.) In addition, a glossary containing many Christian and Lutheran specific terms is included. It also includes more difficult vocabulary words and information on important people. Words that look like *this* are defined there.

Memorization:

Always start the memorization early before it is due. It is easier to memorize something, and it will have more value to you if you understand what it is you are memorizing. That is why they are summaries and highlights from the lessons. If you understand the lesson, then you should understand the memorization.

Workbook flow:

The first four sections should be done first and in order. The reasons are that they lay the foundation for: 1) why a person should study the Bible and the Catechism, 2) what the Catechism is and who Luther is, 3) how the Bible is laid out and understood, and 4) who God is and what He has done. After that, the workbook is designed so each section, up and until Section 10, can be independently completed from the others. Therefore, it is not necessary to complete them one after another. Section 10 summarizes all of the ideas learned in the prior nine sections. So to complete it, you will most likely have to have completed the prior sections. Section 11 also refers to some of the prior sections, and it gives the final understanding on how to live as a Christian. Section 12 goes beyond the basic teachings of the Catechism. To effectively understand it, a person must understand all of the other sections. Section 12 should not necessarily be a requirement for confirmation class, but adults will find it helpful.

Even though it is permissible and possible to change the order of this workbook, I do not recommend it unless you are doing a refresher. I have designed it to flow in a logical manner, and I selected each section to be put in its particular order to build each level carefully. Each subsequent section builds on the previous one and prepares you to learn the next. In that way, careful consideration was done to ensure a progressive understanding from "I know nothing of the Bible, the Catechism or why I should be a Christian" to "I understand and believe the basic Christian doctrine of the Bible."

SECTION 1 – DOES GOD EXIST?

LESSON 1: DO YOU BELIEVE GOD EXISTS?

Before doctrine even matters, we must determine if God, or even a god, exists. The vast majority of people who go through this study will already accept or otherwise believe in the existence of, or the possibility of, God. However, some may not. So, this is the first question you must answer now:

1. Does God exist? (____) yes, (____) no, (____) maybe

The next question is equally important:

2. Why do YOU believe your answer (what are YOUR reasons for YOUR Yes / No / Maybe)?_____
    _____
    _____
    _____
    _____

These questions are so important because if God does not exist then everything is decided based on human will and human desire. Furthermore, everything that we do will ultimately have no lasting consequences for us because we can "opt out" through death. So then, our biggest concern becomes avoiding the penalties for what we do on this earth and gaining power, prestige or money. It also means that this workbook will only become an exercise in understanding Lutheran doctrine. However, if God does exist, then this is an exercise in understanding Who He is and What He expects. Also, what happens when we die? How should we live? What is my purpose?

To begin looking into this, there are really two places (outside of the Bible) that we can learn that there is a God. The first is inside of us and the second is outside in the natural world. We will begin by first looking inside of ourselves.

LESSON 2: GOD MAKING HIS PRESENCE KNOWN FROM INSIDE OF US

> **Memorization:** Romans 2:14–15 –
> *For when Gentiles, who do not have the law, by nature do the things in the law, these, although not having the law, are a law to themselves, who show the work of the law written in their hearts, their conscience also bearing witness, and between themselves their thoughts accusing or else excusing them.*

Catechism Material: Question 92 (pp. 104–105) –

1. Name five things that you KNOW are wrong to do (e.g., steal):
    a. _____
    b. _____
    c. _____
    d. _____
    e. _____
2. What is the name of the thing inside of us that tells us right from wrong?_____

3. Without telling them your answers, ask two or more people to name five things that they KNOW are wrong to do:

Person 1 _____   Person 2 _____

1) _____   1) _____

2) _____   2) _____

3) _____   3) _____

4) _____   4) _____

5) _____   5) _____

How do their answers and your answers compare? Are they similar to or the same responses that you gave?

_____

_____

4. List the other people's responses in regard to agreeing or disagreeing with KNOWING that those things are wrong to do.

Agree with   Disagree with

_____   _____

_____   _____

_____   _____

_____   _____

_____   _____

5. Do the answers given for questions 3, 4 and 5 surprise you? Why or why not? _____

_____

_____

_____

The conscience is one of the things that show that there is a God because of how universal the human beings' feelings are towards identifying the things people KNOW are wrong. While there are many different viewpoints on political ideology or religious ideology, there is very little difference in, for example, KNOWING that stealing is wrong. There is little difference in KNOWING that murder is wrong and on down the line. That concept is shown on a grand scale when you compare laws across different countries. To say that the laws are ALL the same would be misleading and a lie. Also, the definition of say "murder" can also vary between nations because of what a lawful killing is. It can even vary between people in the same nation.

So, if God gave us a conscience, why then is there any differences in laws at all? The Bible says:

Titus 1:15 – To the pure all things are pure, but to those who are defiled and unbelieving nothing is pure; but even their mind and conscience are defiled.

1 Timothy 4:1–2 – Now the Spirit expressly says that in latter times some will depart from the faith, giving heed to deceiving spirits and doctrines of demons, speaking lies in hypocrisy, having their own conscience seared with a hot iron.

In Titus, it states that when a person is unbelieving both their mind and their conscience are "defiled" and no longer "pure." Think of a glass of water. If you put a bit of sand in the water, it will eventually settle at the bottom. It will not look very good, but if you started with drinkable water, it would still be drinkable, just not completely good. Or instead, put salt in the water. A little is just fine, but too much and it becomes salt water like the ocean. It may look clear and fine, but it is actually poisonous for you. Both are very different things, and just like they are different, as human beings we are all polluted in different ways (sand or salt). Therefore, our consciences are polluted in different ways, but the base (the water) is the same. So, our consciences are similar with some differences.

The other passage is from Timothy, and it talks about a conscience "seared with a hot iron." If you have ever burned something on your body, it hurts, a lot. But then the skin boils over and a callous forms, scarring occurs, and if it is really bad, the nerves are damaged. That deadens the feeling that you have in that spot for a time or permanently. The point here is that if we or anyone repeatedly does something that they know is wrong, they will develop a scar or a callous that will prevent them from feeling bad about it. That feeling of KNOWING something is wrong gets less and less until it is either completely gone or buried under so much rubble that it does not bother them anymore.

6. Give an example of something a person could believe or a type of person whose conscience is polluted (for example someone who believes it is good and right to oppress others):_____

_____

Give an example of how you could "sear" your conscience: _____

_____

_____

LESSON 3: GOD MAKING HIMSELF KNOWN FROM OUTSIDE OF US

> **Memorization:** Romans 1:20 –
> *For since the creation of the world His invisible attributes are clearly seen, being understood by the things that are made, even His eternal power and Godhead, so that they are without excuse.*

God created a big beautiful world in the middle of nothing. Furthermore, that nothing that surrounds the Earth is so big and dotted with stars, planets, black holes, and the whole host of the cosmos, that the Earth is infinitesimally small in comparison. It is this earth and that universe that so many psalmists, poets, writers, artists, scientists, astrologers, and many more have attempted to capture and understand for thousands of years. It is a testimony that is so big and so plain that generation after generation, culture after culture have written about one god or another derived from the nature and the world around them. From the Native Americans to the Incans, to the Chinese, the Arabs, the Africans, and many, many more, they have all come up with a god or deity to worship (many times many more than one). It is a testimony that still persists today despite the onslaught of evolution and aliens, so that some of those who believe in evolution also believe in the spirits or being spiritual. It is so big that religions and cults are still being created today based off of their idea of God.

Catechism Material: Question 92 (pp. 104–105)

1. Name a culture, people, or religion that believes in god(s) besides Christianity._____
   Can you name more than one?_____

2. Name a god that you know of from that or another culture or belief. _____
   Can you name more than one? _____

3. Are all the gods that have been believed in the same? (____) Yes   (____) No

4. Do all the gods that have been believed in have the same characteristics?_____
   _____

5. Give a reason why something in this world points you or another to believe in a god. _____
   _____

6. What characteristics would you give to God by looking at the world?_____
   _____

SUBSECTION: EVOLUTION

1. Does the theory of evolution prove that God does not exist? (____) Yes   (____) No
   Why or why not? _____
   _____
   _____
   _____

Lesson 4: The "Father" of Evolution

> **Memorization:** Hebrews 3:4 –
> *For every house is built by someone, but He who built all things is God.*

This lesson is intended to go through some of the current techniques and evidence presented by those scientists and believers in evolution. It is not intended to be exhaustive, and I encourage you to really think and look into other techniques and evidence presented by evolutionists for yourself.

The *theory of evolution* is attributed to **Charles Darwin** (1809–1882), and he is considered to be the "Father" of evolution. He published his theory of evolution in the book called *The Origin of Species* (1859). It is in this book that Darwin presents his ideas on evolution and what he describes as "natural selection." *Natural selection*, as he describes it, is as organisms (plants, animals, etc.) multiply and grow, they compete with various others over habitat and food (i.e., limited resources). As they do this, certain of these organisms obtain various traits through reproduction. Those traits that help the organism survive (because they give the organism an edge over the others) would survive as the others died off due to their inability to obtain habitat or food or to reproduce. Thus, over time, nature would naturally select the most qualified animals to survive, and the least qualified would die out. That would then lead to evolution or the changing of organisms over time due to small changes over a very long time.

This theory of "Natural Selection," and thus evolution, is derived from his voyage on the HMS Beagle which started in 1831. He started out this trip as a naturalist with the job of documenting the various fauna and animal life as he visited many parts of the world. One of the most well-known and significant places he observed was the Galapagos Islands which are near South America. It was there that he observed finches that appeared to be of the same species but had varying sizes and differently formed beaks. He noted that each of those beaks enabled their respective birds to gather food differently and in a specialized way.

After taking this trip, he spent many years considering his findings. Then a man named Alfred Wallace presented Darwin with his work on the subject and asked Darwin to write a forward for him. Darwin, seeing the similarity in work, then rushed to put together his findings first. Thus, *The Origin of Species* was written and published in 1859.

1. Who is the "Father" of evolution?_____
2. What is the definition of evolution? _____
    _____
3. What is the definition of natural selection? _____
    _____
    _____
4. What is the name of the book that the "Father" of evolution wrote?_____
5. How did the "Father" of evolution get his ideas? _____
    _____

Lesson 5: Complex Systems

Evolution and specifically the success of Natural Selection depend upon traits (i.e., any part of an organism, e.g., eye, hand, foot, blood, etc.) being beneficial (i.e., increases its ability to reproduce, obtain habitat, or obtain food). If a new trait that is formed in an organism is not immediately beneficial in that organism's lifetime, then the trait will not take dominance in nature and thus not survive. In other words, if the new trait does not increase surviv-ability in the organism, then it is not natural for it to be selected. Thus, complex traits that require more than one step in change do not fit within the confines of Natural Selection. Charles Darwin wrote this:

> *Organs of extreme perfection and complication.* To suppose that the eye, with all its inimitable contrivances for adjusting the focus to different distances, for admitting different amounts of light, and for the correction of spherical and chromatic aberration, could have been formed by natural selection, seems, I freely confess, absurd in the highest possible degree. Yet reason tells me, that if numerous gradations from a perfect and complex eye to one very imperfect and simple, each grade being useful to its possessor, can be shown to

exist; if further, the eye does vary ever so slightly, and the variations be inherited, which is certainly the case; and if any variation or modification in the organ be ever useful to an animal under changing conditions of life, then the difficulty of believing that a perfect and complex eye could be formed by natural selection, though insuperable by our imagination, can hardly be considered real. (Origin of Species, Chapter 6)

It is in this paragraph and others that Darwin admits that complex organs (which can be applied to any part of the body or structure of the organism) cannot have evolved through natural selection as one part. That is, an eye as we now know it would be impossible to be generated by an organism through one change. Furthermore, every organ or trait must be beneficial through each succession of change for it to be selected through natural selection. <u>Therefore, if an organ or trait cannot be useful in one step, then Natural Selection, indeed evolution, falls apart.</u>

It is not hard to believe that natural selection would select the eye if we look at the whole eye. However, natural selection has to select each part of the eye one at a time, so what are the parts of the eye?

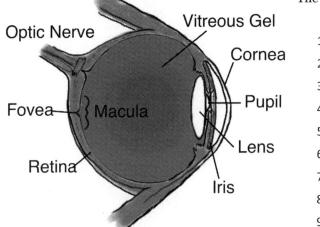

The eye in that diagram[1] is not too complicated; there are 9 parts:

1. _____
2. _____
3. _____
4. _____
5. _____
6. _____
7. _____
8. _____
9. _____

However, even this is simplified as those parts have parts including the iris with its muscles to increase and decrease the size of the pupil or that "the mammalian retina consists of neurons of >60 distinct types, each playing a specific role in processing visual images."[2] But do not forget the blood vessels in the eye which carry the red blood cells, white blood cells and the liquid that carries them. The eye, which may start out as nine simplified parts, gets massively more complicated as each part is investigated. Indeed, this can be applied to the many different organs, parts and even cells that are inside of anybody. The complexity of the eye was barely understood by Charles Darwin when he authored his book. Moreover, its complexity is barely covered here, and I have mentioned more than 70 elements. Therefore, due to the sheer number of elements and complexity, it would be impractical to explain why the eye is too complex to evolve through natural selection in this workbook. Instead, a simpler structure is in order.

One of the simplest organisms in the world is bacteria. Bacteria is also made up of several different parts. Some bacteria have a part called a flagellum. A *flagellum* is the tail used by the bacteria to allow it to move through its environment. On the next page is a picture of a bacterium.[3] The flagellum is the tail, and the zoomed-in portion shows the components that make the tail move.

1   Diagram based on image taken from the National Eye Institute – Diagram of the Eye https://nei.nih.gov/health/eyediagram
2   Richard Masland The Neuronal Organization of the Retina, 2012 http://www.cell.com/neuron/fulltext/S0896–6273(12)00883–5
3   Image based on information/pictures taken from the "Structure and Function of Bacterial Cells" – http://textbookofbacteriology.net/structure_2.html

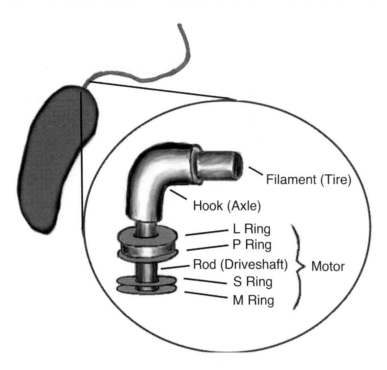

Filament (Tire)

Hook (Axle)

L Ring
P Ring
Rod (Driveshaft) } Motor
S Ring
M Ring

The components of the tail are what are known as having *"irreducible complexity."* That means that if one part is taken out of the organ or machine, it cannot work. An appropriate (albeit simplified) comparison to help illustrate the functions and the parts of the flagellum is a car. The filament (or tail) is like the tire on a car. The rod with all the rings is the motor, and the hook is the driveshaft that connects the motor with the tire. Without any one of those parts the flagellum would not be able to move, just like without any one of those parts a car would not be able to move. This particular example illustrates that multiple parts would have to evolve at the same time for it to function. It is contrary to multiple small changes because if a change has no benefit, it will not make it "natural" to select those changes over others. In the cases of the flagellum and the eye, changes in their structures with no benefit would have to be selected, which is contrary to the concept of natural selection.

For further studies in "irreducible complexity" refer to *Refuting Evolution 2* by Jonathan Sarfati, Ph.D. and Michael Matthew (available online at www.creation.com or http://creation.com/refuting-evolution-2–chapter-10–argument-irreducible-complexity).

1. The eye is made up of how many "big" parts? _____
2. Can those parts be broken down into even smaller parts? (___) Yes   (___) No
3. What is a flagellum? _____

    _____

4. How many parts are there to a flagellum? _____
5. What is the definition of "irreducible complexity"? _____

    _____

6. How does "irreducible complexity" argue against "natural selection"? _____

    _____

    _____

    _____

Lesson 6: The Fossil Record

Evolutionists very highly regard the "human fossil record" as being proof of
the gradual change of humans. It is the set of fossils uncovered that they use to
demonstrate the gradual changes human beings have gone through to become
what they are (i.e., the fossils showing apes becoming human beings). Evolutionists view the many finds of fossils detailing that evolution as pure evidence against
creationism. However, what exactly has been found? One of the prime examples
and most heavily advertised at one time was "Lucy." Lucy is proclaimed to be 3.2
million years old and as having "relative completeness" according to the Smithsonian.[4] What does relative completeness mean? It means out of 207 bones they
found 47 and of those they are mostly fragments. In fact, the vast majority of the
fossils in the fossil records are much less complete, consisting of a bone, a part of
a bone, or parts of a skull. To see the fossil records at the Smithsonian, go here:
http://humanorigins.si.edu/evidence/human-fossils/fossils.

Recreation of Lucy's bones – picture
taken at the Creation Museum
Kentucky

The fossils are also dated using some type of radiometric dating (an example
would be carbon dating). That then puts the fossil in a particular time (radiometric dating will be discussed in the next lesson). By putting the fossil at a
particular time, this allows the scientists to put the fossil in a particular part of
the evolutionary tree. They also look at the bones in order to make an "interpretation" of them and decide what they would look like as a whole organism.
They decide how much muscle tissue, fat, skin color and texture, hair color and
the amount of hair, and in some instances the height and size of appendages
are included. That process is by no means an exact science, and the results
are subject to bias, personal interpretation, and professional training. The
technique for skulls is called Forensic Facial Reconstruction. To learn more, go
to: http://anthropology.si.edu/writteninbone/facial_reconstruction.html

1. What is the "human fossil record"?_____

    _____

2. How many bones did they find of "Lucy" and how many would a complete skeleton have? _____

    _____

3. Evolution currently states that the world has been around for roughly 4.5 billion years (that number has

    increased a lot over the years); does the condition of the "human fossil record" and the number of fossil

    records surprise you? Why or why not?_____

    _____

    _____

    _____

4   Smithsonian National Museum of Natural History – Human Evolution Evidence http://humanorigins.si.edu/evidence/human-fos-
sils/fossils/al-288-1

4. The oldest dinosaur fossil is dated to be 240 million years old;[5] does it surprise you that at the time of this writing they have found many more fossils from dinosaurs (more than 1,900 records) than those that form the human fossil record (102 records)? Why or why not? (If you remember Lucy, the oldest fossil found in the human fossil record is 3.2 million years old.) _____

_____

_____

5. Is everyone's face in this world the same? _____

6. Do some people have deformed faces or skulls? _____

7. Have you seen anyone whose head or face has features of an animal (e.g., monkey, rat, etc.)? _____ If so, what animal did they have features of and what were those features? _____

_____

Do those features make them any less human or intelligent, or mean that they lived long ago? _____

_____

Lesson 7: Understanding Radiometric Dating

Radiometric dating according to dictionary.com is "any method of determining the age of earth materials or objects of organic origin based on measurement of either short-lived radioactive elements or the amount of a long-lived radioactive element plus its decay product." To understand this, think of an apple or some other fruit that has started to rot. Some parts of the apple will still be red, but other parts will be black or discolored. Certain atoms, like carbon (specifically carbon 14), will naturally rot. When they do, they transform into a slightly different type of atom (carbon 14 becomes carbon 12). This rate of decay is constant in a laboratory. So, based on either the amount of rot or comparing the rot to the good part, they determine the age of something. The amount of time it takes for half of the set of atoms to decay is called a "half-life." They utilize different types of atoms to date things because some atoms have a longer decay time than others, so they can theoretically track the age of something to be older using different atoms than carbon, such as potassium.

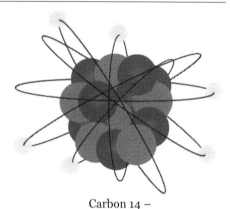

Carbon 14 –
6 Protons, 8 Neutrons and 6 Electrons

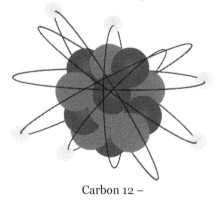

Carbon 12 –
6 Protons, 6 Neutrons and 6 Electrons

There are several assumptions that are required for the test to work. The first assumption is that the predetermined ratios of atoms in a living organism are accurate (they base the ratios they use on information about ratios observed in nature today). The second assumption is that the sample has not been contaminated with outside atoms. (Atoms are the base element, and as such all carbon 14 atoms look the same as any other carbon 14 element; therefore, if some got mixed in, it would be indistinguishable from the original organism's atoms.) The third assumption is that the atoms that are present are all of the atoms that were originally there. (No atoms were stripped away over the course of time.)

5   Oldest Dinosaur Found? By Ker Than, National Geographic News http://news.nationalgeographic.com/news/2012/12/121205-oldest-dinosaur-found-tanzania-science-archaeology/

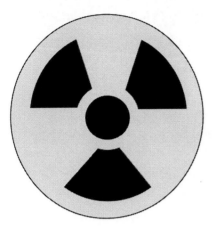

So, in simple terms, all the test requires is that the prediction about the number of atoms to be there is correct and that no atoms were added or subtracted from the mix. In theory, radiometric dating is completely possible, but in actuality and all practicality, it is impossible for several reasons. First, the theory relies upon a constant environment. It is known that the environment has not been constant for two reasons. The first is because this idea is in direct conflict with what they have established as an "ice age" and when meteors struck the earth. Those things changed the atmosphere and the temperature of the earth, thus changing these constants, and this has happened more than once. So, it is impossible to predict what the initial ratio should be due to those events. The second reason why we know the environment has not been constant is because of the events in 1940. We know outside forces can manipulate the ratios in a living organism because after 1940, nuclear bombs and nuclear testing changed the ratio in unpredictable ways[6]. In fact, the only reason we can test things that existed before 1940 is because of the data obtained before 1940.

The second problem that makes radiometric dating only work in theory is because the sample must not have been contaminated. If the sample has been contaminated (by the addition or subtraction of atoms), it will change the dating results. Those results do fluctuate greatly if the atoms are contaminated. Imagine that your phone screen is the fossil sample. (Really, any object works for this example.) How long during normal use can you go before the screen or object is scratched? How long can you go without the screen or object breaking? Some people can go a year or more, others, a few months, especially if it is not protected. Now imagine that you put your phone or object outside unprotected for a year; how well will it do? How about ten years? 100? 1000? How about 3.2 million years? Now keep in mind that if your phone gets scratched, it will break off atoms, and that will change your result. Maybe it will make it older, or maybe it will make it younger.

For more on radiometric dating and how 300-year-old trees became older than 450,000 years, refer to "Is Carbon Dating Accurate" by Professor Walter J. Veith, Ph.D., here: http://amazing-discoveries.org/C-deception-carbon_dating_radiometric_decay_rates

1. What is the definition of radiometric dating (in your own terms)?_____

    _____

    _____

2. What is an example name of a radiometric dating test? _____

3. List the three assumptions that radiometric dating relies on:

    a. _____

    b. _____

    c. _____

4. Why do those assumptions fail in real life?_____

    _____

    _____

    _____

6   According to How Stuff Works Science – "Anything that dies after the 1940s, when nuclear bombs, nuclear reactors and open air nuclear tests started changing things, will be harder to date precisely." – How Carbon-14 Dating Works http://science.howstuffworks.com/environmental/earth/geology/carbon-142.htm

LESSON 8: GOD TELLING US WHO HE IS AND THAT HE EXISTS FROM HIS WORDS AND HIS WITNESSES

> **Memorization:** John 20:30–31 –
> *And truly Jesus did many other signs in the presence of His disciples, which are not written in this book; but these are written that you may believe that Jesus is the Christ, the Son of God, and that believing you may have life in His name.*

Even though nature and our consciences point to there being a god, it does not tell us who that god is, what He is like and for some, it does not convince them that He even exists. For example, there are many gods, such as the Greek gods and goddesses or the god of Muhammad, Allah. The Greek gods and Allah are very different and the people who believe in them understand God very differently. Others refuse the existence of God through the belief in the Theory of Evolution. So, God did two things; first, He showed that He does exist, and second who He is through the use of many witnesses. Those witnesses would go on to write His words and what they saw Him do in a book called the Bible.

The Bible is not merely a collection of fables and stories, but accurate accounts of eye witnesses of real historical events. These events tell us that God exists and what He did to and for the nation of Israel and ultimately for everyone. The Bible begins with the story God told through Moses of how He created the earth. Then it goes in and talks about the people He established and His nation of Israel. Finally, it concludes with Jesus Christ and His Apostles. This book does not simply tell stories, but actual events that occurred to and around real people (e.g., the Apostle Paul, whose tomb is in Rome and Pontius Pilate whose existence is verified through archaeology) and places (like the cities of Jericho and Bethlehem; you can still visit Bethlehem today).

2 Peter 1:16 – For we did not follow cunningly devised fables when we made known to you the power and coming of our Lord Jesus Christ, but were eyewitnesses of His majesty.

Catechism Material: Questions 2 (p. 48) and 92 (pp. 104–105)

1. What is the name of the book that God revealed Himself in?_____
2. Does this book contain made-up stories or real events?_____
3. Where do we turn to know who God is?_____

SECTION 1: REVIEW

1. What are the three ways God makes himself known to us?
    a. _____
    b. _____
    c. _____
2. Our conscience is ALWAYS in alignment with God and His ways: True / False Why?_____
    _____
    _____
    _____
3. Who is the "Father" of Evolution?_____
4. What book did the "Father" of Evolution write?_____

5. What does the term "Natural Selection" mean? _____
_____

6. The eye is (select one):
    a. ____ A simple structure
    b. ____ A complex structure
    c. ____ Evolved through natural selection
    d. ____ Was completely understood by the "Father" of evolution

7. The flagellum is (select one):
    a. ____ An arm
    b. ____ A head
    c. ____ A leg
    d. ____ A tail

8. What is "irreducible complexity"? _____
_____

9. Why is the flagellum an example of "irreducible complexity"? _____
_____

10. True / False – The "Human Fossil Record" is a collection of many complete skeletons clearly showing the progression of human beings from apes to human beings as we now know them.

11. True / False – Every record in the "Human Fossil Record" contains a complete skeleton.

12. True / False – Radiometric dating proves that the Earth is roughly 4.5 billion years old. Why?
_____
_____
_____

13. Of the three ways God makes Himself known to us, which way tells us Who God is and What He has done?
_____

14. The Bible is just a collection of made up stories True / False Why?_____
_____
_____

15. What is the name of a real place you can go to that is talked about in the Bible?_____
_____

16. Read Hebrews 11:1–3. After reading that, should we be surprised when people believe in evolution? Why or why not? _____
_____
_____

Section 2 – The Catechism and Luther

After establishing the existence of a god (or at least the possibility of one), the next step is to look into how to find out who this God is. So, the next two sections are dedicated to the resources that will be used to discover God, including what exactly they are, how to use them and who wrote them. First will be Luther's Small Catechism because it is what this workbook uses as a guide to the Bible.

Lesson 9: The Catechism and Confirmation

> **Memorization:** from Luther's preface to the Small Catechism –
> *Although we cannot and should not force anyone to believe, we should insist and encourage the people. That way they will know what is right and wrong for those among whom they dwell and wish to make their living. For whoever desires to live in a town must know and observe the town laws, because he wishes to enjoy the protection offered by the laws whether he is a believer or at heart and in private a rascal or rogue.*

Luther's Small Catechism was developed because Martin Luther (11/10/1483–2/18/1546) wanted the people within the Christian churches to understand what they believed and why they believed it. It has six parts, and the doctrine is taken from the Bible alone. To begin, we will first look at what the Catechism is, so you know what you are getting into:

Catechism Material: Questions 9–12 (pp. 52–53), 306 (p. 245), and Table of Contents (pp. 7–8)

1. What is a *catechism*? _____

    _____

2. Who wrote the Small Catechism? _____

3. What year did he write it? _____

4. What does the Small Catechism do?
    a. ____ Answer Christian questions
    b. ____ Tell us about the Bible
    c. ____ Sum up the Christian doctrine

5. What are the six chief parts of the Catechism?
    a. _____
    b. _____
    c. _____
    d. _____
    e. _____
    f. _____

6. Why are the six chief parts taken solely from the Bible?_____

    _____

7. Provide the page numbers for each of the following sections:

Name of the Part	Section WITHOUT explanation	Section WITH explanation
The Ten Commandments		
The Creed		
The Lord's Prayer		
Holy Baptism		
Confession		
The Sacrament of the Altar		

Name of the Part	Page Numbers
Table of Duties	
Christian Questions with their Answers	
Luther's Preface	

8. What is Confirmation?
    a. ____ A public rite of the church
    b. ____ A ceremony
    c. ____ Mandatory instruction to be saved

9. Confirmation provides an opportunity for a person to:
    a. ____ Publicly confess their faith
    b. ____ Give a lifelong pledge to Christ
    c. ____ Show that they have been instructed in the Christian faith
    d. ____ Confirm their understanding of the Lord's Supper
    e. ____ All of the above

LESSON 10: WHO IS LUTHER?

> **Memorization:** Martin Luther –
> *"Unless I am convinced by Scripture and plain reason—I do not accept the authority of the popes and councils, for they have contradicted each other—my conscience is captive to the Word of God."*

Martin Luther lived from 1483–1546 and was born in Eisleben, Germany. Eisleben is a small town northwest of Leipzig and southwest of Berlin. His father was a copper miner and worked hard to send him to the University of Erfurt, which was one of the best universities in Germany at the time. It was there that he studied and obtained a Master's degree. It was his father's original and seemingly Martin Luther's original intention to become a lawyer. However, in July 1505 he was caught in a storm. It was due to this storm (and a lightning strike near Luther) that Luther vowed to become a monk/friar if God would save his life. Luther did survive, and so he became a friar much to the chagrin of his father.

What is the difference between a monk and a friar? A monk is a position in the Catholic Church that focuses on God and piety. They are inwardly focused. Martin Luther did not become a monk; he became a friar.[7] There are many similarities between a monk and a friar which do cause confusion. However, friars, while they do pursue God, learning about Him, and striving for piety, also focus on service to the poor and communities around them. A simple contrast is that a friar lives with and works in a community whereas a monk lives outside of the community.

After becoming an Aan friar, Luther was ordained in 1507 and became a professor at the University in Wittenberg. Then in 1510, he was sent to Rome. His visit to Rome was another significant turning point in his life. It was there that he witnessed the corrupt practices of the Roman Catholic Church. The most anger, for him, came regarding the sale of indulgences. It was through these sales that the Catholic Church promised to forgive the sins of the buyer or the person of their choosing (dead or alive). By purchasing said indulgences, the person was able to reduce the amount of time they spent in purgatory. The Catholic Church argued that the "good works" of the saints were more than enough to get them straight into heaven, and therefore their righteousness could be bought from the church.

Martin Luther Exhibit at the Creation Museum in Kentucky

Two years later in 1512 Luther became a Doctor of Theology at Wittenberg, and five years later on October 31, 1517, he posted his *95 Theses* on the door of the church in Wittenberg[8]. The 95 Theses were not intended to fracture the church or to separate Luther from it; rather they were intended as points of discussion. Luther intended upon reforming the church from the heresies that he observed. Based on the Bible, he made the determination of what those heresies were. He demonstrated them as heresies through the use of the Bible and church fathers (the people whom the church looked on as reliable and accurate teachers of the truth). He further published his ideas and teachings through several pamphlets including "On Christian Liberty," "To the Christian Nobility" and others. Luther was able to reach a large population because of the recent invention of the Guttenberg Printing Press. Through this device, his works were able to be reliably and cheaply produced in mass. Moreover, because Luther wrote in the German language, it allowed his message to reach the people of Germany.

It was because of Luther's writings and his opposition to the sale of indulgences that in 1518 Cardinal Cajetan summoned him to Augsburg. It was the intention of the Cardinal to force Luther to recant (take back everything he said against the church and admit his error). However, Luther refused and then fled when he heard that he was to be arrested. Since Luther refused to recant, Pope Leo X (the Pope at the time) excommunicated Luther from the church in 1521. Pope Leo X encouraged and desired the sale of indulgences to finance the building of a new St. Peter's Basilica, and Luther's descent was hurting those sales. Shortly after he was excommunicated, Emperor Charles V called a diet (or meeting) at Worms, called the Diet of Worms. It occurred in Worms instead of Rome

---

7   Martin Luther History – BBC http://www.bbc.co.uk/history/historic_figures/luther_martin.shtml
8   The act of nailing the 95 Theses to the door of the church is contested, but the 95 Theses being distributed is not.

(where the papacy originally wanted it to be held) because of Prince Frederick (also known as Frederick the Wise) who protected Luther. Prince Frederick understood that if Luther went to Rome that Luther would be killed. So, he pressed for Luther to be tried in Germany to determine if a crime had occurred. (In the movie, the Pope attempts to bribe Prince Frederick with a bouquet of roses made of gold and blessed by the Pope. This bouquet is only given out once a year to one prince who showed "heroic loyalty and devotion" to the Catholic Church.)

At Worms, Luther again refused to recant stating, "Unless I am convinced by Scripture and plain reason—I do not accept the authority of the popes and councils, for they have contradicted each other—my conscience is captive to the Word of God." The Emperor, who was aligned with the Pope, declared Luther a heretic and an outlaw. Prince Frederick, therefore, protected Luther and hid him inside of Wartburg Castle.

In 1522, Luther returned to Wittenberg and in 1525 met a former nun named Katharina von Bora, who was smuggled to safety within a barrel. Luther, who had taught against celibacy in the priesthood, married her, and they had six children. During this time (1524–1526) was the Peasants War. The leaders of the war based their revolts on some of the teachings of Martin Luther. However, Luther recognized and supported the authority's right to put down the revolt. Due to this, many of his supporters no longer supported him.

Finally in 1534, Luther completed his translation of the Bible into German. He also wrote many Hymns and a liturgy (order of formal worship service) in German as well. Translating the Bible into German was a huge event because the Roman Catholic Church at the time formally taught and read from the Bible in Latin, which the people did not understand.

Watch the movie "Luther" (2003) by director Eric Till. It is a brief summary of Martin Luther and gives you an idea of the setting and situation at the time of the Reformation.

1. What was Luther originally studying to become?
   a. ____ A businessman
   b. ____ A lawyer
   c. ____ A priest
   d. ____ A scribe

2. What event drove Martin Luther to become a friar?
   a. ____ A lightning storm
   b. ____ A religious epiphany while reading the Bible
   c. ____ His rebellious nature toward his father
   d. ____ It was a random decision

3. Was Luther's father happy with his decision?
   a. ____ Yes
   b. ____ No

4. What were indulgences for (the people)?
   a. ____ They allowed the people to show their dedication to the church
   b. ____ They had no real purpose for the people
   c. ____ They were letters of praise purchased by the people from the pope
   d. ____ They allowed them to purchase forgiveness for their and others' sins

5. How did someone obtain an indulgence?
   a. ____ Through the good works that they did
   b. ____ By giving a certain amount of money to the church
   c. ____ By becoming a monk/priest
   d. ____ By working at the church

6. Why did the Pope and the Catholic Church want and encourage the sale of indulgences?
   a. ____ They were only for the benefit of the people
   b. ____ They were sold to raise money to build St. Peter's Basilica
   c. ____ They encouraged people to attend mass
   d. ____ They helped the Pope keep the Cardinals in line

7. How many Theses did Luther write?
   a. ____ 10
   b. ____ 25
   c. ____ 50
   d. ____ 95

8. What was the main focus of the Theses?
   a. ____ The sale of indulgences
   b. ____ The authority of monks
   c. ____ The rights of the people
   d. ____ The order of service

9. What was Luther's main intention with the 95 theses?
   a. ____ To disgrace the pope
   b. ____ To bring about discussion and abolish the sale of indulgences
   c. ____ To make a name for himself
   d. ____ To bring about discussion about the rights of the people

10. The Bibles used in the Catholic Church, before Luther, were written and read in what language?
    a. ____ English
    b. ____ Dutch
    c. ____ Latin
    d. ____ German

11. What was the language of the people?
    a. ____ English
    b. ____ Dutch
    c. ____ Latin
    d. ____ German

12. What language did Luther write in and translate the Bible into?
    a. ____ English
    b. ____ Dutch
    c. ____ Latin
    d. ____ German

13. What is the name of the prince that protected Luther?

    a. ____ Prince Albert

    b. ____ Prince Frederick

    c. ____ Prince Francis

    d. ____ Prince Aaron

14. What did the Pope try to bribe the prince with?

    a. ____ A golden bouquet of roses blessed by the Pope

    b. ____ Gold coins

    c. ____ A meeting with the emperor

    d. ____ More land to control

15. Where was the hearing for Martin Luther called by the Emperor?

    a. ____ Rome

    b. ____ Diet of Worms

    c. ____ Wittenberg

    d. ____ Diet of Augsburg

16. Why didn't the prince want Luther to go to Rome?

    a. ____ It was too far away

    b. ____ It was too costly

    c. ____ The prince wanted him dead

    d. ____ The Pope and people of the Catholic church planned to kill him

17. What two things did Luther request in order for him to recant? (Mark two.)

    a. ____ Clear reason

    b. ____ Money

    c. ____ A position within the church

    d. ____ Scripture

LESSON 11: LUTHER'S PREFACE – THE "WHY" OF THE CATECHISM

> **Memorization:** from Luther's preface to the Small Catechism –
>
> *Therefore I beg you all for God's sake, my dear sirs and brethren, who are pastors or preachers, to devote yourselves heartily to your office. Have pity on the people who are entrusted to you and help us teach the catechism to the people, and especially the young.*

Despise: when a person more than hates something or someone and avoids it or them; to treat something or someone as being worthless

Catechism Material: Luther's Preface (pp. 246–252)

1.   True / False – Luther was happy with how much doctrine the common person knew.

2.   True / False – Luther did not think it was important for a person to be able to recite The Lord's Prayer or anything from memory.

Martin Luther's Seal (Its explanation is on page 257 of the Catechism)

3. What prompted Luther to write the Small Catechism? (Mark all that apply.)

    a. ____ The common person did not know Christian doctrine

    b. ____ The pastors (bishops/priests) were unqualified to teach the people

    c. ____ The pastors (bishops/priests) were teaching false doctrine

    d. ____ The pastors (bishops/priests) were neglecting the people

4. True / False – Luther wanted people to be taught the Lord's prayer, the Ten Commandments, etc. in the same way year after year. Why or why not? _____

_____

_____

5. What did Luther say should happen to people who are unwilling to learn the catechism? _____

_____

_____

6. True / False – Luther did NOT believe/teach that people should be forced to believe in the Bible or what is taught in the catechism.

7. True / False – After the people learned the Small Catechism, Luther did not care if the people were taught anything more.

8. Luther gave three examples of things that needed to be taught more of, specifically if they were problems in the church. Explain the reasons why Luther believed they should be taught more:

    a. The Seventh Commandment: _____

_____

_____

_____

    b. The Fourth Commandment: _____

_____

_____

_____

    c. The responsibilities of Parents and Rulers (magistrates): _____

_____

_____

_____

9. Luther talks about the "Sacrament," which is to refer to the Lord's Supper, and he felt it was very important to attend. How many times did Luther say that a person could forgo the Lord's Supper a year before they were deemed to be despising it?

    a. ____ 1

    b. ____ 2

    c. ____ 4

    d. ____ 5

    e. ____ 10

10. If a person desires to go to the Lord's Supper, Luther says they would believe this: _____

    _____

    _____

11. True / False – If the people did not go to the Lord's Supper, Luther said the pastor should make it a law

    that they go. What is his reason for why or why not? _____

    _____

    _____

    _____

SECTION 2: REVIEW

1. What does the catechism do? _____

2. What are the six chief parts of the catechism?

    a. _____

    b. _____

    c. _____

    d. _____

    e. _____

    f. _____

3. Why are the six chief parts based solely on the Bible?

    a. ____ It seemed like a good idea

    b. ____ The Bible is the final authority

    c. ____ Everyone agreed on it

4. True / False – Confirmation is a requirement for a person to be saved.

5. True / False – Luther always intended upon becoming a friar.

    If false, what did he originally intend to be? _____

6. Why did Luther object to the sale of indulgences?

    a. ____ He actually did not

    b. ____ He wanted to start a revolution

    c. ____ He was upset the money was not coming to his church

    d. ____ The doctrine they were based on was false

7. True / False – Luther always intended upon breaking away from the Catholic Church when he posted his theses.

8. How many theses did Luther write? _____

9. The Pope set up a hearing for him to recant because Luther wrote those theses. Where was the hearing at?

    a. ____ Wittenberg

    b. ____ Augsburg

    c. ____ Rome

    d. ____ Worms

10. What was the name of Luther's wife?_____

    How was she smuggled to safety?

    a. ____ In the bottom of a boat down a river

    b. ____ In a barrel

    c. ____ Under a stack of hay

    d. ____ In a closed carriage with Prince Frederick

11. What language did Luther translate the Bible into?_____

12. True / False – Luther was adamant that Christians should learn the catechism.

13. What was Luther's response to those who refused to learn the catechism?

    a. ____ He believed and advocated that they be told they deny Christ

    b. ____ He had them thrown into prison

    c. ____ He did not mind it as long as they went to church

    d. ____ He sent them back to the Catholic Church

14. Did Luther believe people should be forced to learn the catechism?

    a. ____ Yes

    b. ____ No

15. Why did Luther want the chief parts of the catechism taught the same, year after year?

    a. ____ It made it easier on him

    b. ____ The people did not have time to learn it more than one way

    c. ____ If Luther wrote anymore then he would have been killed

    d. ____ He wanted to avoid confusion and encourage retention of the material

16. True / False – Luther wanted the people to continue to study and learn even after the small catechism because it did not teach everything.

17. Luther believed that people would earnestly desire the Lord's Supper because...

    a. ____ They were poor, and it was free bread and wine

    b. ____ By participating it would lessen the amount of time they spent in Purgatory

    c. ____ People would understand their sin and need for forgiveness

    d. ____ If they did not come they would be thrown in jail

SECTION 3 – THE BIBLE

LESSON 12: WHAT IS THE BIBLE?

> **Memorization:** 2 Timothy 3:16–17 –
> *All Scripture is given by inspiration of God, and is profitable for doctrine, for reproof, for correction, for instruction in righteousness, that the man of God may be complete, thoroughly equipped for every good work.*

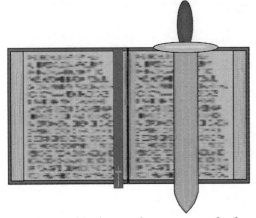

God's Word is sharper than any two-edged sword (Hebrews 4:12).

"Who wrote the Bible? Holy men of God wrote the Bible. The *Prophets* wrote the books of the *Old Testament*, and the *Evangelists* and the *Apostles* wrote the books of the *New Testament*"[9] (2 Peter 1:21)

"For what purpose did God give us the Bible? God gave us the Bible to make us 'wise unto <u>salvation</u> through faith which is in Christ Jesus,' and to <u>train us in holy living</u>."[10] (2 Tim. 3:15–17 and Ps. 119:105)

"What use should we make of the Bible? We should diligently and reverently <u>read and study</u> the Bible, <u>listen</u> attentively when it is read and explained, <u>believe</u> it, and live according to it."[11] (John 5:39, Luke 11:28, Luke 2:19 and John 14:23)

The book in the Bible called Song of Songs is also called Song of Solomon. The first four books of the New Testament are also called the *Gospels*.

Catechism Material: Questions 2–5 (pp. 48–51) and Books of the Bible Appendix (pp. 253–254)

1. Give another name for the Bible: _____

2. The Bible is separated into two parts:

    a. _____

    b. _____

3. What does the first part tell us about? _____

4. What does the second part tell us about?_____

5. Who wrote the Bible? _____

6. Match the following people with the parts that they wrote:

    a. Evangelists

    b. Prophets   ____ The Old Testament

    c. Apostles   ____, ____ The New Testament

7. What are the two reasons God gave us the Bible?

    a. _____

    b. _____

---

9   Question 8 from "A Short Explanation of Dr. Martin Luther's Small Catechism" Concordia Publishing House, 1943
10 Question 12 from "A Short Explanation of Dr. Martin Luther's Small Catechism" Concordia Publishing House, 1943
11 Question 13 from "A Short Explanation of Dr. Martin Luther's Small Catechism" Concordia Publishing House, 1943

8. What is *"Verbal Inspiration"*?_____

_____

9. What passage is the best proof for "Verbal Inspiration" from the Bible?_____

What is your reasoning for the one you picked?_____

_____

_____

_____

_____

10. The Bible (contains / is) God's own word.

11. The Bible (contains / is) truth.

12. The Bible:

a. ____ Has some errors that need to be found out

b. ____ Is completely inerrant (without errors)

13. True / False – Every word in the Bible is true.

14. The Old Testament was originally written in _____ and the New Testament was written in _____.

15. True / False – The translations of the Bible into English are completely without error.

16. What is the key to understanding Scripture? _____

17. In order to understand the Holy Scripture, we must use human logic or human reasoning. However, human reasoning should be_____ of the text.

18. If what we believe and KNOW to be true is different from what we are reading in the Bible, what should we do?

a. ____ Impose our view onto the Bible

b. ____ Carefully determine if we read the Bible correctly

c. ____ Continue reading to obtain a better understanding of the concept

d. ____ After we have done b and c, and have determined there is a difference, throw out our understanding and accept what the Bible has said as the real truth.

19. It is (OK / wrong) to deny the sacredness or the truth of the Bible.

20. What are the four ways we should use the Bible?

a. _____

b. _____

c. _____

d. _____

21. How many books are in the Old Testament? _____

22. What is the Pentateuch?_____

_____

23. How many and who are the Major Prophets?_____

_____

24. How many books are in the New Testament?_____

25. What are the first four books of the New Testament called?_____

SUBSECTION: LAW AND GOSPEL

Lesson 13: An Introduction to Law and Gospel

> **Memorization:** Galatians 3:24 –
> *The law is our tutor to bring us to Christ, that we might be justified by faith.*

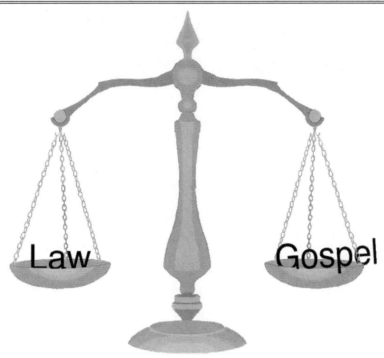

Catechism Material: Questions 6–8 (pp. 51 and 52) and 84–85 (pp. 100–101)

1. What two things must be distinguished between as we read the Bible?

    a. _____

    b. _____

2. God teaches us to do good works in three ways through the Law; what are those three ways?

    a. _____

    b. _____

    c. _____

3. The Law tells us what sin is. What two things does God do in regard to sin?

    a. _____

    b. _____

4. What is the Gospel? _____

_____

5. What are the four things God gives us in the Gospel?

    a. _____

    b. _____

    c. _____

    d. _____

6.   Write Law or Gospel next to the appropriate descriptions:

    a.   _____ teaches what we are to do and not to do

    b.   _____ teaches what God has done and still does for our salvation

    c.   _____ shows us our sin and wrath of God

    d.   _____ shows us our salvation and the grace of God

    e.   _____ must be proclaimed to sinners who are troubled because of their sins

    f.   _____ must be proclaimed to all people, especially impenitent sinners

7.   The answer to the question "Why do I need to be saved?" is found in what?

    a.   ____ The Law

    b.   ____ The Gospel

8.   The answer to the question "How can I be saved?" comes through what?

    a.   ____ The Law

    b.   ____ The Gospel

Lesson 14: The Law

> **Memorization:** Matthew 5:48 –
> *Therefore you shall be perfect, just as your Father in Heaven is perfect.*

"What is the *Law*? The Law is that doctrine of the Bible in which God tells us how we are to be and what we are to do and not to do."[12] (Lev. 19:2, Ex. 34:11, Deut. 6:6–7)

> What does God mean by promising grace and every blessing to those who love Him and keep His commandments? God will graciously reward in body and soul all those who love Him and keep His Commandments.[13] (1 Tim. 4:8 and Gen. 32:10)

Read question 14, pages 54–55. In that question and answer it talks about three types of law in the Old Testament. Those three types are the Moral Law, Ceremonial Law, and Political Law which we will also call the Civil Law. This distinction is important, and the majority of the Catechism when it talks about the "Law" is referring to specifically the Moral Law. The reason for this is that the Political/Civil Law and the Ceremonial Law are no longer observed. The reason that the Ceremonial Law is completely fulfilled, and therefore the sacrifices and feasts are no longer required, is because of Hebrews 10:11–18:

> *And every priest stands ministering daily and offering repeatedly the same sacrifices, which can never take away sins. But this Man, after He had offered one sacrifice for sins forever, sat down at the right hand of God, from that time waiting till His enemies are made His footstool. For by one offering He has perfected forever those who are being sanctified.*

> *But the Holy Spirit also witnesses to us; for after He had said before,*

> *"This is the covenant that I will make with them after those days, says the LORD: I will put My laws into their hearts, and in their minds I will write them," then He adds, "Their sins and their lawless deeds I will remember no more." Now where there is remission of these, there is no longer an offering for sin.*

---

12   Question 15 from "A Short Explanation of Dr. Martin Luther's Small Catechism" Concordia Publishing House, 1943
13   Question 84 from "A Short Explanation of Dr. Martin Luther's Small Catechism" Concordia Publishing House, 1943

The *Ceremonial Law* was the Law concerning the ceremonies for paying for sins. Therefore, when it says "there is no longer an offering for sin" and "for by one offering He has perfected forever those who are being sanctified," it is saying that all of the Ceremonial laws have been fulfilled and have ended. It is because those sacrifices and ceremonies were a "shadow of things to come" (Colossians 2:16–17). That shadow was pointing to Christ. Therefore, no further sacrifices are needed nor required because Jesus' one sacrifice was the fulfillment and completion of all sacrifices.

Curb – Keeping the world on the road   *Mirror* – Showing us who we really are and what we are really like   *Guide* – Showing Christians how to live their lives

However, in regard to the *Moral Law*, God states that "I will put My laws into their hearts, and in their minds I will write them." This refers to the portion of the law that the 1943 version of the Catechism refers to: "The Law is that doctrine of the Bible in which God tells us how we are to be and what we are to do and not to do." It is that duty, responsibility, and commandment that we have from God in how we act, think, talk, and do to both our neighbor and God. Furthermore, for those who do not believe nor trust in Jesus' sacrifice, the consequences and requirements of the Moral Law still exist (Hebrews 10:26–28).

Finally, that leaves the *Political/Civil Law*. This is the law that was given to the Israelites primarily through Moses which governed the day-to-day life of the people of Israel. It also included the physical consequences and legal requirements of the nation and its laws. However, that nation, as it was, ceased to exist. Therefore, those rules and regulations are no longer enforced. That does not mean that we cannot learn from these laws in how a godly government should act.

Catechism Material: Questions 13–14 (pp. 54–55), 23 (p. 60), 44 (p. 73), 70, and 72–77 (pp. 94–97)

9. God gave His Law in three ways:
    a. He wrote it on our hearts; what is that referring to? _____
    b. He gave it to us through a mediator; who was that mediator? _____
    c. He wrote it on stone tablets; what did He write? _____

10. There are three types of Law that God gave; what are they?
    a. P_____ (aka the civil law)
    b. M_____ (the Ten Commandments)
    c. C_____ (concerns religious sacrifices and rights)

11. Define the following terms:
    a. Political/Civil Law: _____

    _____

    b. Moral Law:_____

    _____

    c. Ceremonial Law: _____

    _____

12. The following are examples of the different types of law. Write "P" for Political/Civil Law, "M" for Moral
    Law and "C" for Ceremonial Law next to the examples of each:
    a. ____ Matthew 19:19 – "'Honor your father and your mother,' and, 'You shall love your neighbor as
       yourself.'"
    b. ____ Exodus 20:25 – "And if you make Me an altar of stone, you shall not build it of hewn stone;
       for if you use your tool on it, you have profaned it."
    c. ____ Leviticus 20:2 "Again, you shall say to the children of Israel: 'Whoever of the children
       of Israel, or of the strangers who dwell in Israel, who gives any of his descendants to Molech,
       he shall surely be put to death. The people of the land shall stone him with stones."
    d. ____ Leviticus 26:1 – "'You shall not make idols for yourselves; neither a carved image nor
       a sacred pillar shall you rear up for yourselves; nor shall you set up an engraved stone in your
       land, to bow down to it; for I am the Lord your God."
    e. ____ Deuteronomy 21:20–21 – "And they shall say to the elders of his city, 'This son of ours is
       stubborn and rebellious; he will not obey our voice; he is a glutton and a drunkard.' Then all the
       men of his city shall stone him to death with stones; so you shall put away the evil from among
       you, and all Israel shall hear and fear."
    f. ____ Exodus 29:36 – "And you shall offer a bull every day as a sin offering for atonement. You
       shall cleanse the altar when you make atonement for it, and you shall anoint it to sanctify it."

13. For the following types of Law, state whether or not it is currently enforced and why or why not:
    a. Political/Civil Law:_____

    _____

    _____

    b. Moral Law:_____

    _____

    _____

    _____

    c. Ceremonial Law: _____

    _____

    _____

14. There are three functions of the Law (i.e., the Moral Law); what are they? Then match each one to its purpose.

Function	Purpose
a. _____	____ Helps keep order in the world
b. _____	____ Shows us our sin
c. _____	____ Tells Christians how to live

15. Which part of the law tells us how God expects us to live (which is how we should live)?
    a. ____ The Political/Civil Law
    b. ____ The Moral Law
    c. ____ The Ceremonial Law

16. As Christians what should our reaction to following the Law be?
    a. ____ We should eagerly want to do it because it is God's will
    b. ____ We should hate and reject it because it is impossible for us to follow it

17. What gives us that reaction to following the law?
    a. ____ Our sinful nature
    b. ____ Our desire to please God
    c. ____ The Holy Spirit

18. How well do we need to follow the law in order to save ourselves or to be righteous?
    a. ____ Perfectly
    b. ____ Better than other people
    c. ____ Just enough to be a good person
    d. ____ It does not really matter how well we follow it

19. Who is required to perform the Law as described in the previous question?
    a. ____ Adults
    b. ____ Children
    c. ____ All people (born and unborn, young and old, the genius and the physically or mentally handicapped, including and especially me)

20. In what ways do we need to follow the law (Mark all that apply.)?
    a. ____ In our thoughts
    b. ____ In our deeds
    c. ____ In our desires
    d. ____ In our words

21. Can we keep any or all of God's Commandments?
    a. ____ Yes
    b. ____ No

22. If we do not follow the law, what is the consequence that God threatens?
    a. ____ A timeout
    b. ____ A slap on the wrist
    c. ____ A lecture
    d. ____ Earthly punishment, physical death, and eternal condemnation

23. Read James 2:10. (True / False) That passage tells us that no matter what part of the law we break we are guilty of breaking it all.

24. Based on what you have learned about the Moral Law, who must follow it (question 11), how well they must keep it (question 10), and in what ways that they must keep it (question 12), who then can save themselves by keeping the law? Why can they or can they not do it?_____

_____

_____

_____

25. Which Bible passage supports your answer to the previous question?
   a.   ____ Genesis 32:10
   b.   ____ Romans 3:23
   c.   ____ Exodus 34:11
   d.   ____ Deuteronomy 6:6–7

26. When we do follow God's Law, even though it cannot be done perfectly, what does God promise?_____

   _____

   _____

   If God does not give us those things, can we accuse God of wrongdoing? Why or why not? (Genesis 32:10)

   _____

   _____

   _____

Gospel – The truth of our Savior that sets us free from sin, guilt, and eternal condemnation.

Lesson 15: The Gospel

> **Memorization:** John 3:16 –
> *For God so loved the world that He gave His only begotten Son, that whoever believes in Him should not perish but have everlasting life.*

The Law, as you learned, tells us over and over again how we do not measure up to it. It is more than that though, because God is perfect. So in reality, you do not measure up to Him. The Gospel portion of the Bible is in direct contrast to the Law. Instead of focusing on how we are not perfect and cannot do the will of God, it focuses on this aspect of God:

> *1 Timothy 2:3–4 – For this is good and acceptable in the sight of God our Savior, who desires all men to be saved and to come to the knowledge of the truth.*

The old English meaning of the word *Gospel* is "the good news." The good news in the Bible is that God has set us free from our sin and reconciled Himself to us. It is also the good news about how God did this and how we can be saved, and instead of being separated from him forever (Hell), go to and be with Him forever (Heaven). This lesson will be split into three sections: How did God save us, how do we become a part of God's family, and how does God sustain us in His family.

How did God save us?

God saved us through sending His "only begotten Son." He sent His Son, Jesus, to be born of a virgin (Matthew 1:23), whose name was Mary (Luke 1:26–37). This Son of God was God and was man, i.e., human (John 1:1, 14). This Jesus then, after fulfilling the whole will of God (John 8:28) and thus the whole Law, died on a cross as the true sacrifice for our sins (Hebrews 10:8–14). But this not being enough, He rose again from the dead, thus conquering death and allowing us to be raised as well (1 Corinthians 15:12–19). Because Jesus died, rose again, and lives forever, He can and does intercede for us (Hebrews 7:25) and pours out the forgiveness of sins on His believers. We then cannot do anything to add to or supplement this forgiveness to grant us salvation (Galatians 3:1–4).

How do we become a part of God's Family?

God sends to us His Holy Spirit to convert us and strengthen our faith through the Holy Spirit's work of *Sanctification*. The Holy Spirit utilizes the *Means of Grace*. The Means of Grace includes Word (i.e., the Bible) and Sacrament (i.e., Holy Baptism "which now saves us" [1 Peter 3:21] and Holy Communion [through which we receive Christ's body and blood for the remission of sins {Matthew 26:26–28}]) to accomplish those goals. But more than that, God and the Holy Spirit utilize people, specifically preachers (pastors), whom they have personally selected (Jeremiah 3:15) to spread the good news of the Gospel. As it says in Romans 10:14–15:

> *How then shall they call on Him in whom they have not believed? And how shall they believe in Him of whom they have not heard? And how shall they hear without a preacher? And how shall they preach unless they are sent? As it is written:*
>
> *"How beautiful are the feet of those who preach the gospel of peace,*
> *Who bring glad tidings of good things!"*

How does God sustain us in His family?

After saving us, God has not left us to fend for ourselves but instead takes care of every bodily need (Matthew 6:25–27). But more than that, He sustains our faith (Hebrews 12:1–2), corrects us (Hebrews 12:6), and continually gives us the forgiveness of sins (1 John 1:8–10). Even more than that, He gives us His body and blood through the word and sacrament of Holy Communion that we might receive the forgiveness of sins in a physical and personal way (Matthew 26:26–28).

Catechism Material: Questions 42–43 (p. 72)

1. True / False – According to the Gospel Jesus is both God and man.
    What verse(s) support your answer? _____

2. True / False – Jesus was crucified, buried, and his body is still in the ground.
    What verse(s) support your answer? _____

3. True / False – Even though Jesus died, we still need to do good works in order for us to get into heaven.
    What verse(s) support your answer? _____

4. What are the three ways that God/the Holy Spirit works faith in us?

    a. _____

    b. _____

    c. _____

5. How does God sustain us after He brings us into His family? Give examples. _____
    _____
    _____

6. In your own words, explain how Jesus saved you and everyone: _____
    _____
    _____
    _____

SECTION 3: REVIEW

1. The Bible:
    a. _____ Contains some truths
    b. _____ Contains stories
    c. _____ Is God's Words
    d. _____ Tells us how to save ourselves

2. The Bible is made up of two sections:
    a. _____
    b. _____

3. What are the two things that must be distinguished between in order to understand the Bible?
    a. _____
    b. _____

4. What are the three types of law and their definitions?
    a. _____ : _____
        _____
    b. _____ : _____
        _____
    c. _____ : _____
        _____

5. What are the three functions of the law and their definitions?
    a. _____ : _____
        _____
    b. _____ : _____
        _____
    c. _____ : _____
        _____

6. True / False – It is enough to just keep most of the law to get into heaven.

7. Who can be saved by keeping the law?
    a. _____ Really good people
    b. _____ Infants
    c. _____ No one
    d. _____ Those who do not know the law

8. How are we brought to faith?
    a. ____ Through the Bible
    b. ____ Through a Pastor's sermons based on the Word
    c. ____ Through the Holy Spirit
    d. ____ Through Baptism
    e. ____ All of the above

9. How did God save us?_____

_____

_____

10. Who intercedes for us?
    a. ____ Our parents
    b. ____ Jesus
    c. ____ The Saints
    d. ____ God the Father

11. Imagine you are in a conversation with someone and they make the following statements. Write "L" for Law or "G" for Gospel to indicate whether you should respond with the Law or Gospel:
    a. ____ God will let me into heaven because I'm a good person.
    b. ____ How can anyone ever love me after what I did?
    c. ____ Does God forgive me?
    d. ____ How do I know when I've done enough to get into Heaven?
    e. ____ I'm really glad I'm not like that person!

12. For your previous responses write out a quick response:
    a. _____

    _____

    _____

    b. _____

    _____

    _____

    c. _____

    _____

    _____

    d. _____

    _____

    _____

    e. _____

    _____

    _____

SECTION 4 – GOD, HIS CREATIONS, AND HIS WORK OF SALVATION

LESSON 16: WHO IS GOD? – THE HOLY TRINITY

> **Memorization:** Deuteronomy 6:4 –
> *Hear, O Israel: The LORD our God, the LORD is one!*

God has three persons: The Father, The Son, and The Holy Spirit. They are all equally God and equally distinguishable from each other. They are also able to move and exist in the three separate places at the same time (The Baptism of Jesus in Luke 3:21–22: Jesus [the Son of God], the dove [the Holy Spirit], and the voice from heaven [God the Father]). In this way, it is right to pray and call upon each distinct person individually. However, they are not three gods, but one God, and to call upon God is to call upon them all as a single Deity (Deuteronomy 6:4). Moreover, when you pray to one person of the Trinity, you are in effect praying to all three.

Begotten: The offspring or child of (the naturally born child of)
Proceeds: Originates or comes from
Divine Attributes: Characteristics that can only belong to God.

The clover is a symbol for the Trinity with each leaf representing a member of the Godhead (Catechism p. 276).

Catechism Material: Questions 93–95 (pp. 105–108)

1. The catechism talks about God and 13 of His different attributes. Write down the attribute and match it to the passage where God identifies Himself as such.

	Attribute	Bible Passage
a.	_____	____ Genesis 17:1
b.	_____	____ Psalm 90:1–2
c.	_____	____ John 4:24
d.	_____	____ Malachi 3:6
e.	_____	____ 1 John 4:8
f.	_____	____ Deuteronomy 32:4
g.	_____	____ 2 Timothy 2:13
h.	_____	____ Psalm 145:9
i.	_____	____ John 21:17
j.	_____	____ Leviticus 19:2
k.	_____	____ Exodus 34:6–7
l.	_____	____ Jeremiah 23:24
m.	_____	____ Titus 3:5

2. Pick one or two of those attributes that stand out to you and explain why. _____
_____
_____

3. God is made up of three persons, but is one person. This is similar to a triangle that has three equal sides, but is one shape. It must have three equal sides because each person in the trinity is equal to the other.

Step 1: Below is an equilateral triangle; write the names of each of God's persons one on each side.

Step 2: Each person has a special work that they accomplish. Write that special work next to their name.

Step 3: Draw arrows through the triangle from the originating person to the person that comes from them.

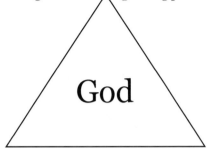

4. What does it mean that God is the "Holy Trinity"?_____

_____

5. Christians believe in:

    a. ____ Three Gods

    b. ____ One God with three persons

SUBSECTION: THE PERSONS OF THE TRINITY – GOD THE FATHER

Lesson 17: God the Father

> **Memorization:** Isaiah 64:8 –
> *But now, O LORD, You are our Father; We are the clay, and You our potter; And all we are the work of Your hand.*

There are two ways the term "father" is used in the Catechism. The first way refers to God being the loving parent. In this way, God is the loving parent of God the Son, whom He begot (Hebrews 1:5), and all Christians, whom He adopted (Romans 8:15). God is not the loving parent of the whole human race because He is not the loving parent of the condemned (John

8:37–47). The second way the term "father" is used refers to the fact that He is the Creator Father. God created me and the whole human race, and in that sense, He is everyone's father. However, He is not the creator of God the Son because God the Son was with God the Father in the beginning and thus was not created (John 1:1–3).

Catechism Material: Questions 96–98 (pp. 109–110)

1. God the Father is called "Father" because He is the loving parent of... (Mark all that apply.)
    a. ____ God the Son
    b. ____ Christians/Me
    c. ____ The whole human race

2. God the Father is called "Father" because He is the creator of... (Mark all that apply.)
    a. ____ God the Son
    b. ____ Christians/Me
    c. ____ The whole human race

3. Read Galatians 3:26. How do I or anyone become God's child so that He is my or their loving parent and Father?_____

4. Jesus and Christians are the children of God. However, Jesus is a(n) _____ child of God while Christians are _____ children of God. (Fill in the blanks with "begotten" and "adopted.")

5. God the Father's special work is creation. What exactly did He create?
    a. ____ The Earth
    b. ____ Everything on the earth
    c. ____ The universe
    d. ____ All things visible and invisible

    What verse tells you that? _____

6. Who was begotten from God the Father?_____

7. Who proceeded from God the Father? _____

Lesson 18: God the Father's Special Work of Creation
Read Genesis Chapter 1 and Genesis Chapter 2 verses 1–3.

God judges things based on His own nature of perfection. So when He determines that something is good, based on His perception from His nature, it must be without mistake or flaw (it must be perfect). Another way to think of it is that the Hebrew word used can also mean "pleasant." God is only pleased by things that are perfect. Therefore, in order to be pleased, the thing that God created must have been perfect.

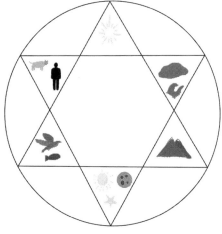

The six pointed star of creation is also the Jewish Star of David (Catechism p. 282).

A Complete Creation:
God, when He formed the earth and all that was in it, created it as a *complete creation*. Everything God created was *fully formed* (with all of its parts and appendages, e.g., arms, legs, eyes, etc.), *fully functional* (fully capable of completing every task God had given to it). That is, there were full-grown trees producing fruit to provide for Adam and Eve. Adam and Eve were "old" enough to tend the earth, subdue the animals and name them (Genesis 2). However, in reality, they were only days old. So while they were only infants according to time, they were complete adults according to their creation. It is like when Jesus turned water into wine (John 2:1–10). Wine takes time to ferment and some even more time to become really good (years). However, when Jesus made the best wine at the feast, it happened at His word (instantly).

Catechism Material: Questions 97–98 (pp. 109–110) and 103–105 (pp. 114–115)

1. God created the world in _____ days, and on the _____ day, He rested.

2. How did God define the word "day" in Genesis?
    a. ____ Evening and Morning
    b. ____ He did not
    c. ____ As a time only He can understand

3. What did God create everything out of?
    a. ____ Existing atoms
    b. ____ Nothing
    c. ____ Dirt
    d. ____ Cosmic dust

4. What did God use to create everything?
    a. ____ His physical strength
    b. ____ His mind
    c. ____ His word
    d. ____ Pieces of Himself

5. When God created everything, He created it all "complete." What are the two terms used to help us understand what it means to be complete? Define them.
    a. _____ : _____
        _____
    b. _____ : _____
        _____

6. For each day, write down what was created:

    Day 1:   Day 4:
    _____

    Day 2:   Day 5:
    _____

    Day 3:   Day 6:

7. After each day what was God's response to what He created?
    a. ____ That it was terrible
    b. ____ That it was OK
    c. ____ That it was good

8. In order for God to say something is "good" it must also be:
    a. ____ Good enough
    b. ____ Simple
    c. ____ Perfect
    d. ____ Workable

9. What did God do on the seventh day?_____

10. Compare Day 1 to Day 4, Day 2 to Day 5, Day 3 to Day 6. How are they similar?_____
    _____
    _____

11. God instructed everything to reproduce "after their own kind." What does that statement mean?_____
_____
_____

12. Can a fish have a lizard offspring or a lizard produce a bird? Why or why not?_____
_____
_____

13. Read Psalm 36:6. Who still sustains the world and everything in it?_____
    Who sustains you?_____

Lesson 19: Theistic Evolution

(All references can be found in Genesis 1 unless otherwise noted.)

Theistic evolution refers to the teaching that God utilized evolution when He created the world. This is the attempt by some to combine what the evolutionists teach with their faith in God and what they see in Scripture. Traditionally this is done by utilizing 2 Peter 3:8 which states, "But, beloved, do not forget this one thing, that with the Lord one day *is* as a thousand years, and a thousand years as one day." In this, they argue that God is outside of time and therefore the time (specifically the word *day*) in Genesis could be expanded to be millions or billions of years. Furthermore, it argues from the standpoint that God COULD have used evolution as the method to create life on the earth, and based on the evidence they see God DID use evolution. This doctrine or theory is called the *Day-Age Theory*. God could have used this because He is capable of creating or using whatever method He desires.

First off, the Holy Scriptures do teach that God is outside of time and is therefore eternal. Secondly, God is not limited and COULD use any method of creation that He desired. "Any method" therefore must include the use of evolution. However, whether or not God did ACTUALLY use evolution is another matter entirely. If we read the Bible, we understand that while, yes, God is outside of time and, yes, God COULD have used evolution, He did not. This doctrinal teaching and combination DO NOT work for several reasons.

To start, let us examine the time constraints listed in Genesis. Yes, the term "day" is used in Genesis for each day of creation. If it was left at that, it could be interpreted to be millions or billions of years. However, the term day is <u>qualified</u> every time it is used in the creation story. It is qualified with the words "evening and morning." It is by those words that we know that it is a traditional and humanly understood day (one revolution of the earth). Well, one could argue that the earth just rotated REALLY slow to make one revolution. However, when we observe a planet turning slowly (or you can experience it for yourself in the summer and winter), that the side in the day gets hotter and hotter and the side that is night gets colder and colder. Therefore, all life would either be cooked or burned to death on one side or frozen on the other.

Continuing the theme of time in Genesis chapter 2:4–6, it tells us that no rain had fallen on the earth during creation. Rain (that is water) is a fundamental building block of all life. Without rain to feed the plants, they could not grow, and life could not exist. Even the lakes and streams would dry up due to the constant beating of the sun on the land. Therefore, if the days were really millions or billions of years, life would have to have grown without rain and water, which is impossible.

Finally, as you will learn in depth later, sin is the cause of both spiritual and physical death (Romans 5:12–14). Sin did not come into the world until Adam and Eve sinned. Therefore, there could not have been death before Adam and Eve. As you learned, "Natural Selection" by very definition requires that the weak or less fit die so that the strong or more fit survive. That means, according to evolution, there must have been millions and billions of years' worth of death to make it possible. That is impossible because of other scriptural truths. Death did not occur until after Adam and Eve were formed and fell (Romans 5:12–14). Evolution cannot be combined with Scripture.

Catechism Material: Questions 104–105 (pp. 114–115)

1. Theistic evolution attempts to combine:
   a. ____ Faith and science
   b. ____ Evolution and the Bible
   c. ____ Milk and cookies
   d. ____ God and man

2. True / False – God is outside of time, so the word "day" could mean any length of time.

3. True / False – We especially know that the word "day" in Genesis means one literal day (or one revolution of the earth) because it is qualified.

4. What is the term "day" qualified with in Genesis?_____

5. If the earth revolved one time, but lasted millions or billions of years, what would happen to the life on earth?
   a. ____ Nothing
   b. ____ Growth would be accelerated
   c. ____ It would be killed either by freezing or burning

6. When did it rain on the earth?
   a. ____ On day 1
   b. ____ On day 2
   c. ____ On day 6
   d. ____ After God finished His creation

7. True / False – Life can exist without rain.

8. True / False – Evolution cannot exist or happen without death.

9. Adam and Eve sinned and caused what to enter into the world?
   a. ____ Life
   b. ____ Death
   c. ____ Happiness
   d. ____ Work

10. Evolution and the Bible can be combined. Why or why not? _____

_____

_____

_____

_____

Lesson 20: God the Father's Creation – Man (i.e., the Human Race)

> **Memorization:** Isaiah 44:24 –
> *Thus says the LORD, your Redeemer, And He who formed you from the womb:*
> *"I am the LORD, who makes all things, Who stretches out the heavens all alone, Who*
> *spreads abroad the earth by Myself."*

Which is the foremost visible creature? The foremost visible creature is <u>man</u>, because in the beginning God Himself especially formed his body, gave him a rational soul, made him ruler over the earth, and, above all, created him in His image.[14] (Gen. 2:7, Gen. 1:26–27)

Catechism Material: Questions 101–103 and 106–112 (pp. 112–118)

1. What day did God create humanity?
    a. ____ First
    b. ____ Third
    c. ____ Fourth
    d. ____ Sixth

2. God said that He used a specific base element to create Adam before breathing life into him. What was it? _____

3. Read Genesis 2:18–24. What was Eve made from? _____

God the Father's hand of creation (Catechism p. 278)

4. What were the only two genders God made when He created the Human Race?
    a. _____
    b. _____

5. How many of each gender did He Create? _____

6. According to Genesis 1:28, God gave the human race two instructions. What were they?
    a. _____
    b. _____

7. Can two people of the same gender fulfill both of those instructions? Why or why not? _____

_____

_____

8. Does God still create each individual human being?
    a. ____ Yes
    b. ____ No
    Which Bible passage tells you your answer? _____

9. Who then has created you and assigned you your gender? _____

10. Adam and Eve were created in the image of God.

    How well did they know God?

        a. ____ Not so well

        b. ____ Like we know Him now

        c. ____ Perfectly

    How well did they know God's will?

        a. ____ Not so well

        b. ____ Like we know it now

        c. ____ Perfectly

    How well did they do God's will?

        a. ____ Not so well

        b. ____ Like we do it now

        c. ____ Perfectly

    How happy were they in that situation?

        a. ____ Not so happy

        b. ____ As happy as we are now

        c. ____ Perfectly happy

11. Do human beings still have God's image now?

        a. ____ Yes

        b. ____ No

12. What does that mean for the ability of human beings to know God, to know, do and be pleased with His will? Human beings will naturally... (circle the correct answer)

        a. (Not know / Know) who God really is

        b. (Not know / Know) the true will of God

        c. (Not be / Be) pleased with God's will

        d. (Go against / Do) the will of God

13. The image of God was lost when Adam and Eve sinned. Read Genesis 2:15–17 and 3:1–8. What was the sin that they committed?_____

    _____

14. Who has begun to regain the image of God albeit imperfectly?

        a. ____ Everyone

        b. ____ Christians

        c. ____ Good people

        d. ____ People who go to church

15. To whom will the image of God be fully restored to?_____

    When will this restoration fully occur?_____

16. Given what you have learned about God, why is it impossible for the term "image of God" to refer to Adam and Eve's physical appearance? _____

    _____

    _____

17. Who takes care of me and all human beings?_____

18. What are the two ways that God provides for me and all human beings?

     a. _____

     b. _____

19. Why does God provide for me and all human beings?_____

_____

20. What should I do in response to God's care? (Mark all that apply.)

     a. ____ Thank and praise Him

     b. ____ Obey Him

     c. ____ Be good stewards of the earth

21. Being a good steward of earth means... (Mark all that apply.)

     a. ____ Not polluting the earth

     b. ____ Not being wasteful

     c. ____ Recycling

     d. ____ Valuing and caring for all animals and life

22. According to Genesis 2:15, one of the responsibilities God gave to human beings is to tend and keep the garden (that is the earth). If we litter, pollute, or cause animals to go extinct, have we kept this command? Why or why not?_____

_____

23. What is the thing that has caused evil and suffering in the world?

     a. ____ Freewill

     b. ____ Sin

     c. ____ Death

24. Who brought sin into the world?

     a. ____ God

     b. ____ Satan

     c. ____ Human beings

25. If God takes care of me and all human beings, why do bad things happen to me and everyone else?

     a. ____ God really does not take care of us.

     b. ____ Because we are sinful and our sin causes them.

Lesson 21: God the Father's Creation – The Angels

> **Memorization:** Psalm 103:20 –
> *Bless the LORD, you His angels, Who excel in strength, who do His word, Heeding the voice of His word.*

Which are the foremost invisible creatures? The <u>angels</u> are the foremost invisible creatures.[15]

What does the Bible tell us about the good angels? The Bible tells us that the good angels:

A. Are <u>holy spirits</u> *confirmed in their bliss*; (Heb. 1:14, Matt. 25:31, Matt. 18:10)

B. Are of great number and great power; (Luke 2:13, Dan. 7:10, Ps. 103:20, 2 Kings 19:35, 2 Kings 6:15–17)

C. Praise God, carry out His commands, and serve the Christians, especially the children.[16] (Ps. 103:20–21, Heb. 1:14, Ps. 91:11–12, Luke 2:13–14, Acts 12:5–11, Dan. 6, Luke 16:22)

---

15   Question 108 from "A Short Explanation of Dr. Martin Luther's Small Catechism" Concordia Publishing House, 1943

16   Question 110 from "A Short Explanation of Dr. Martin Luther's Small Catechism" Concordia Publishing House, 1943

What does the Bible tell us about the evil angels, or devils? The Bible tells us that the evil angels, or devils,

A. Are spirits who were created holy, but sinned and are *forever rejected* by God; (2 Peter 2:4)

B. Are cunning, powerful, and of great number; (Eph. 6:12, Mark 6:9, 2 Cor. 11:13–14)

C. Are enemies of God and of man and endeavor to destroy the works of God.[17] (John 8:44, 1 Peter 6:8–9, Gen. 3:1–5, Job 2, Matt. 4:1–11)

The word "angel" as it is used in the Bible means messenger. In and of itself the word "angel" does not refer to a good or evil being, rather to a spiritual being. We have divided these spiritual beings into "angels" and "demons" to help us understand and talk about the good and bad ones.

Angels are heavenly (i.e., spiritual) beings that God has created. Some of those angels disobeyed God and were cast out of heaven. Angels are like us in that they are servants of God (Revelation 22:9), but they are unlike us because Christ did not redeem them (Hebrews 2:16) nor did He spare them (2 Peter 2:4). Therefore, we should not worship or pray to them. To do so would be like telling the hammer to build you a house when the real person you should be talking to is the carpenter (that is God). It would also break the First Commandment.

Legion: A great number of persons or things. (A Roman legion had 6000 persons.[18])

Catechism Material: Questions 99–100 (pp. 110–112)

1. Who is the foremost invisible creature?_____

2. What does the word "angel" mean?_____

3. For the following examples, read the Bible Passage and state what the angel's name is if we know it, who the angel talked to, and what the news of the angel was.

    a. Luke 1:1–20:_____

    _____

    _____

    b. Luke 1:26–38:_____

    _____

    _____

    c. Matthew 28:1–8:_____

    _____

    _____

4. There are two factions of angels; what are they?

    a. ____ Fallen and spiritual

    b. ____ Strong and weak

    c. ____ Good and evil

---

17   Question 111 from "A Short Explanation of Dr. Martin Luther's Small Catechism" Concordia Publishing House, 1943

18   Organization of the Imperial Legion http://www.unrv.com/military/legion.php

5. How did some of the angels become evil?_____

_____

6. Who is the ruler of the good angels? _____

7. What are the evil angels called? _____

8. Read Mark 3:20–26. Who does God allow to command the evil angels?_____

9. Read Mark 5:1–13. If God commands an evil angel to do something, do they have to do it?
     a. ____ Yes
     b. ____ No

10. Who then should we rely on if we are confronted or tormented by evil angels? _____

11. True / False – There are not many evil angels.

12. True / False – There are legions of good angels.

13. True / False – Angels, good or evil, have no real power to do anything or harm us.

14. Read Psalm 91:11–12. What is one of the ways that good angels are used by God today?_____

_____

15. Read John 8:44. What are the two main attributes of Satan and his kind?
     a. _____
     b. _____

16. Why is Satan and his evil angels the enemy of God and human beings? How do they try and accomplish this?

_____

_____

_____

17. Read 2 Peter 2:4. Did God forgive or spare any of the angels that rebelled against Him?
     a. ____ Yes
     b. ____ No
Ultimately what will happen to the evil angels?_____

_____

18. Do we need to fear the evil angels then? Why or why not?_____

_____

_____

19. Should we pray to angels for protection or for anything? Why or why not?_____

_____

_____

20. True / False – God redeemed the angels that rebelled against Him.

21. True / False – God redeemed people who believe even though they rebelled against Him.

22. Match the term with their definition:

Term	Definition
a. Confirmed in Bliss	____ They cannot be saved and are rebellious.
b. Forever rejected	____ They can no longer rebel against God.

SUBSECTION: THE PERSONS OF THE TRINITY – GOD THE SON

Lesson 22: Son of God AND Son of Man

> **Memorization:** Luther's explanation of the Second Article –
> *I believe that Jesus Christ, True God, begotten of the Father from eternity, and also true man, born of the Virgin Mary, is my Lord.*

Jesus has many names (see Isaiah 9:6). All of His names are appropriate and can be used interchangeably to refer to Jesus or pray to Him. However, some names are more appropriate than others at times, but only because His different names emphasize Jesus' different attributes. It is like a person named Jonathan Adam Smith. His friends may call him "John," his parents "Jonathan" (or "Jonathan Adam" when he is in trouble), his co-workers "Adam," his subordinates "Mr. Smith," and the government "Jonathan Adam Smith." Are any of these names wrong? No. They all appropriately refer to a man named Jonathan Adam Smith. The only difference is context and how people know him. The same is with Jesus and His names.

What two natures, then, are united in Christ? The <u>divine</u> and the <u>human</u> natures are united in Christ, <u>both natures together forming one undivided and indivisible person</u> (***personal union***).[19] John 1:14, 1 Tim. 3:16, Col. 2:9, Is. 9:6, Matt. 28:20, Acts 3:15, and 1 John 1:7).

These two natures (the divine and human) are what the Catechism is referring to when it talks about Jesus being "***True God***" and "***True Man***." Furthermore, Jesus is wholly and completely God and Man at the same time without divisions or schisms (i.e., True God AND True Man). (It is His *Personal Union*.)

Catechism Material: Questions 115, 116 and 118–123 (pp. 120–127)

1. Read John 1:1–4. Who was in the beginning with God?
    a. ____ Spirits
    b. ____ Life
    c. ____ The Word
    d. ____ Man
    Was this being also God?
    a. ____ Yes
    b. ____ No

2. Read John 1:14–15. What happened to this being?
    a. ____ Became flesh
    b. ____ Died
    c. ____ Came to earth as a spirit
    d. ____ Left to create another world
    How did this happen?
    a. ____ God the Father Created Him
    b. ____ God the Father begot Him
    c. ____ God became Him completely
    d. ____ It is impossible to know

Christmas Rose – Jesus is the fulfillment of the ***Messianic Prophecy*** (Catechism p. 282).

(Question 2 continued.)

Based on your answers, what does this make this being?

    a.   ____ The Holy Spirit

    b.   ____ God the Father

    c.   ____ God the Son

Why?_____

_____

3.   Read John 1:16–17. What is the name of this being? _____

4.   The Son of God has the name, Jesus. What does Jesus mean?_____

5.   The Son of God also has the name, Christ. What does Christ mean?_____

6.   What are some of the other names of the Son of God? _____

_____

7.   Why do these divine names matter?

    a.   ____ They do not

    b.   ____ The Catechism says so

    c.   ____ They are in the Bible

    d.   ____ They tell us about the person that owns them, and those attributes only belong to God

8.   List the five attributes given to Jesus in the Catechism.

    a. _____

    b. _____

    c. _____

    d. _____

    e. _____

9.   How do those attributes compare to God's? (Refer to Lesson 16, The Holy Trinity) _____

_____

10. Jesus also did divine works. Read the following Bible passages and say what miracle or divine work He did or will do.

    a. Luke 7:47–48: _____

_____

    b. John 9:1–7: _____

_____

    c. Luke 8:40–42, 49–56:_____

_____

    d. John 5:1–9: _____

_____

    e. Hebrews 1:1–2:_____

_____

    f. 2 Timothy 4:1: _____

_____

(Question 10 continued)

    g. Hebrews 1:3:_____

_____

11. Read John 5:19–23.

    True / False – When people do not honor Jesus they do not honor God.

    True / False – Jesus does the work of His Father.

    Who is Jesus' Father?_____

    What does that make Jesus?

        a. ____ A god

        b. ____ The Son of God

        c. ____ Only a carpenter's son

        d. ____ Only a man

12. Jesus was also born of a woman. What was the woman's name?_____

13. Read Matthew 1:23. What unique attribute would this woman have?_____

    How is it impossible for her to have that attribute and be pregnant at the same time?_____

_____

    Read Luke 1:26–37. How then did she become pregnant?_____

_____

14. Give one Bible passage where Jesus is called a man by a believer. _____

15. True / False – Jesus has a body and soul.

    What Bible passage(s) support your answer?_____

16. What are some of the human feelings Jesus had?_____

_____

17. Did Jesus die?

        a. ____ Yes

        b. ____ No

18. What are the two natures joined in Jesus?

        a. _____

        b. _____

19. What does it mean then that Jesus is True God and True Man?_____

_____

20. What are the two reasons Jesus had to be True God?

        a. _____

        b. _____

21. What are the two reasons Jesus had to be True Man?

        a. _____

        b. _____

22. Read Hebrews 2:9 and fill in the blanks with either "Man" or "God".

    If Jesus had not been True _____ then He could not have died. If He had not been True _____ then He could not have saved everyone.

Lesson 23: *The Threefold Office of Christ*

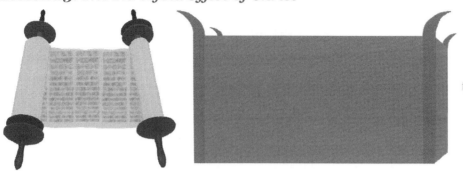
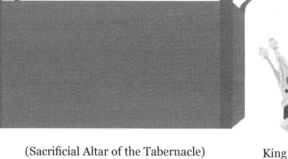

(*Torah* Scroll)
Prophet – Jesus taught and gave the Words of God

(Sacrificial Altar of the Tabernacle)
Priest – Jesus was the true sacrifice for sins.

King – Jesus rules over heaven and earth.

Audible: heard and able to be understood with the ear

Catechism Material: Question 125 (pp. 127–130)

1. What three offices did/does Jesus hold?

    a. _____

    b. _____

    c. _____

2. In the past how did Jesus fulfill His office of Prophet? Match the passage to the fulfillment.

Passage	Fulfillment
a. John 3:2	____ He preached using His audible voice
b. Mark 1:38	____ He sent some of His disciples including the 12 to preach
c. Luke 9:1–3, 10:1	____ He used miracles to affirm His preaching

3. Presently Jesus fulfills His office as a prophet by:

Passage	Fulfillment
a. Matthew 28:18–20, Romans 10:14–15	____ Sending pastors and missionaries to preach the Gospel
b. Romans 10:17	____ Using His Holy Word (what He said and taught was written down in the Bible for us to read today)

4. As a priest Jesus does/did three things. What two things has He accomplished in the past?

    a. _____

    b. _____

    What one thing does He still do today as a Priest for Christians? _____

    _____

5. What does Jesus do/will do as King over the following kingdoms?

    a. *Kingdom of Power*: _____

    _____

    b. *Kingdom of Grace*: _____

    _____

(Question 5 continued)

    c.   *Kingdom of Glory*:_____

_____

6.   Who are the residents/citizens of:

    a.   The Kingdom of Power?_____

    b.   The Kingdom of Grace? _____

    c.   The Kingdom of Glory?_____

Lesson 24: *Christ's State of Humiliation*

> **Memorization:** Isaiah 53:5 –
> *But He was wounded for our transgressions, He was bruised for our iniquities; The chastisement for our peace was upon Him, And by His stripes we are healed.*

Christ's **State of Humiliation**, according to the catechism, was when Jesus limited His Divine powers. Some of the effects of Jesus limiting His power meant that He had to sleep and eat. He also endured being mocked, judged, tempted, and crucified even though He could have stopped or prevented all of them.

Catechism Material: Questions 127 and 129–132 (pp. 130–133)

1.   Christ's State of Humiliation was when Jesus... (Mark all that apply.)

    a.   ____ Was mocked

    b.   ____ Was disfigured

    c.   ____ Limited His Divine Powers

    d.   ____ Slept

2.   How was Jesus conceived?_____

3.   Who gave birth to Jesus? _____

4.   During Jesus' earthly life He endured many things. Pick three of them and state what they were, give an example of how He suffered in that way, and a Bible passage that illustrates it.

    a. _____ , _____

    _____

    b. _____ , _____

    _____

    c. _____ , _____

    _____

5.   Read the following passages and then state how Jesus suffered under Pontius Pilate.

    a.   Matthew 27:27–29: _____

    _____

    b.   Mark 15:19: _____

    c.   John 19:1: _____

    _____

6. Read Luke 23:4. Did Pontius Pilate find a fault or actual reason to do those things to Jesus?
   a. ____ Yes
   b. ____ No

   Read Mark 15:15. Why did Pontius Pilate do those things to Jesus? _____
   _____

7. After all Jesus' sufferings, what happened to Him?
   a. ____ He was released
   b. ____ He was made king of Israel
   c. ____ He was crucified on a cross and died
   d. ____ He conquered and killed those who betrayed Him

8. How do we know that Jesus really died?
   a. Mark 15:43–45: _____
   _____

   b. John 19:31–34: _____
   _____

9. Read Mark 15:33–47, Luke 24:1–7, and Psalm 16:10. What happened to Jesus' body after He was killed?
   (Mark all that apply.)
   a. ____ He was taken down before the Sabbath
   b. ____ His bones were broken
   c. ____ He was buried in a tomb until the third day
   d. ____ His body did not decay (see corruption)

10. Read John 18:36. If Jesus was not in a state of humiliation, could Pontius Pilate have done those things?
    a. ____ Yes
    b. ____ No

11. Read Matthew 26:50–53. If Jesus was not in His State of Humiliation, could they have even taken Him?
    a. ____ Yes
    b. ____ No

12. Read John 10:17–18. Who put Jesus into His State of Humiliation? _____

13. Read Matthew 26:54. Why did Jesus keep His State of Humiliation on?
    a. ____ To glorify Himself
    b. ____ To fulfill the Scriptures
    c. ____ To show His craftiness
    d. ____ To ambush them all

14. Read 1 Peter 2:23–24. Ultimately because of His State of Humiliation, He did
    what regarding our sins? _____
    _____
    _____
    _____

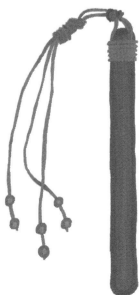

Roman Flagrum – It is the
tool used by the Romans when they
scourged/whipped someone.

Lesson 25: Christ's State of Exaltation and Second Coming

> **Memorization:** 2 Peter 3:10, 13 –
> *But the day of the Lord will come as a thief in the night, in which the heavens will pass away with a great noise, and the elements will melt with fervent heat; both the earth and the works that are in it will be burned up... Nevertheless we, according to His promise, look for new heavens and a new earth in which righteousness dwells.*

Millennialism in brief:

The Lutheran Church and the Bible do not teach *Millennialism*. However, Millennialism is well established in many denominations. Some of those denominations include the Baptists, the Mormons, and the Jehovah's Witnesses. It is essentially a belief that there will be 1000 years of peace and prosperity on the earth (typically involving Jesus reigning here on earth). What that looks like, when it is supposed to happen and how it is supposed to happen varies between the different churches (there are many versions of Millennialism). Lutherans reject the idea, finding that it is not scripturally based (as your catechism notes) and as Jesus stated, "My kingdom is not of this world" (John 18:36).

Catechism Material: Questions 141 and 143–149 (pp. 138–145)

1. Christ's *State of Exaltation* was when Jesus...
    a. ____ Ascended into Heaven
    b. ____ Did miracles
    c. ____ Died
    d. ____ After He became True Man and True God and died, now fully and always uses His divine powers

2. Why did Christ descend into Hell when He died?
    a. ____ To proclaim His triumph
    b. ____ To preach the Gospel to them and thus save them
    c. ____ To be punished
    d. ____ To wage war with the Devil

3. True / False – Christ's descent into Hell was a part of His State of Exaltation.

4. True / False – Christ's resurrection is not a part of Jesus' State of Exaltation.

5. How do we know that Christ rose from the dead?
    a. ____ We do not know
    b. ____ The Bible says so
    c. ____ His witnesses tell us so in the Bible
    d. ____ b and c

6. Give a Bible passage that tells of Jesus' death and resurrection. _____

7. Match the reason Jesus' resurrection is important with the Bible passage.

Bible Passage	Reason Resurrection is Important
a. John 14:19	____ Jesus is the Son of God
b. Romans 4:25	____ His doctrine is the truth
c. Romans 1:4	____ The sacrifice was accepted for our reconciliation with God
d. John 8:28	____ All believers will rise to eternal life

8.   Read 1 Corinthians 15:12–19. Why is it important that there is a resurrection of the dead and that Jesus was raised from the dead?_____

_____

_____

9.   How long after Jesus was raised from the dead did He ascend into heaven?
   a.   ____ 10 days
   b.   ____ 14 days
   c.   ____ 30 days
   d.   ____ 40 days

10.   Who watched Jesus ascend into heaven?
   a.   ____ Everyone
   b.   ____ No one
   c.   ____ The disciples
   d.   ____ His family

11.   According to John 14:2–3, why did Jesus ascend into heaven? _____

_____

12.   True / False – Jesus sat at the right hand of God and is no longer on the earth.

   Why or why not?_____

_____

_____

13.   Because Jesus is at the right hand of God, He has _____ and _____ over the Kingdoms of Power, Grace, and Glory.
   a.   ____ Authority, power
   b.   ____ Strength, wisdom
   c.   ____ Dominion, strength

14.   Will Jesus come again?
   a.   ____ Yes
   b.   ____ No

   If He will come again, when will it be?_____

15.   How should we live then? (Read Matthew 24:42–51)
   a.   ____ Doing whatever we want as quickly as possible.
   b.   ____ Live in poverty with no pleasures in life.
   c.   ____ Prepare for the second coming by having faith and living a life of faith.

16.   Match the following Bible passages to the description of Jesus' second coming:

Bible Passage	Description
a. Mark 13:32	____ Christ will come visibly
b. Titus 2:13	____ Christ will Judge the world and not establish a new earthly kingdom
c. Luke 21:27	____ It will be on a specific day that we do not know
d. 2 Peter 3:10–13	____ Before He comes turmoil on the earth will increase
e. Matthew 25:31–32	____ Christ's return should be met with hope and joy by every Christian
f. Matthew 24:4–14	____ This world will be destroyed, and a new heaven and earth will be made

17.   True / False – Millennialists teach that Jesus will establish an earthly reign for 1000 years.

18. Read John 6:10–15. How does the Millennialist view compare with the people of that passage and what was Jesus' response? _____

_____

Also read 2 Peter 3:10–13. When Jesus comes the second time what will happen to the world?_____

_____

How do those two passages compare with the idea of an earthly reign and Millennialism?_____

_____

_____

19. Some people teach that Jesus has already come. Based on what you have learned and Revelation 1:7, is that true? Why or why not? _____

_____

_____

_____

Lesson 26: Salvation (The Son of God's Work of Redemption)

> **Memorization:** Luther's explanation of the Second Article –
> *I believe that Jesus Christ, True God, begotten of the Father from eternity, and also true man, born of the Virgin Mary, is my Lord, who has redeemed me, a lost and condemned person, purchased and won me from all sins, from death, and the power of the devil; not with gold or silver, but with His holy precious blood and with His innocent suffering and death.*

Use what you have learned in Parts A–D of this Lesson.

Catechism Material: Questions 126 (p. 130), 133–140 (pp. 134–137), and 150 (pp. 145–146)

1. The Son of God has two natures. What are they?
    a. _____
    b. _____

2. Why must He be True Man in order to save us? (Mark all that apply.)
    a. ____ So that He could know our suffering
    b. ____ So that He could be born under the law
    c. ____ So that He could die
    d. ____ So that He could reign on earth

3. Why must He be True God in order to save us? (Mark all that apply.)
    a. ____ So that He could keep the Law perfectly
    b. ____ So that He could defy God the Father's judgment against us
    c. ____ So that He could overcome death and the Devil
    d. ____ So that He could save everyone and not just Himself

Jesus is the sacrificial lamb for us (Catechism p. 280).

4. Christ's work of redemption required two distinct states. What were those two states?

    a. _____

    b. _____

5. Why did the Son of God need to enter into a State of Humility to save us? (Mark all that apply.)

    a. ____ So that He was under the Law

    b. ____ So that He did not fight back when He was falsely tried and executed

    c. ____ So that He did fulfill all the Scriptures

    d. ____ So that He did take on all our sins

6. Why did the Son of God need to enter into a State of Exaltation to save us (Mark all that apply.)

    a. ____ To proclaim His triumph

    b. ____ To rise from the dead

    c. ____ To intercede for us continually

    d. ____ To rule everything

7. If the Son of God had not been True Man and True God, could He have saved us? Why or why not?

_____

_____

_____

8. If the Son of God had not entered into a State of Humiliation and then into a State of Exaltation, could He have saved us? Why or Why not? _____

_____

_____

9. Who exactly did Jesus die for?

    a. ____ Everyone past, present, and future

    b. ____ The Angels

    c. ____ Those who are good enough

    d. ____ Believers

Give a Bible passage that supports your answer. _____

10. Is there a restriction then based on race, age, or sin that restricts who can be saved? Why or why not?

_____

_____

_____

11. True / False – Jesus only died for those who believe in Him.

Why or why not? (Support your answer with a Bible passage.) _____

_____

_____

12. From what three things has Jesus redeemed, that is saved, you, me, and everyone from?

    a. _____

    b. _____

    c. _____

13. Read 2 Thessalonians 1:3–9. If Jesus had not died for you, or if you do not believe and trust in His salvation, what will happen to you when you die?_____
_____

14. Since Jesus redeemed us from death, how is it that we still die?
   a. ____ Only those who truly believe will live forever in this world.
   b. ____ Jesus saved us from spiritual death in Hell and will raise our bodies up on the last day to save them from eternal physical death.

15. What did Jesus redeem you with? _____
_____

16. Jesus did this because...
   a. ____ He was forced to
   b. ____ He wanted to show how great He was
   c. ____ Of His love, and it was voluntarily done for our sakes
   d. ____ He was angry

17. Read John 3:18. Since Jesus has died for all and paid for all sins, will everyone be saved? Who will be saved?
_____
_____

18. How did Jesus save us from our sins? Fill in the blanks:

| Conceived | True God | Third | Perfectly | Conquered | True Man |
| Crucified | Right Hand | Law | Born | Whole World | |

Jesus is both _____ and _____. That happened because He was _____ by the Holy Spirit and _____ of the Virgin Mary. Because He had both attributes, he was able to be under the _____ and keep it _____. These attributes also allowed Him to be able to bear not just the sins of one person, but for the _____. In order to pay the price of every sin, He humbled Himself to be _____ on a cross. He showed that He _____ death and the devil by being resurrected on the _____ day. He now sits on the _____ of God in power and glory.

LESSON 27: FAITH, AND THE PERSONS OF THE TRINITY – GOD THE HOLY SPIRIT

> **Memorization:**
> Luther's Explanation of the Third Article – *I believe that I cannot by my own reason or strength believe in Jesus Christ, my Lord, or come to Him; But the Holy Spirit has called me by the Gospel, enlightened me with His gifts, sanctified and kept me in the true faith.*
>
> *And*
>
> 1 Corinthians 12:3b – *No one can say that Jesus is Lord, except by the Holy Spirit.*

Means of Grace:

The *Means of Grace* can rightly be understood as: the way God creates or strengthens faith and gives salvation to the people of the world. As you will soon learn, Holy Baptism and Holy Communion give us the forgiveness of sins, and they create or strengthen faith. There is one more thing that is a Means of Grace as well. It is the Word of God. It is through these means that the Holy Spirit works to create faith.

"Born Again":

Question 160 talks about *"regeneration"* and *"conversion."* That can also refer to being *"born again,"* but Lutherans often use the other terms to avoid confusion. The term "born again" is used in different ways throughout the different denominations of Christendom. The way "born again" is commonly used outside of the Lutheran Church refers to an act by a person so that they accept Jesus as their Savior. If someone asks you if you were "born again," that is what they are asking you.

When a person is "born again," according to them, the Holy Spirit comes to an individual and prompts them to make a choice to accept or reject Jesus as their Savior. That is different than what is taught by Lutherans. Lutherans believe that we are "born again" by the Holy Spirit's work alone, and because of His work we can reject Jesus as our Savior or because of the Holy Spirit and the faith created in us we remain in Jesus. In other words, others teach that human intervention is needed for a person to be saved. Lutheran teaching is that only the Holy Spirit and the work of God saves us and creates faith in us with no action on our part required to make that happen.

An illustration of the difference is this: Some non-Lutherans believe that Jesus comes to the door and knocks. At this point, a person has the responsibility and ability to either open the door (accept) or to keep the door shut (reject) Jesus as their Savior. Lutherans believe that a person is dead and Jesus comes along and makes them alive. A dead person has no ability to say, do, or hear and respond to anything or anyone. Therefore, the work is God's alone to make a person alive. Once a person is alive, they can reject the work of God and commit spiritual suicide (reject) or they can remain alive. Even this act of remaining alive is not their choice because God sustains them. Another way that a person can reject God is by resisting the Holy Spirit. This is like when a person covers their ears and saying "La, la, la, la, la…" to prevent them from hearing the truth.

Catechism Material: Questions 154–168 (pp. 148–157)

1. What are the four reasons why we know the Holy Spirit is God?

   a. _____

   b. _____

   c. _____

   d. _____

2. Match the Holy Spirits *divine attributes* or works to the appropriate Bible passage:

Bible Passage	Divine attribute/work
a. Titus 3:5	____ Omnipresence
b. Hebrews 9:14	____ Omniscience
c. Psalm 139:7–10	____ From Eternity
d. Job 33:4	____ Holy
e. Isaiah 63:10	____ Creation
f. 1 Corinthians 2:10	____ Sanctification

3. The word *sanctification* is used in two ways, the wide and narrow sense. Match the correct definition to the correct sense.

                Term   Definition

    a. Sanctification (Wide)   ____ The whole work of the Holy Spirit (bringing us to faith and enabling us to lead a godly life)

    b. Sanctification (Narrow)   ____ The Holy Spirit directing and empowering a believer to lead a godly life.

4. What is the difference between the two ways the word sanctification is used? _____

   _____

   _____

5. The Bible gives many attributes to those who are sinners and lost. Those attributes include being spiritually illiterate (Isaiah 29:12), spiritually deaf (Isaiah 29:18), spiritually blind (Matthew 23:26), spiritually dead (Ephesians 2:1), and actually an enemy of God (Romans 8:7). Pick two of those attributes, and including spiritually dead, explain why each attribute you picked makes it impossible for you to believe in Jesus or come to Him.

    a. _____

       _____

    b. _____

       _____

    c. Spiritually Dead: _____

       _____

6. Based on what you learned, can you take credit for coming to faith? Why or why not? _____

   _____

   _____

7. Based on what you learned, can you take credit for all the good things you do or for following/doing what God wants and expects you to do? Why or why not? _____

   _____

   _____

8. How does the Holy Spirit bring us to faith?

    a. ____ By performing miracles

    b. ____ By calling us by the Gospel

    c. ____ By striking people with lightening

    d. ____ By forcing them

9. True / False – When The Holy Spirit enlightens someone with His gifts, it means they will be able to and will speak in tongues. Why or why not? _____

   _____

   _____

10. What does it mean that the Holy Spirit has "enlightened me with His gifts"? _____

   _____

   _____

11. What is a "Means of Grace"? _____

_____

12. What three things are a "Means of Grace"?

    a. _____

    b. _____

    c. _____

13. What actions do you take when the Holy Spirit regenerates or converts you?

    a. ____ I accept Jesus

    b. ____ I reject Jesus

    c. ____ I read the Bible

    d. ____ I do nothing; it is solely the work of the Holy Spirit

14. If you have been converted, what must you do because the Holy Spirit prompts you?

    a. ____ Go to church

    b. ____ Live a new life, striving to overcome sin and do good works

    c. ____ Accept Jesus

    d. ____ Do nothing

15. What four things does the Holy Spirit change in you so that you lead this new life?

    a. _____

    b. _____

    c. _____

    d. _____

16. What are good works? (Mark all that apply.)

    a. ____ Following the Ten Commandments

    b. ____ Being nice to all people

    c. ____ Things that are done for the glory of God

    d. ____ Doing something for the benefit of our neighbor

17. Can you do good works in God's sight without being a Christian? Why or why not? _____

_____

_____

18. When a person is converted, how do they stay in the Christian faith?

    a. ____ Once they are converted they cannot go back

    b. ____ They do many good and gracious works

    c. ____ The Holy Spirit keeps them in the faith

    d. ____ No one knows how

19. True / False – The Holy Spirit wants all people to be converted and saved.

20. Why are some people not converted and saved? _____

_____

_____

21. Who is responsible for a person being saved?
    a. _____ That individual
    b. _____ Me
    c. _____ God
    d. _____ No one

22. Who is responsible for a person being condemned?
    a. _____ That individual
    b. _____ Me
    c. _____ God
    d. _____ No one

SECTION 4: REVIEW

Part 1: The Holy Trinity (An Overview)

1. God is made up of three persons. What are the names of those three persons?

    a. _____

    b. _____

    c. _____

2. True / False – Because God is made up of three persons, Christians believe in three Gods.

3. What does the term "Holy Trinity" mean? _____

    _____

4. What are divine attributes?_____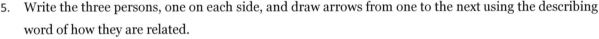

    _____

    Name 3 of them:

    a. _____

    b. _____

    c. _____

5. Write the three persons, one on each side, and draw arrows from one to the next using the describing word of how they are related.

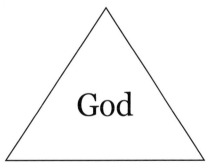

Part 2: God the Father – His Work and His Creations

6. What is God the Father's special work? _____

7. God the Father is called "the Father" because He is the Father of the following three things. In what way (i.e., how) is He the Father of each of them?

    a. God the Son: _____

    b. The whole human race: _____

    c. Christians: _____

8. What is the difference between how God is the Father of the whole human race and Christians?

    _____

    _____

9. How many days did it take for God to create the world and everything in it?

    a. ____ 4

    b. ____ 5

    c. ____ 6

    d. ____ 7

10. For each day write out what God created/did:

    1: _____

    2: _____

    3: _____

    4: _____

    5: _____

    6: _____

    7: _____

11. What is the foremost visible creature God created? _____

12. What is the foremost invisible creature God created? _____

13. The term "complete creation" means that something is both fully _____ and fully _____.
    What does the term "complete creation" mean? _____

    _____

14. What does the term "Theistic Evolution" mean? _____

    _____

15. True / False – Theistic evolution agrees with the Bible. Why or why not? _____

    _____

    _____

16. When God created man (i.e., the human race), He created them in His own image. What does that mean?

    a. ____ They were perfect

    b. ____ They had divine powers

    c. ____ They commanded the Angels

17. What are the two genders that God created?

    a. _____

    b. _____

18. Does God still create each human being?

      a.   ____ Yes

      b.   ____ No

19. Does God still care for each human being?

      a.   ____ Yes

      b.   ____ No

20. Who brought sin into this world?_____

21. What does it mean to be a good steward of the earth? _____

_____

22. Should we pray to Angels for anything? Why or why not?_____

_____

23. Can the Angels who rebelled be saved? Why or why not?_____

_____

24. Who is the leader of the evil Angels?_____

Part 3: God the Son – His Work and His States

25. What is God the Son's special work? _____

26. How did God the Son accomplish His special work?_____

_____

27. Who did He accomplish the special work for?_____

28. What are the two natures of God the Son and how did He obtain them?

      a. _____ , _____

           _____

      b. _____ , _____

           _____

29. In the Gospel of John, the writer refers to a being known as "the Word"; who is "the Word"? _____

30. Who is Jesus?

      a.   ____ Only a man

      b.   ____ Only a great prophet

      c.   ____ The Son of God

31. What is the name of Jesus' mother?_____

32. What is the name of Jesus' Father?_____

33. What unique attribute did Jesus' mother have and how did it prevent normal child conception?

_____

_____

34. How then did Jesus' mother become pregnant with Him?_____

_____

35. What thing could the Son of God accomplish by becoming human?
    a. ____ He could get married
    b. ____ He could be under the Law in our place
    c. ____ He could feel the things we do
    d. ____ We could see Him

36. What is the importance and effect of Jesus having divine attributes?_____
    _____

    Name 2 divine attributes of Jesus:
    a. _____
    b. _____

37. Jesus holds the "Threefold Office of Christ," and in one of those offices, Jesus is a ruler. What are the names of the three kingdoms He rules over and who are their residents/citizens?
    a. _____ , _____
    b. _____ , _____
    c. _____ , _____

38. Name each of the offices of the "Threefold Office of Christ" and then state how Jesus did, does, and/or will fulfill each of them:
    a. _____ , _____
    _____
    b. _____ , _____
    _____
    c. _____ , _____
    _____

39. Jesus had/has two states, what are those two states?
    a. _____ (During Jesus' time on earth before He descended into Hell)
    b. _____ (After Jesus' descent into Hell)

40. Which state is He currently in? _____

41. Why did Jesus endure the first state, and what did He accomplish by enduring it?_____
    _____
    _____

42. Who put Jesus into that first state?_____

43. Where is Jesus now? (Mark all that apply.)
    a. ____ In Heaven
    b. ____ On Earth
    c. ____ In Hell
    d. ____ At the right hand of God
    e. ____ Right next to you

44. Jesus tells us He will come again.

    a.   How will He come again?_____

    b.   Why will He come again?_____

    c.   When will He come again?_____

    d.   What is Millennialism?_____

    e.   Is Millennialism consistent with Scripture? Why or Why not?_____

        _____

        _____

Part 4: God the Holy Spirit – His Work and Our Faith

45. What is the special work of the Holy Spirit? _____

    a.   How is that work described in the "wide" sense?_____

        _____

    b.   How is that work described in the "narrow" sense?_____

        _____

    c.   What is the difference?_____

        _____

46. True / False – We come to faith and then the Holy Spirit comes to us.

47. Can we take credit for coming to faith? Why or why not? _____

    _____

    _____

48. The Holy Spirit uses the "Means of Grace." What are the three "Means of Grace"?

    a.   _____

    b.   _____

    c.   _____

49. What does the term "Means of Grace" mean?_____

    _____

50. Can we take credit for the good works that we do? Why or why not?_____

    _____

    _____

51. Can an unbeliever do good works in the sight of God? Why or why not?_____

    _____

52. Who is responsible for a person being saved?_____

53. Who is responsible for a person being condemned?_____

SECTION 5 – THE TEN COMMANDMENTS

At the back of the book is Appendix I. It lists out the "Do's and Don'ts" of the Ten Commandments. These are all of the ways that you keep and break each of those commandments. Review them and use it as a reference as you go through this section.

LESSON 28: AN INTRODUCTION TO THE COMMANDMENTS

> **Memorization:** Matthew 22:36–40 –
> *"Teacher, which is the great commandment in the law?" Jesus said to him, "You shall love the Lord your God with all your heart, with all your soul, and with all your mind.' This is the first and great commandment. And the second is like it: 'You shall love your neighbor as yourself' On these two commandments hang all the Law and the Prophets."*

Catechism Material: Questions 13–18 (pp. 54–55), 24 (p. 61), 46–47 (p. 73), and 72 (p. 95)

1. How many commandments are there?
    a. ____ 5
    b. ____ 7
    c. ____ 10
    d. ____ 12

2. Who is our neighbor?
    a. ____ Our friends
    b. ____ Everyone
    c. ____ Our family
    d. ____ Only the people we like
    e. ____ Those with power or money

3. The first three commandments are in regard to our relationship with:
    a. ____ Our Neighbor
    b. ____ God
    What Bible passage summarizes the first three commandments?_____

4. The last seven commandments are in regard to our relationship with:
    a. ____ Our Neighbor
    b. ____ God
    What Bible passage summarizes the last seven commandments?_____

5. What is the fulfillment of the Law?
    a. ____ Kindness
    b. ____ Friendship
    c. ____ Empathy
    d. ____ Love
    What Bible Passage tells us the fulfillment of the law? _____

6. What does it mean to love our neighbor?
    a. ____ To be nice to them
    b. ____ To care for them
    c. ____ To not ignore them
    d. ____ To treat them as we would like to be treated

    Which passages tells us what it means to love our neighbor? _____

7. Who are the Ten Commandments for?
    a. ____ Christians
    b. ____ Unbelievers
    c. ____ Everyone including me

8. Each explanation of the commandment begins with "We should fear and love" God.

    a. Read Hebrews 10:28–31. From that passage should you fear (i.e., be terrified of) God if you do not
        keep his commandments? Why or why not?_____

        _____

        _____

    b. Read Proverbs 3:12. From that passage, God is compared to us as a loving Father. Why should
        we fear (i.e., respect) God in regard to His commandments?_____

        _____

        _____

        _____

    c. Read 1 Corinthians 13:1–3. From that passage, if I kept the commandments of God without Love,
        would I have truly kept the commandments? Why or why not? _____

        _____

        _____

        _____

LESSON 29: THE FIRST COMMANDMENT

> **Memorization:** Luther's explanation of the First Commandment –
> *You shall have no other gods.*
> *What does this mean? We should fear, love, and trust in God above all things.*

Catechism Material: Questions 19–22 (pp. 56–60)

9. One of God's attributes is that He is *Triune* (i.e., He is the Holy
    Trinity). This means that there are three distinct persons in one
    divine being. What are the names of the three distinct persons?

    a. _____

    b. _____

    c. _____

God is the "Alpha" (beginning) and the
"Omega" (end) (Catechism p. 275).

10. This is the only commandment where the explanation includes "trust" as well as to fear and love God. Read Psalm 91 and give examples of how we should trust in God:

   a. _____

   b. _____

   c. _____

11. Continuing in Psalm 91, what does God promise to do for those who trust in Him? _____

   _____

   _____

12. What does the first commandment forbid? _____

13. What are the four ways a person can have another God?

   a. _____

   _____

   b. _____

   _____

   c. _____

   _____

   d. _____

   _____

14. Match the passage to what it is an example of:

   a. Acts 15:18–20   ____ Believe in a god that is not God

   b. Psalm 52:7   ____ Join in worship of another god

   c. Acts 19:23–28   ____ Worship the Triune God only

   d. Deuteronomy 6:4   ____ Trust in something other than God

15. What are the three ways that we keep the first commandment?

   a. _____

   _____

   b. _____

   _____

   c. _____

   _____

16. Give two examples of how you could break the first commandment:

   a. _____

   b. _____

17. Give two examples of how you can keep the first commandment:

   a. _____

   b. _____

LESSON 30: THE SECOND COMMANDMENT

> **Memorization:** Luther's explanation to the Second Commandment –
> *You shall not misuse the name of the Lord your God.*
> *What does this mean?*
> *We should fear and love God so that we do not curse, swear, use satanic arts, lie, or deceive by*
> *His name, but call upon it in every trouble, pray, praise, and give thanks.*

"What is God's name? A: Every name by which God has made Himself known, such as God, Lord, Almighty, Jesus Christ, Holy Ghost." (Jer. 23:6, 32:18, Matt. 1:21, Ex. 3:13–14, Deut. 28:58, Is. 43:15, 44:6, 47:4) "B: Every statement in which God tells us about Himself."[20] (Ex. 20:24)

Catechism Material: Questions 25–34 (pp. 61–67)

1. God has given Himself many names. Give three examples of God's name and the Bible passage where He gives it:

    a. _____ , _____

    b. _____ , _____

    c. _____ , _____

2. There are five different ways God's name can be misused. Name them and then match them to a definition of what it means to do it:

    Term

    a. _____ or
    _____

    b. _____

    c. _____

    d. _____

    e. _____ or
    _____

    Definition

    ____ Speaking evil of God or mocking Him or using His name to call down punishment on us or others

    ____ Taking an oath using God as a witness

    ____ Using God's name to teach false doctrine by saying it is His Word or revelation or pretending to be a Christian

    ____ Using God's name without thought

    ____ Using God's name to perform or pretend to perform supernatural things with the help of the devil.

3. When is swearing using God's name permitted?
    a. ____ To bring glory to God
    b. ____ When we want to
    c. ____ For the welfare of our neighbor
    d. ____ Both a and c

4. When you curse someone or something what are you doing?
    a. ____ Wanting it or them to do well
    b. ____ Wishing and asking for it or them to have evil happen to them
    c. ____ Praying for its or their protection

5. What does it mean to *blaspheme*?

    a. ____ To mock God, His name, or His Word

    b. ____ Be thankful to God

    c. ____ Make fun of someone

    d. ____ Lie about something

6. Now that you have defined the five ways God's name can be misused, give two examples on how you could misuse His name for each:

    a. 1 _____

        2 _____

    b. 1 _____

        2 _____

    c. 1 _____

        2 _____

    d. 1 _____

        2 _____

    e. 1 _____

        2 _____

7. There are four ways we keep this commandment. Name and match them to their definition.

Term	Definition
a. _____	____ Talking to God with our voice, our heart, and our soul
b. _____	____ Recognizing all the things God does for us
c. _____	____ Asking God for help when we need it
d. _____	____ Singing and honoring God in our hearts, our minds, and with our voice

Now that you have defined the four ways to keep the second commandment, give two examples on how you could keep the second commandment for each:

    a. 1 _____

        2 _____

    b. 1 _____

        2 _____

    c. 1 _____

        2 _____

    d. 1 _____

        2 _____

8. God tells us that He will deliver us in the day of trouble. Read 2 Corinthians 12:7–10. Did God take away the physical problem that bothered Paul? If not, how did God deliver Paul from His trouble?_____

_____

_____

_____

9. What kind of troubles should you pray to God about? _____

    _____

    _____

10. Read 1 Thessalonians 5:16–18. How often should we give thanks?

    a. ____ Sometimes

    b. ____ Once a day

    c. ____ A couple times a week

    d. ____ Only during worship

    e. ____ Always and in everything

11. According to 1 Thessalonians 5:16–18, how often should we pray?

    a. ____ Sometimes

    b. ____ Once a day

    c. ____ A couple times a week

    d. ____ Only during worship

    e. ____ Always, without ceasing

12. Read Psalm 3:1–6 and Matthew 6:25–34. Why is it that we should pray, praise, give thanks, and call upon

    God in trouble as often as we do?_____

    _____

    _____

    _____

13. Read Matthew 6:5–7 and Luke 11:9–13 and answer the following questions:

    a. God tells us in these passages that He is our Heavenly Father. What does that mean about how

        and what we should pray?_____

        _____

        _____

    b. How should we pray?_____

        _____

        _____

    c. Should we trust God to give us what we need when we pray to Him? Why or Why not?

        _____

        _____

        _____

        _____

LESSON 31: THE THIRD COMMANDMENT

> **Memorization:** Luther's Explanation of the Third Commandment –
> *Remember the Sabbath day by keeping it holy.*
> *What does this mean?*
> *We should fear and love God so that we do not despise preaching and His Word, but hold it*
> *sacred and gladly hear and learn it.*

Ceremonial Law versus Moral Law of Sabbaths:

It is important to distinguish the Third Commandment Moral Law from the Ceremonial Law. Remember the Ceremonial Law is in regard to the feasts, sacrifices, and religious practices of the time. The Sabbath day religious practice is defined in Leviticus 23 along with many other religious practices. It defines that there shall be no work on the Sabbath day (Leviticus 23:3). If this portion is part of the Ceremonial Law, and not the Moral Law, we should expect to find Jesus fulfilling the Ceremonial Law of Sabbaths and showing what it really points to. In fact, we do in Hebrews 4, which will be discussed in the next portion.

Sabbath **Rest:**

Physical Rest: Rest that occurs when we stop working; rest from physical labors.

Spiritual Rest: Rest which is found in God's Word which gives us comfort during times of distress and stress, the assurance of forgiveness and salvation, and the promise of the true rest to come.

True Rest: The ultimate rest which is found when we enter into Heaven and no longer have to strive against sin, the world, or the devil.

The religious leaders at the time of Jesus combined the Moral Law and the Ceremonial Law of the Third Commandment into an outward commitment to physical rest. They set up many rules and regulations about rest including how far one could go from their house or what they could do on the Sabbath day (Matthew 12:1–14). In that way, they could outwardly appear pious and holy. However, this outward keeping of the Law was not the original intent of the Third Commandment. Rather the intent of the Third Commandment (in particular the Ceremonial Law of it) was and is to point to the ultimate rest we would find in Christ. It is Christ who will give us the true rest when we get to heaven (Hebrews 4).

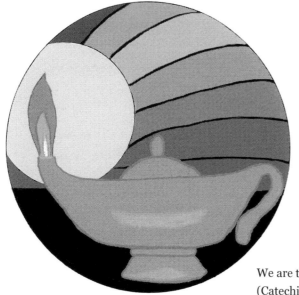

The question then becomes how does one find that true rest? It is through the knowledge of Christ which is found in the Word of God. Worship on one day or another is an important part of this Commandment because it is there that we receive the Word of God and Sacrament. However, attending a worship service once a week does not exempt a person from independent study and devotion throughout the week (Joshua 1:8). We equally despise the Sabbath day by making it only a religious weekly obligation rather than a frequent search for knowledge and rest in God's word. In other words, the moral implication of this commandment is that we must diligently seek the true rest through God's Word and Worship.

We are the light and that light comes from the light of God's Word (Catechism p. 280).

What about physical rest? In the passage of Exodus where the law is given (Exodus 20:8–11), there is a mention of both honoring the Sabbath to keep it holy AND physical rest. So while the commandment is ultimately about the true rest, which in fact is the physical and spiritual rest we receive through Christ, this commandment also tells us how to rest on this earth. Part of that rest includes a personal physical rest from labors. Just as God rested from His labors on the seventh day of creation, we too should find time to rest from our labors. Not as an outward religious rest to be paraded around among the masses. Rather a personal physical rest to allow a person to focus on Christ and renew us for the coming days. In this way, the commandment, through God's instruction in Exodus 20:9–11, also uniquely cares for us physically as well. "The Sabbath was made for man, and not man for the Sabbath" (Mark 2:27).

Spreading the Word of God:
Part of keeping the Third Commandment is the requirement that "we should diligently spread the Word of God." As a Pastor that concept can be easily understood, they get up and preach the Word and reach out to the community and those in the church with it. But as individual Christians and even children, how does one accomplish such a task? As an individual Christian or younger person, you may feel as though you do not readily know or understand the Word of God. How can you preach and teach others, if you do not know the Word of God? This is where an important distinction between the sheep of the flock and the shepherds of the flock must be made. The sheep are not shepherds and will not be held accountable as such. Moreover, the shepherds are not sheep and will not be held accountable as such (James 3:1). Rather God has established the office of the Shepherds, and today they are known as Pastors to teach and preach (Jeremiah 3:15).

So what about the sheep? What should the individual Christians young and old, new and veteran do? They are responsible for being the "light" and the "salt" of the earth (Matthew 5:13–16). They are also responsible to "always be ready to give a defense to everyone who asks you a reason for the hope that is in you" (1 Peter 3:15). However, how can you live such a life if you do not know or understand the Ten Commandments? How can you give an answer if you have not studied or been taught? That is why you must study (independent study) and be taught to know (through worship and Pastoral direction) the Word of God and so keep the Sabbath day Holy.

Catechism Material: Questions 35–40 (pp. 67–72)

1. In the Old Testament what day was the Sabbath day?
   a. ____ Friday
   b. ____ Saturday
   c. ____ Sunday
   d. ____ Monday

2. The Sabbath being on that particular day in the Old Testament was a part of the Ceremonial Law (Leviticus 23:1–3). If the specific day was a part of the Ceremonial Law, would you expect it to be required of us to observe the Sabbath on that day? Why or why not? _____

   _____

   _____

   _____

3. Observing a Sabbath day is a part of the Moral Law. That being said, would you expect it to still be required of us to observe a Sabbath day? Why or Why not? _____

_____

_____

4. Why does the church usually worship on Sundays? _____

_____

5. True / False – God still requires us to worship together.

6. We break the Third Commandment by despising the preaching of God's Word. In what three ways can we break the Third Commandment? Give an example of each.

a. _____ , _____

_____

b. _____ , _____

_____

c. _____ , _____

_____

7. According to the Catechism (Question 40 pp. 70–72), there are seven ways we keep the Third Commandment. Below is that list. Give an example for each one on how to keep them.

a. Hold the preaching of the Word Sacred: _____

_____

b. Gladly hear the Word: _____

_____

c. Gladly learn the Word: _____

_____

d. Gladly meditate on the Word: _____

_____

e. Honor the teaching and preaching of the Word: _____

_____

f. Support the teaching and preaching of the Word: _____

_____

g. Diligently spread the Word of God: _____

_____

8. According to Matthew 5:13–16 and 1 Peter 3:13–17, how do individual Christians spread the Word of God?

_____

_____

_____

9. What was the purpose of the Sabbath day in the Old Testament?

a. _____ Rest

b. _____ Worship

c. _____ Both a and b

10. What is the purpose of the Sabbath day today?
    a. ____ Rest
    b. ____ Worship
    c. ____ Both a and b

11. If going to church becomes simply a ritual habit (i.e., something we just do because you always go to church on a particular day at a particular time), are you really keeping the Third Commandment? Why or why not?

_____

_____

_____

_____

12. If we only go to church and do not study or have devotions in the Bible outside of the worship on a particular day, have we kept the Third Commandment? Why or why not? _____

_____

_____

_____

Lesson 32: The Fourth Commandment

> **Memorization:** Luther's explanation of the Fourth Commandment –
> *Honor your father and your mother.*
> *What does this mean?*
> *We should fear and love God so that we do not despise or anger our parents and other authorities, but honor them, serve and obey them, love and cherish them.*

Why does God add the promise "that it may be well with you and that you may live long on the earth" (Eph. 6:3)? By this promise God <u>impresses upon us the importance and benefit</u> of honoring our parents and superiors and urges us to obey this Commandment willingly.[21]

This Commandment is not set in isolation from the others, and in fact, is married to the others. Acts 5:29 states, "We ought to obey God rather than men." At first, this may be in direct contradiction to the Fourth Commandment because the apostles were not doing what the leaders of the time asked. However, as we learned in the introduction to the Commandments, we must love our neighbors as ourselves. Those in authority are also our neighbor. Therefore, if we do what goes against God to "honor" or obey those in authority, we do not love them. Loving them includes being a "Light to the world" and being the "Salt of the earth" (as you learned in the last lesson). In this case, it means

The Fourth Commandment refers to all those in authority, not just parents.

showing them how God has taught us to live and doing it in humbleness and love. Furthermore, we must in all ways try to do what they have asked or as much as we can without breaking the other commandments. To do it in this way is indeed an act of love and not of defiance. (In no way is this liberty or freedom to disobey those in authority.)

21   Question 35 from "A Short Explanation of Dr. Martin Luther's Small Catechism" Concordia Publishing House, 1943 (scripture from KJV substituted with NKJV)

Why do we and should we honor, obey, and love our parents, the government, and all those in authority?

The Fourth Commandment does not give a requirement for our parents to earn our love, respect, or honor. It does not also give a requirement that we must agree with or respect them before we obey them. Likewise, the government is not required to be godly and agree with our opinions for us to graciously allow them to enforce the law. Rather the Fourth Commandment simply states "do this because I the Lord your God have commanded it." As Luther writes in his large catechism:

> Young people must therefore be taught to revere their parents as God's representatives, and to remember that, however lowly, poor, feeble, and eccentric they may be, they are their own father and mother, given them by God. They are not to be deprived of their honor because of their ways or their failings. Therefore, we are not to think of their persons, whatever they are, but of the will of God, who has created and ordained them to be our parents. ...

> You are to esteem and prize them as the most precious treasure on earth. In your words you are to behave respectfully toward them, and not address them discourteously, critically, and censoriously, but submit to them and hold your tongue even if they go too far. You are also to honor them by your actions (that is, with your body and possessions), serving them, helping them, and caring for them when they are old, sick, feeble, or poor; all this you should do not only cheerfully, but with humility and reverence, as in God's sight. ...

> The same may be said of obedience to the civil government, which as we have said, is to be classed with the estate of fatherhood, the most comprehensive of all relations. In this case a man is father of not of a single family, but of as many people as he has inhabitants, citizens, or subjects. Through civil rulers, as through our own parents, God gives us food, house and home, protection and security. Therefore since they bear this name and title with all honor as their chief glory, it is our duty to honor and magnify them as the most precious treasure and jewel on earth.[22]

Catechism Material: Questions 48–51 (pp. 74–76)

1. The Fourth Commandment is not just about our Mother and Father, but about all those who are in authority. Give examples of authorities in the following categories:

Family	School	Government	Work	Church

2. Name four people who have authority over you besides God:

   a. _____

   b. _____

   c. _____

   d. _____

---

22   Luther's Large Catechism on the Fourth Commandment taken from the Book of Concord

3. In what two ways can we despise our parents or those who are in authority?

    a. _____

    b. _____

4. What are the five ways that we keep the Fourth Commandment?

    a. _____

    b. _____

    c. _____

    d. _____

    e. _____

5. In regard to the following examples, how was the child's parent (authority figure) dishonored, honored, or both?

    a. Mom tells the child to go clean his room and they say they will, but then never does. _____

    _____

    _____

    _____

    b. Mom tells the child to do their homework and they say they will and they do. _____

    _____

    _____

    _____

    c. Dad tells the child to do the dishes. However, the child refuses to respond and does not do it.

    _____

    _____

    _____

    d. Dad tells the child to stop playing video games and they refuse, but then they stop. _____

    _____

    _____

    _____

6. Of the four scenarios in the previous question, how should you respond to your parents or anyone in authority?

    _____

    _____

    _____

7. Who are our parents and those in authority representative of?

    a. ____ The rule of law

    b. ____ Love

    c. ____ God

8. Considering your answer to the previous question, why is it important to honor and respect those in authority?

    _____

    _____

9. True / False – It is okay to use bad language against our parents.

10. True / False – We should not get mad with an authority figure if we do not get what we want.

11. What should our attitude towards those in authority be when they ask us to do something?

    a. _____ Gladly do it

    b. _____ Do it out of obligation

    c. _____ Resentment

12. Read Matthew 5:41. The word "compel" means that the order came from an authority. Based on that verse, if someone in authority (or even if they are not) asks you to do something that is not sinful, how should you do it?

    a. _____ Refuse

    b. _____ Only do what they ask

    c. _____ Do enough to make them think you did a good job

    d. _____ Go above and beyond what they ask

13. God has given us parents and other authorities as _____?

    a. _____ Obligations

    b. _____ Gifts

14. What do our parents have to do to earn our respect, honor, and love?

    a. _____ Please us

    b. _____ Work hard

    c. _____ Nothing

    d. _____ Love us

15. If our parents or government do something that we do not like or ask us to do something we do not like, how should we respond? _____

    _____

16. If our parents or anyone in authority treats us badly, how should we respond and treat them? _____

    _____

17. Read Leviticus 19:32. How should you treat the aged (or your elders)? _____

    _____

18. For the following examples state if the authority is asking you to go against God's Law. Then explain how they are or are not. Finally state what you should do in that situation.

    a. Your parents are neglecting to take you to church on a regular (e.g., weekly) basis. _____

       _____

       _____

       _____

    b. Your pastor tells you that you need to do more good works and give more to the church or you will not get into heaven. _____

       _____

       _____

    c. Your boss tells you to "mislead" or "omit" certain product problems for an item you are selling.

       _____

       _____

       _____

19. Consider the promise attached to this commandment and then consider one of the following: A loving parent corrects their child and asks them to do things; this teaches a child how to live, what to value, and ultimately how to be successful. At work, a boss who wants their business to succeed corrects bad employee behavior and encourages good behavior. The government in order to keep order and peace in its borders creates and enforces laws. Pick one of those statements you agree with and explain why and how this is a fulfillment of the promise God gives for the Fourth Commandment.

_____

_____

_____

_____

SUBSECTION: THE FIFTH COMMANDMENT

Lesson 33: *The Fifth Commandment*

> **Memorization:** Luther's explanation of the Fifth Commandment –
> *You shall not murder.*
> *What does this mean?*
> *We should fear and love God so that we do not hurt or harm our neighbor in his body, but help and support him in every physical need.*

Genocide: Murdering a large group of people due to their race, religion, ethnicity, or political affinity.

Catechism Material: Questions 52–54 (pp. 77–80)

1. What is genocide?_____

_____

2. The Catechism gives four ways to commit actual murder. What are they? Match them with their definitions.

Term	Definition
a. _____	____ Killing someone without the lawful authority to do so
b. _____	____ Killing someone because of their age, mental capacity, health condition, etc.
c. _____	____ Killing the unborn
d. _____	____ Killing oneself

Murder begins in the heart.

3. Abortion is considered murder. Read the following passages and then explain why they show that an unborn baby is a living human child and not just tissue.

a. Luke 1:39–44: _____

_____

_____

(Question 4 continued.)

    b.   Psalm 51:5: _____

_____

_____

    c.   Jeremiah 1:4–5: _____

_____

    d.   Exodus 21:22–25: _____

_____

_____

4.   While abortion in itself is wrong, the catechism gives one exception. What is that exception?
      a.   ____ When it is an unplanned pregnancy
      b.   ____ In instances of rape
      c.   ____ When the life of the mother is in danger
      d.   ____ When the child is not wanted

(The exception given here is because of the sinful world we live in. It is important for both parents to consider their options and talk their options over with a doctor and pray about it.)

5.   Read 1 Corinthians 6:15–20. Based on the fact that, as Christians, our bodies belong to Christ and are the temple of the Holy Spirit, do we have the right to take our own life (i.e., commit suicide)? Why or Why not?

_____

_____

6.   Actually murdering someone is not the only way to break this commandment. How else can we break this commandment?
      a.   ____ Tolerating our neighbor
      b.   ____ Being nice to our neighbor
      c.   ____ Hating our neighbor

Give a passage that supports your answer: _____

7.   Read Acts 17:24–28. God created us so that we should seek Him. When an unbeliever commits suicide, or if someone helps another person commit suicide, what in effect have they done?_____

_____

_____

8.   God gives the authority (and even the responsibility) to those in the government to *kill* people sometimes. It is given as a matter of judgment and it is different than *murder*. Read the following passages and match them to the reasons why they apply to this topic.

Passage	Explanation
a. Genesis 14:14–16	____ God gives the responsibility to punish people to the government, which includes killing them.
b. Exodus 22:2	____ God establishes that soldiers in war are allowed to kill in order to remove evil from the land (i.e., soldiers kill, not murder).
c. Romans 13:4	____ God establishes that if you are defending yourself or your home (while you are in it) against someone, you are not guilty of murder.
d. Deuteronomy 20:16–18	____ God tells us it is okay to use deadly force (kill) to protect the life of your neighbor. (Note: This is the last resort.)

9. Considering what you have just learned, who has the right to kill? (Mark all that apply.)
   a. ____ God
   b. ____ The Government and its representatives acting lawfully
   c. ____ Everyone
   d. ____ A person acting in the defense of theirs or another's life

10. There are three ways in which we keep the Fifth Commandment. Match the appropriate verse to the way we keep the Fifth Commandment.

Verse	How we keep the Fifth Commandment
a. 2 Corinthians 7:1	____ Help and support our neighbor in every bodily need.
b. Romans 12:20	____ Be merciful, kind, and forgiving.
c. Ephesians 4:32	____ We avoid and do not use any drugs or substances that harm the body or mind, and help our neighbor to do the same.

11. *"Bodily need"* refers to anything that is necessary to sustain and protect a person's body (e.g., food). Give a few examples of bodily needs.

   a. _____
   b. _____
   c. _____

Lesson 34: Anger

> **Memorization:** Psalm 4:4 –
> *Be angry, and do not sin. Meditate within your heart on your bed, and be still. Selah*

Anger frequently and easily leads to sin, but to say that to be angry is to sin is overly simplified. God at various times in the Bible was angry. At times, He also acted out of anger. Consider Numbers 11:1: "Now when the people complained, it displeased the LORD; for the LORD heard it, and His anger was aroused. So the fire of the LORD burned among them, and consumed *some* in the outskirts of the camp." Moreover, God tells us to "be angry and do not sin" (Ephesians 4:26). So then, a distinction between types of anger must be established. If all anger was sin, then God would have sinned by being angry, and by telling us to be angry He is telling us to sin.

How was and is God righteous in His anger?

Read Numbers 11:1. God is righteous in His anger because He is perfect and His anger is aroused by sin. (God was angry at the Israelites because they complained against Him; i.e., they did not keep the First or Second Commandments.) God in His anger then executed His judgment against sin through an immediate punishment. (The fire of the LORD burned among them.) So, should sin anger us? Yes, but unlike God, we have no right to execute judgment against whoever sinned against us. Why not? It is because we are all sinful (Romans 3:23) and therefore deserve judgment as well. If our neighbor sins against us, then any judgment we impose on them ought to be imposed on us (Matthew 7:1). Secondly, God tells us that judgment is for Him (Romans 12:9) and His representatives to execute (Romans 13:4).

What is our responsibility towards those who anger us?

Even in anger, we must LOVE our neighbor as ourselves. To love our neighbor as ourselves means that we must forgive them as God forgave us. Furthermore, we must recognize our place in relation to our neighbor. A king, for instance, is responsible for discouraging and ultimately punishing those who wrong one another and even him. If you are not a king or one in authority, then you cannot take on that responsibility. Even as a king, or as one in authority, remember what Jesus said: "For the Son of Man did not come to destroy men's lives, but to save them" (Luke 9:56). As a person in authority, your job is to correct and bring them closer to Christ, not to just hurt or harm them. It is also similar to the individual. Your responsibility is to point out the error in humbleness and love, to bring them closer to Christ.

A path to dealing with anger:

The first step when we get angry is first to identify why we are angry. For example, if we get angry because we did not get our way, then the sin is ours. The sin is ours because we are really mad because of covetousness. However, if we are angry because someone destroyed our property, then anger is not necessarily a sin. This is the hardest step because of our sinful nature which seeks to justify us instead of to find fault in ourselves. The next steps that follow are more based on your ability to control your anger and less based on a specific order. In most instances, however, it is best to distance yourself from both the person and the situation until you can manage your emotions and words. More often than not, it will require you to forgive whoever angered you before you readdress the person. Ultimately, like the parable of the two servants (Matthew 18:21–35), we have no right to demand or inflict retribution against those who do us wrong because God has forgiven us all of our debts. Therefore, if you take "justice" into your own hands with your words or actions, it is sinful. Remember their sin is judged by God, and their crimes are judged by the government/courts, not us. Finally, when and if you are able to, go and tell them their sin in private with the express intent to gain a brother (Matthew 18:15–20), remembering that you too are just as sinful as they are.

1. True / False – Anger in and of itself is a sin.
2. True / False – Even when we are angry, our responsibility is to love our neighbor, which includes the one that angered us.
3. True / False – God has never been angry.
   If God has been angry, how is God righteous in His anger? _____
   _____
4. True / False – It is up to us to exact judgment when someone does something to us or sins against us.
5. Who has the right to impose judgment on someone who did us wrong or made us angry?
   a. ____ Me
   b. ____ God
   c. ____ The proper authorities
   d. ____ b and c
6. If you are an authority and in charge, what is your responsibility when someone does something wrong?
   a. ____ Use my power to get even.
   b. ____ Make sure everyone knows what they did.
   c. ____ Use appropriate consequences to try and achieve a change in behavior.
   d. ____ Ruin their livelihood.

7. Explain what you should do if you get angry with someone: _____

_____

_____

_____

_____

LESSON 35: THE SIXTH COMMANDMENT

> **Memorization:** Luther's explanation of the Sixth Commandment –
> *You shall not commit adultery.*
> *What does this mean?*
> *We should fear and love God so that we lead a sexually pure and decent life in what we
> say and do, and husband and wife love and honor each other.*

In Genesis 1:28, God said to man, that is Adam and Eve, "Be fruitful and multiply, fill the earth and subdue it." This shows that from the very beginning and before Adam and Eve sinned, God intended men and women to have sex. It is through this mechanism that God intended for human beings to fill the earth.

Homosexuality:

The Bible clearly and definitively teaches that homosexuality is a sin (1 Corinthians 6:9). However, homosexuality is placed equally next to stealing, coveting, drunkards, etc. (1 Corinthians 6:10) as far as being a sin and condemning a person to hell. What this means is that we, as Christians, cannot persecute a homosexual for being homosexuals. If we did this, we must persecute ourselves in the same way (Matthew 7:1–3). The important context here is that we are all equally deserving of condemnation, but we are tempted by and commit different sins. If you covet, if you steal, if you commit a sexual sin (such as adultery), if you hate or murder, if you do not keep the Sabbath day or any other sin, you commit an equal sin as being a homosexual. Therefore, love your neighbor as yourself and treat those homosexuals around you as you would treat yourself. This means that you recognize that like you, they need a Savior from their sins. You recognize that, like you, they need to turn from their sins and not do them anymore. You need to recognize that even if they do turn to God they, like you, struggle with their sins to not do them anymore. You need to recognize that, like you, God "desires all men to be saved and come to the knowledge of the truth" (1 Timothy 2:4). Therefore, do not persecute them for their sins, but do not join or encourage them in them either (John 17:14–19). Rather be a light to them with your lives (Matthew 5:13–16).

Catechism Material: Questions 55–58 (pp. 81–85)

1. What are the four ways we keep the sixth commandment according to the Catechism?

    a. _____

    b. _____

    c. _____

    d. _____

2. The Catechism states that sexuality is a good gift from God. This means that we:

    a. ____ Should treat sex as a dirty thing.

    b. ____ Not talk about sex.

    c. ____ Regard sex between two married persons as natural and good.

    d. ____ Experiment with sex and sexuality.

3. According to Titus 2:11–12, how should we deal with our sinful sexual urges?

    a. ____ Indulge them

    b. ____ Deny them

4. Read 1 Corinthians 7:9. What is one of the ways that we can control sexual urges in a godly way?_____
    _____

5. God instituted marriage when the Bible says, "Therefore a man shall leave his father and his mother and be joined to his _____." (Genesis 2:24) What goes in the blank?

    a. ____ Animal

    b. ____ Husband

    c. ____ Wives

    d. ____ Whoever and whatever he pleases

    e. ____ Wife

6. Romans 7:1–3 outlines the length of a marriage. What is its proper length?

    a. ____ Until death

    b. ____ At least ten years

    c. ____ Until they do not love each other anymore

    d. ____ Until one becomes sick

7. There are two instances in which divorce is permitted. In both those cases, the marriage is broken without a formal divorce. What are those two instances? (Mark the two correct answers)

    a. ____ Lack of fun or love

    b. ____ Adultery

    c. ____ Lack of money

    d. ____ *Desertion*

    What are the two passages that support your answer?_____

8. True / False – It is only considered adultery if someone actually has sex with another person outside of marriage.

9. The Catechism lists 12 ways we can commit adultery. List them:

    (1) _____   (7) _____

    (2) _____   (8) _____

    (3) _____   (9) _____

    (4) _____   (10) _____

    (5) _____   (11) _____

    (6) _____   (12) _____

10. Adultery is the opposite of "keeping the marriage bed pure." How do you keep the marriage bed pure?

_____

_____

11. Read 1 Corinthians 6:15–20. When we have sex with someone who is not our spouse or have sex without being married, who are we really sinning against? _____

12. According to 1 Corinthians 6:9–10, homosexuals will not inherit the kingdom of God. According to that passage, what is the punishment for adulterers?
    a. ____ Sexually transmitted diseases
    b. ____ A bad life
    c. ____ The same as homosexuals

13. Considering your previous answer, which sin is worse?
    a. ____ Homosexuality
    b. ____ Adultery
    c. ____ Both are equally bad

14. Should we persecute homosexuals around us?
    a. ____ Yes
    b. ____ No

    Why or why not?_____

    _____

    _____

15. When we encounter someone who is a homosexual, how should we treat them? (Mark all that apply.)
    a. ____ We should love them as ourselves
    b. ____ We should shun them
    c. ____ We should tell them how much worse they are than us
    d. ____ We should not encourage or join them in their sin

16. Read Ephesians 5:3–4. What does it tell us about our language and conduct as it relates to the Sixth Commandment? _____

    _____

    _____

17. Read Genesis 39:6–15. How does Joseph keep the Sixth Commandment? _____

    _____

    _____

    _____

18. What kind of physical places and places on the Internet can you stay away from to help you keep this commandment?_____

    _____

    _____

LESSON 36: THE SEVENTH COMMANDMENT

> **Memorization:** Luther's explanation to the Seventh Commandment –
> *You shall not steal.*
> *What does this mean?*
> *We should fear and love God so that we do not take our neighbor's money or possessions, or get them in any dishonest way, but help him to improve and protect his possessions and income.*

Catechism Material: Questions 59–60 (pp. 85–87)

1. For the following examples, use the following terms to describe what type of stealing it is: *robbery* (stealing with violence), *theft* (stealing without violence) or *fraud* (stealing by lying).

    a. _____ You take a bag of potato chips from the store.

    b. _____ You are a sales person, and you lie about the product capabilities to get someone to buy it.

    c. _____ You go to a restaurant and get a cup for water, but instead, take soda from the soda fountain.

    d. _____ You walk into a gas station and use a gun to demand the cashier give you money.

    e. _____ Your house is broken into, and you lie to the insurance company about what was taken to get more money from your claim.

    f. _____ You take the purse from an old lady and knock her down in the process.

2. Read Genesis 29:15–25. How did Laban break the Seventh Commandment? _____

    _____

    _____

3. There are three ways that we are to help our neighbor. What are they?

    a. _____

    b. _____

    c. _____

4. If you see someone breaking into another person's car, house, boat, store, etc. what is one way that you can keep the Seventh Commandment?

    a. ____ Walk away

    b. ____ Call the police

    c. ____ Call your friend

5. Who owns every store or business?

    a. ____ Sometimes a person

    b. ____ Shareholders

    c. ____ My neighbor

6. Considering the answer to the previous question, would you be keeping the Seventh Commandment if you did nothing while your friend stole something from a store? Why or why not? _____

    _____

    _____

7. What should you do if your neighbor left his front door or garage open?
    a. ____ Pray no one takes advantage of it
    b. ____ Close it / tell them about it
    c. ____ Do nothing

8. How can you care for your neighbor's property if you find something that they accidentally dropped, left, or lost? (Mark all that apply.)
    a. ____ Return it
    b. ____ Turn it in to someone who can return it (e.g., the police)
    c. ____ Take it for yourself
    d. ____ Leave it there and hope someone else does not steal it

LESSON 37: THE EIGHTH COMMANDMENT

> **Memorization:** Luther's explanation to the Eighth Commandment –
> *You shall not give false testimony against your neighbor.*
> *What does this mean?*
> *We should fear and love God so that we do not tell lies about our neighbor, betray him, slander him, or hurt his reputation, but defend him, speak well of him and explain everything in the kindest way.*

Gossiping, lying, and telling secrets all break the Eighth Commandment.

The Eighth Commandment deals with lying. Like the rest of the commandments, it cannot be taken in isolation. Consider if two people, Bob and Jim, got into a fight. Jim picked the fight because he never liked Bob and wanted to beat him up. Bob ran next to your house to get away and hide. Jim comes storming up to your house asking if you have seen Bob. If you took the Eighth Commandment in isolation, you MUST tell Jim where Bob is because you would be lying otherwise. However, if you did so would you be keeping the Fifth Commandment (You shall not murder)? As you remember from the Fifth Commandment, we are supposed to protect our neighbor and "help him in every bodily need." Each of these commandments about our neighbor is supposed to tell us how to love our neighbor. If we are not doing those things, then we are breaking the commandments.

Now, let us take a different approach. Bob just robbed Jim, and Jim was chasing Bob to get his stuff back. Would you be keeping the Eighth Commandment if you lied to him now? What else should you do? How about calling the police? When the police do come, you are then under obligation by the Eight Commandment to tell them about what happened. In that way, you are protecting the one who was hurt. By not telling the police what you saw, you are lying and ultimately not loving your neighbor as yourself.

Catechism Material: Questions 61–62 (pp. 87–89)

1. Read 2 Kings 5:20–27. Who did Gehazi lie to? _____
    Gehazi also broke another commandment; which one was it?
    a. ____ The Third Commandment
    b. ____ The Fifth Commandment
    c. ____ The Sixth Commandment
    d. ____ The Seventh Commandment

    Which of the three ways did he break the Commandment you picked in the previous question? _____
    What was Gehazi's punishment?_____

2. Breaking the Eighth Commandment can be simplified into three ways: lying (not telling the truth outside of court), gossiping (telling secrets or harming a person's reputation), and bearing false witness (lying in court). Read the following Biblical examples and state which way they broke the Eighth Commandment.
    a. Acts 6:8–11:_____
    b. Acts 6:12–15:_____
    c. 1 Samuel 22:6–18 (Doeg): _____
        How did the priest keep the Eighth Commandment? _____
        _____
    d. Acts 5:1–5: _____
        What was Ananias' punishment? _____

3. Likewise, there are three ways to keep the Eighth Commandment by defending our neighbor from false accusations (Defending), praising our neighbor (Praising), and putting the best construction on our neighbor's words and actions (Best Construction). Identify which of these three ways each example shows.
    a. _____ Your neighbor gets upset and yells at you because branches blew into his yard after a storm. Your response is that he must just be having a tough day.
    b. _____ Your neighbor has an old car that he has worked hard to restore. Your friend is jealous and states "the car probably doesn't run." You speak up and say it is very nice and you saw him driving it yesterday.
    c. _____ Your brother breaks your mom's favorite vase and blames your sister. You tell your mom the truth about what happened.

4. If something is true, but it is not flattering or good, do you have a right to say it? Why?_____
    _____
    _____

5. How should a Christian respond when someone is talking bad about another person?
    a. ____ Not say anything
    b. ____ Defend the person and speak about their good qualities
    c. ____ Join in

6. Read Joshua 2:1–7. Did Rahab break the Eighth Commandment? Why or why not? _____
    _____
    _____
    _____

LESSON 38: THE NINTH AND TENTH COMMANDMENTS

> **Memorization:** Luther's explanation of the Ninth and Tenth Commandments –
> *You shall not covet your neighbor's house.*
> *What does this mean?*
> *We should fear and love God so that we do not scheme to get our neighbor's inheritance or house, or get in a way which only appears right, but help and be of service to him in keeping it.*
>
> *And*
>
> *You shall not covet your neighbor's wife, or his manservant or maidservant, his ox or donkey, or anything that belongs to your neighbor.*
> *What does this mean?*
> *We should fear and love God so that we do not entice or force away our neighbor's wife, workers, or animals or turn them against him, but urge them to stay and do their duty.*

The Ninth and Tenth Commandments both deal with when a person covets something that is not theirs. Coveting and the mere desire for something are not the same things. *Coveting* can be defined as a sinful desire for something based on the belief that it is "not fair" that they have it instead of us. Coveting can also be defined as a desire that believes that we have the "right" to take something that does not belong to us. A final definition of coveting is a desire that believes that we can take or obtain something regardless of who it really belongs to.

Both of these commandments could be combined to state simply "You shall not covet your neighbor's stuff." But God lists out specific things and separates these two commandments to impress upon us the importance of not coveting. Also by doing so, he impresses upon us the different types of things we can covet. The Ninth primarily deals with a person's inheritance and their non-living property (e.g., TV's, jewelry, *intellectual property*, house, inheritance, etc.). The second has to do with living things that belong to them legally (e.g., through marriage), contractually (e.g., employees), relationships (e.g., friends) and personal ownership (e.g., animals).

Catechism Material: Questions 63–68 (pp. 89–92)

1. For the following examples, state if it is covetousness or not and why.

    a. My friend has an awesome video game system, and I want one too. _____

    _____

    b. She doesn't deserve to have such a nice phone; it should be mine. _____

    _____

    c. It's not fair that he has such a big house. _____

    _____

(Question 1 continued.)

  d.   They have a lot of money so they should be giving more to the poor instead of spending it on such extravagant things. _____

  _____

  e.   The store sells such an awesome camera. I'm going to save up and buy one. _____

  _____

  f.   That person should work for me because they do not deserve such a great employee. _____

  _____

  _____

2. Read the story of Ahab and Naboth (1 Kings 21:1–16).

  a.   At first, did Ahab covet Naboth's property?_____

  b.   At what point did Ahab's desire for Naboth's property become covetousness? _____

  _____

  c.   What did Jezebel do to Naboth to allow Ahab to get the property?_____

  _____

  d.   Ahab and Jezebel broke several commandments, and it all began with covetousness. What commandments did they break and how?_____

  _____

  _____

3. Read the Parable of the workers in the vineyard (Matthew 20:1–16). This is an example of covetousness. Explain how it is. _____

  _____

4. Read Job 1:1–3, 13–21.

  a.   How wealthy was Job? _____

  b.   How much did Job lose? _____

  c.   What was Job's response to what happened to him? _____

  _____

  d.   In Job's response, he recognized that all of his possessions came from God and he could not complain against God for taking them away. When our neighbor has more or something we want, who gave it to them?_____

  e.   Job eventually complains against God and claims that he is righteous and did nothing to deserve his property being taken from him. Ultimately God responds to Job for his self-righteousness. Read Job 38:1–7. God says that:

    i.   ____ Job had a right to complain

    ii.   ____ God establishes Himself as the creator of all

  f.   Consider your own stuff. If you own something, what is your expectation with it?

    i.   ____ I can use it how I want to

    ii.   ____ I can give it to whom I want to

    iii. ____ I can do with it whatever I want to

    iv.   ____ All of the above

(Question 4 continued.)

    g. If you build a business and it makes lots of money, do you have the same rights?

        i. ____ Yes

        ii. ____ No

    h. If God is the creator of all things (and thus the owner of all things), does He have the same rights as you give yourself?

        i. ____ Yes

        ii. ____ No

    i. So, if God gives us one thing and our neighbor something else, do we have any right to complain against God or covet what they have? Why or why not? _____

_____

_____

    j. If God has then created us, does the "profit" we make really belong to us or to God? Why or why not?

_____

_____

_____

5. God desires us to be content with what we have. This can be incredibly difficult. Read Matthew 6:25–33. Why should we be content? _____

_____

_____

6. True / False – In summary keeping the Ninth and Tenth Commandments means that we are content with all that we have (both living and non-living) and we should help our neighbor keep and protect all that he has.

7. True / False – In summary, breaking the commandment means that we only sinfully desire to obtain our neighbor's property openly.

Why or why not? _____

_____

LESSON 39: CLOSE OF THE COMMANDMENTS

> **Memorization:** Luther's conclusion to all the commandments –
> *What does God say about all these commandments?*
> He says *"For I, the LORD your God, am a jealous God, visiting the iniquity of the fathers upon the children to the third and fourth generations of those who hate Me, but showing mercy to thousands, to those who love Me and keep My commandments." (Exodus 20:5–6)*
> *What does this mean?*
> *God threatens to punish all who break these commandments. Therefore we should fear His wrath and not do anything against them. But He promises grace and every blessing to all who keep these commandments. Therefore, we should also love and trust in Him and gladly do what He commands.*

Catechism Material: Questions 69–74, 76 (pp. 93–96), and 84 (p. 100)

1. (Fill in the blanks.) The Catechism states that God is "Holy," this also means that He is perfect. Because He is perfect He _____ sin and insists on _____ obedience.

2. If God is perfect and He created perfect human beings (Adam and Eve) in a perfect world, are His expectations unreasonable?

   a. ____ Yes

   b. ____ No

3. (Fill in the blank.) As you learned God created everything including us, therefore He rightly owns everything. That is why He will not _____ the love and honor we owe Him with anything or anyone else.

4. What are the four ways we can break the commandments?

   a. _____

   b. _____

   c. _____

   d. _____

God expects us to keep His commandments, but He promises grace and hope to those who trust in Him.

5. When we break God's Commandments what should we expect?

   a. ____ Nothing to happen

   b. ____ Good things

   c. ____ Punishment

6. What three types of punishment should we expect?

   a. _____

   b. _____

   c. _____

7. True / False – If parents do evil and teach their children the same, we would expect God to punish them.

8. True / False – If parents follow the commandments and teach their children the same, we would expect God to bless them.

9. Based on what you have learned about the Ten Commandments, have you kept them perfectly?

   a. ____ Yes

   b. ____ No

   What then would you expect from God?

   c. ____ Good things from Him

   d. ____ His punishment

10. If God expects perfection, can we be more than perfect to make up for our imperfections?

    a. ____ Yes

    b. ____ No

11. Read Isaiah 64:6. What are our good works or righteousness like?_____

12. How then can we save ourselves?

    a. ____ By working really hard

    b. ____ We can't

    c. ____ By being better than someone else

13. What have we done to earn salvation?

    a. ____ We've been good people

    b. ____ We were nice to our neighbor

    c. ____ Nothing

14. Who do we look to as our Savior then? _____ because He has taken our punishment for us.

SECTION 5: REVIEW

1. The Ten Commandments are what type of Law in the Bible?

    a. ____ Moral

    b. ____ Civil/Political

    c. ____ Ceremonial

2. True / False – In order to break one of the Commandments, we have to do or not do something physically.

3. What are the four ways we can break the commandments?

    a. _____

    b. _____

    c. _____

    d. _____

4. If we do not keep the Ten Commandments, according to the close of the commandments, should we be afraid of God's wrath?

    a. ____ Yes

    b. ____ No

5. What is the punishment we deserve, and God will give us, for breaking the commandments? _____

_____

6. Is there any way we can make up or atone for the times that we have broken the commandments? Why or why not? _____

_____

_____

_____

7. Who has taken the punishment we deserve? _____

8. As a Christian, what should our main motivator to keep the Ten Commandments be? _____

_____

_____

_____

9. Write out the Ten Commandments:

1) _____

2) _____

3) _____

4) _____

5) _____

6) _____

7) _____

8) _____

9) _____

10) _____

10. The following are examples of breaking one of the commandments. Identify which commandment was broken by writing the number of the commandment.

a. ____ Stealing a candy bar

b. ____ Blaspheming God's name

c. ____ Gossiping

d. ____ Not going to church regularly

e. ____ Coveting my neighbor's inheritance

f. ____ Having sex outside of marriage

g. ____ Telling a friend's secret

h. ____ Hating someone

i. ____ Telling a crude joke

j. ____ Coveting your friend's car

k. ____ Not doing what your boss tells you to do

l. ____ Making money is more important than studying God's Word

SECTION 6 – OUR SINFULNESS AND HOW WE SHOULD INTERACT WITH EACH OTHER

LESSON 40: SIN

> **Memorization:** Romans 3:23 –
> *For all have sinned and fall short of the glory of God.*

The first sin was when Adam and Eve ate the fruit of the tree of the knowledge of good and evil (Genesis 3).

Original sin, as is taught in the Catechism, is also part of the concept known as the *"total depravity of man."* The "total depravity of man" means that human beings have been corrupted to the core and are incapable of pleasing God, going to Him of their own free will, and following His commandments. This corruption began with Adam and Eve and is passed on through conception. Therefore, everyone is guilty and deserving of death from the time they are conceived, even before they commit an actual sin that we can observe (Psalm 51:5, Romans 5:12, and Isaiah 64:6). However, this does not make Adam and Eve worse sinners than us. Rather we show ourselves to be like them through our sinful nature and actual sins.

Human nature refers to each person's natural (what they are born with) or usual desires. In other words, it is how human beings usually act unless an outside force stops or changes their behavior.

Sinful nature is the concept that people are born with the natural inclination towards sin, and it is inherited from their parents all the way from Adam. It makes it impossible for a person to please God or follow His commandments unless they are reborn by the Holy Spirit.

Read Luke 10:30–36. It is the parable of the Good Samaritan. It is important when talking about sin to recognize that we do not just commit sin by doing something. In the example of the Good Samaritan, both the Priest and the Levite did not beat or rob the person, yet they committed sin in the matter. They broke the Fifth Commandment (You shall not Murder). How did they break it? They broke it through what is known as a *"sin of omission."* That means that they did not do what they should have done which was to care for their neighbor in every bodily need.

Catechism Material: Questions 78–83 (pp. 98–100)

1. What is sin?_____
2. What is the type of the Law that we break?
    a. ____ The Civil Law
    b. ____ The Moral Law
    c. ____ The Criminal Law

3. Read Genesis 2:15–17, 3:1–7. What was the Law God gave to Adam and Eve that they disobeyed?_____

    _____

    What is the name of the being that tempted Adam and Eve? _____

4. Adam and Eve disobeyed God because...
    a. ____ The serpent made them
    b. ____ God forced them
    c. ____ They, of their own will, disobeyed God

5. What are the two types of sin? Match it with its correct definition.

Term	Definition
	____ When we sin by not keeping one of the Ten Commandments
a. _____	____ Is the sinfulness that we are born with making us only slightly sinful
b. _____	____ Is the sinfulness that we are born with, making us completely sinful

6. How are the two types of sin different? _____

    _____

7. Are there any differences in the consequences between the two types of sins? Why or why not? _____

    _____

    _____

    _____

8. According to the catechism, Original Sin has brought two things, left us without two things, and causes us to commit things. What has it...
    a. brought?_____
    b. left us without? _____
    c. caused us to commit?_____

9. What kind of sin is inherited from Adam and Eve? _____

10. Describe the term "total depravity of man." _____

    _____

    _____

11. Who should we blame for making it impossible for us to keep God's commandments?
    a. ____ God
    b. ____ Adam and Eve
    c. ____ Ourselves, because we are like Adam and Eve, and they are our father and mother

12. Who has made it possible for us to keep God's commandments as Christians (albeit imperfectly)?
    a. ____ God
    b. ____ Adam and Eve
    c. ____ Ourselves

13. True / False – Until we actually commit sin, we do not deserve God's punishment.

    Why or why not? _____

    _____

    _____

14. How does one commit a sin of "omission"? _____

_____

15. What are the four ways we commit actual sin?

    a. _____

    b. _____

    c. _____

    d. _____

16. What is another word for sin? _____

LESSON 41: CONFESSION AND ABSOLUTION

> **Memorization:** 1 John 1:8–9 –
> *If we say that we have no sin, we deceive ourselves, and the truth is not in us. If we confess our sins, He is faithful and just to forgive us our sins and to cleanse us from all unrighteousness.*

In the United States, confession is even protected by state law in varying ways.

Catechism Material: Questions 261–268 (pp. 217–223), and Confession (pp. 26–29)

1. What does it mean to confess? (Mark all that apply.)

    a. ____ Acknowledge

    b. ____ Lie

    c. ____ Hide

    d. ____ Admit

2. What is the first part of confession? _____

_____

3. What sins should we confess before God?

    a. ____ The ones we know

    b. ____ The ones we don't know

    c. ____ The ones we feel guilty for

    d. ____ All of them, known and unknown

A confessional is used in the Catholic Church for private confession.

4. What Bible passage tells us that we do not know all the sins that we have done?

    a. ____ Psalm 51:1–4

    b. ____ Psalm 19:12

    c. ____ Matthew 5:23–24

    d. ____ Proverbs 28:13

5. When you confess your sins to God, which Bible passage tells us for certain that God forgives us our sins?

_____

6. True / False – We should confess the sins we have committed against our neighbor to them.

7. Which passage tells us which sins to confess to our neighbor?
    a. ____ Psalm 51:1–4
    b. ____ Psalm 19:12
    c. ____ Matthew 5:23–24
    d. ____ Proverbs 28:13

8. True / False – We must tell our pastor every sin we have ever committed in order to be forgiven.

9. Can a person be forced to go to private confession?
    a. ____ Yes
    b. ____ No

10. The second part of confession is the absolution. What is absolution? _____
    _____

11. When your pastor pronounces the absolution on you, are your sins really forgiven?
    a. ____ Yes
    b. ____ No

12. How can a pastor's word of forgiveness do such a great thing?
    a. ____ The power comes from God's Word, not the Pastor's
    b. ____ The Pastor is the medium by which God speaks His forgiveness (in God's stead)
    c. ____ The Pastor has been commanded to forgive the people's sins
    d. ____ All of the above

13. Read Psalm 32:3–4. We often feel guilty for doing something wrong (for committing sin). What were the physical effects the psalmist felt? _____
    _____

14. Some examples of symptoms we can feel when we do something wrong include guilt, depression, anxiety, sadness, anger, etc. What kinds of feelings have you had when you have done something wrong?
    _____
    _____
    _____

15. Read Psalm 32:5. Where did the Psalmist find relief?
    a. ____ Through forgiveness
    b. ____ After he had suffered enough

16. Read Psalm 103:11–14. How far has God removed our sins from us? _____
    _____

17. What then is the purpose and benefit of private confession with a pastor?
    a. ____ Absolute forgiveness of our sins
    b. ____ Consolation or relief from guilt
    c. ____ There is none
    d. ____ Both a and b

18. True / False – We should have confidence in the secrecy of our confession to our Pastor because they have taken a pledge not to share our sins with others.

19. True / False – There are laws in the United States that protect the confidentiality of confession.

LESSON 42: THE OFFICE OF THE KEYS AND EXCOMMUNICATION

> **Memorization:** Matthew 16:19 –
> *And I will give you the keys of the kingdom of heaven, and whatever you bind on earth will be bound in heaven, and whatever you loose on earth will be loosed in heaven.*

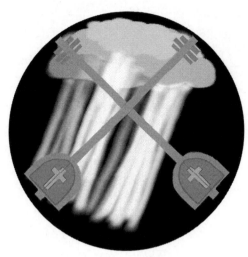

The Keys of Heaven are given to Christians, pastors, and the church as a whole to forgive and retain sins.

Repentance:

Repentance according to Question 274 of your catechism states that there are two aspects to it. One that a person is "sorry for their sins" and two that the person "believes in the Lord Jesus Christ as their Savior." Another aspect to repentance is the evidence of it. A person who is truly sorry for their sins will turn from their sins which includes that they will strive and "want to do better" (Luther's explanation of the *Office of the Keys*, p. 224). This is important because the expectation is that after a person is forgiven or goes through the process of excommunication that the sin(s) that they were performing will stop or at least be fought against. That is why Jesus, when He forgave the adulteress, said, "Your sins are forgiven you, go and sin no more" (John 8:1–11 [paraphrased]). It is also why Paul said to the Romans, "Shall we continue in sin that grace may abound? Certainly Not!" (Romans 6:1–4). Therefore, true repentance is observed when a person turns from their sin(s) and fights against them.

Due Process of the Keys:

The term "*due process*" refers to the legal requirements in the United States that governs legal processes. It specifically refers to the legal process someone has a right to before and after they are convicted of a crime. Examples of the parts of due process include the right to a speedy trial, the right to be represented by an attorney, and the right to be considered innocent until proven guilty. The binding or retaining of a person's sins, which ultimately leads to excommunication from the church, also has a "due process." This due process of the keys is outlined in Matthew 18:15–20.

The due process outlined in Matthew includes individual Christians and then the whole congregation (i.e., the visible church they are a part of). This process has one ultimate goal, and it falls along the lines of God's desire that "all men to be saved and to come to the knowledge of the truth" (1 Timothy 2:3–4). That goal is that the person should repent and be saved from their sins. It is by no means a reason or process to exact revenge, get rid of people that we do not like in the church, or to get rid of people who disagree with us. It is to keep the congregation from falling into sin. It is also to fulfill where it says "But when we are judged, we are chastened by the Lord, that we may not be condemned with the world" (1 Corinthians 11:32). That is why this process is done out of and through love and not anger. It is also why we are to receive the sinner back with open arms, joy, love, and peace when they do repent (2 Corinthians 2:3–11). That is to occur unconditionally upon repentance and NOT conditionally upon *penance* (an act that shows a person is truly sorry for their sins and thus deserving of forgiveness). Furthermore, it is only binding when it is carried out according to the Scriptures (i.e., in accordance with the due process of the keys). If it is not, it may be rightly ignored, and those who carried out the unjust condemnation are subject to judgment and condemnation (Matthew 7:1–2 & Treatise on the Power and Primacy of the Pope).

The Pastor's Role:

The Pastor also plays a key role in this due process of the church. He is responsible for the church he serves. If he sees a person openly sinning, without repentance, he is responsible for starting and seeing to it that the church follows through with the process, but not retaining sins by himself (e.g., Paul and the church at Corinth—1 Corinthians 5 and 2 Corinthians 2:3–11). In this way, he prevents the individual from spreading the sin throughout the church and allowing the person to condemn themselves by their sin. Furthermore, until the person has repented, the pastor must refuse to serve them at the Lord's Supper and give them forgiveness (which would not be forgiveness because of their unrepentant heart). Finally, if and when the person repents, they instruct and make sure that the church receives back the person who had been excommunicated.

The Individual Christian's Role:

To understand the individual role of the Christian in this matter, it is best to understand their position in the church. An individual Christian is a sheep. As they go about grazing in the field and they see a fellow sheep wandering away from the flock, they should not follow, but try and stop them. If that fellow sheep refuses, the first should tell the shepherd (the pastor of the church) about it. In real life, this means, as it is laid out in Matthew, the role of the individual Christian is not to go out looking for other people's sins. Rather, they should live their lives as Christians, and if an instance comes up, then they should act within their respective role (bring the sin to the attention of the person sinning or to the pastor). Remember, everyone sins, and we are not the judges of anyone's sins (God alone is). Furthermore, as an individual, a Christian has no authority to excommunicate someone on their own. Only God, and the Church through the due process of the keys, has that power.

Catechism Material: Luther's Explanation of the Keys, Questions 269–276 and 279–284 (pp. 224–234)

1. What does the term "Office" mean when used in the term "Office of the Keys"?
    a. ____ The workspace where the pastor works
    b. ____ An authority or power
2. What is the authority or power of the keys?
    a. ____ To forgive sins
    b. ____ To open the church doors
    c. ____ To *retain sins* (withhold forgiveness)
    d. ____ Both a and c
3. Jesus calls this power and authority the Keys. What do these particular Keys open and shut?
    a. ____ Heaven
    b. ____ Church doors
    c. ____ Your house
4. The Keys are given three different times to three different audiences. Match the audience with the passage.

Passage	Audience
a. John 20:19–23	____ Peter (the individual Christian)
b. Matthew 16:15–19	____ The Church
c. Matthew 18:15–20	____ The disciples (the apostles / Pastors)

5. How are the keys to be applied to repentant believers?
    a. ____ Retain their sins
    b. ____ Forgive their sins
    c. ____ Forgive their sins after they show they are truly sorry

6. When the keys are used to forgive sins, is everyone forgiven?

    a.   ____ Yes

    b.   ____ No one is forgiven because only God can forgive sins

    c.   ____ No, only the repentant believers are forgiven

7. What are the two things that define a "repentant believer"?

    a.   _____

    b.   _____

8. When a person is repentant, what effect will it have on their lives and the sin they repented of? _____
_____

9. Read James 2:19. True / False – A person who is not sorry for their sins is still forgiven if they believe in Jesus.

10. When will a person who is not sorry for their sins be forgiven?

    a.   ____ When they are sorry for their sins, turn away from their sins (repent), and believe in Jesus as their Savior

    b.   ____ When they ask for forgiveness

    c.   ____ When they believe in Jesus

11. After a person repents what do they do naturally?

    a.   ____ Sing

    b.   ____ Do good works

    c.   ____ Dance

12. Read Matthew 18:34–35. What happens if we do not forgive someone who asks for it?

    a.   ____ God will not forgive us our sins

    b.   ____ Nothing

    c.   ____ We will have to do good works

13. What is the passage that talks about the "due process" of the church? _____

14. If at the end of this "due process" the person repents, what happens?

    a.   ____ Nothing

    b.   ____ They are disciplined

    c.   ____ They are forgiven and welcomed as a brother (into full fellowship)

15. When a person is found to be unrepentant at the end of this "due process," what happens?

    a.   ____ They are forgiven

    b.   ____ Nothing

    c.   ____ They are excommunicated

16. What does it mean to excommunicate someone? _____
_____

17. What is the purpose of excommunication and the due process of the church? _____
_____
_____

18. What is the requirement of the church if the excommunicated person repents?

    a.   ____ Nothing

    b.   ____ Forgive them

    c.   ____ Allow them to come back to church

    d.   ____ b and c

19. For the process of excommunication to be binding it must be done:
    a. ____ In compliance with God's Word
    b. ____ In compliance with what the church wants
    c. ____ In compliance with what the pastor wants

20. True / False – If the due process of the Keys is not followed appropriately in accordance with God's Word, those who carried it out are subject to judgment.

21. The pastor also plays a role in excommunication. (Mark all that apply.)
    a. ____ Starts the due process of the church if the church has not
    b. ____ Encourages the church to forgive if the person has become repentant
    c. ____ Refuses the unrepentant person at the Lord's Supper
    d. ____ Protects the congregation by not allowing the unrepentant person from being with the church

22. When a person is excommunicated, what are the consequences? (Mark all that apply.)
    a. ____ Their sins are not forgiven
    b. ____ They cannot go to church
    c. ____ They cannot read the Bible
    d. ____ They cannot take Communion
    e. ____ They cannot talk with the Pastor

23. True / False – The process of excommunication must be done carefully, because if we do it improperly, Jesus will not forgive us our sins. (Read Matthew 6:14–15)

24. True / False – The ultimate purpose of excommunication is to punish someone.

25. True / False – The ultimate purpose of excommunication is to show someone their sin so that they will repent and be saved.

LESSON 43: FORGIVENESS

> **Memorization:** Matthew 6:14–15 –
> *For if you forgive men their trespasses, your heavenly Father will also forgive you. But if you do not forgive men their trespasses, neither will your Father forgive your trespasses.*

We are all in the same boat:

It is important to consider that every one of our sins are sins against God, while only some of our sins are against our neighbor. So if we place our sins on a scale, the number of sins and the weight of our sins are always greater towards God than towards our neighbor. Therefore, when our neighbor sins against us, it is impossible for their one or more sins to outweigh the sins we have committed against God. So, if we believe and understand that God has forgiven our sins towards Him, then we must by weight and number, forgive the small number of sins our neighbor sins against us. Again, it is impossible for the sins of our neighbor against us to outweigh the sins we have committed against God. (Matthew 18:21–35)

Our mountain of sin towards God always outnumbers our neighbor's sin towards us.

Forgiveness versus enabling:

There is a very real difference between forgiving someone and enabling them. For example, if parents have a child named Sam, and Sam grows up to become a drug addict and is now an adult. Due to Sam's drug addiction, he does not have a job and needs help. So Sam lives at home and steals from his parents to support his drug addiction. So, the parents keep God's will and forgive Sam for the theft. The parents also continue to try and get Sam help. However, Sam continues to steal, and steal, and steal all the while either refusing or pretending like he is going to get help. The parents, by forgiving Sam and allowing him to live with them and steal from them, are not pleasing God by their actions. What the parents are doing is, in fact, unloving and unkind. They continue to enable Sam to sin by not allowing there to be consequences and by not removing temptation from Sam. That goes against God's desire because the parents (in their role) are allowing Sam to continue to sin (1 Samuel 3:11–14). Forgiveness does not always mean there are no consequences. For example, God forgave David for his adultery with Bathsheba, but the earthly consequence was that the child they had would die (2 Samuel 12:1–15).

Sometimes, because of a person's temptation to sin in a particular way is so strong, it is important to remove that temptation from them. In the case of Sam, an appropriate (but very difficult) way to remove the temptation is by the parents removing Sam from their house. They still forgive Sam, but that does not mean that they should let him live with them at their house. They still forgive Sam, but that does not mean that they like his decisions or what he has become. They forgive Sam, but they do not approve of or accept what he is doing.

If you tell your friend a secret and they tell someone else, does God want you to forgive them? Yes. Does this mean you accept or approve of what they did? No. Should you keep telling them your secrets? Whether you should or should not keep telling them depends on the circumstances. Should you still be friends? Again, the answer is maybe or maybe not depending on the circumstances. In this world, it is extremely difficult always to know the best response in regard to earthly consequences. There are no black and white answers for every situation. However, if you decide that you cannot continue to be friends with someone (or you separate yourselves from someone), God still says "pray for your enemies" (Matthew 5:43–48). The point is that even if you cannot be a person's friend or helping hand anymore or for a time, pray that God does well for them.

Forgiveness and our sinful nature:

As was talked about at the beginning of this section, we have a responsibility to forgive our neighbor when they sin against us. Due to our sinful nature and the sin that was committed against us, this is sometimes easier said than done. In fact, our natural response is to withhold forgiveness and keep a grudge. While God does not give us an out to just not forgive them, He does give us support. He does give us His Word and His promise to answer our prayers (Section 7). Therefore, it is appropriate to ask God to forgive our neighbor for us and to help us get to the point where we can forgive them.

Aside from forgiving them, it is often difficult to just not be mean to them. Our sinful nature wants us to demand and exact revenge or retribution for what they did. That is not appropriate nor God-pleasing (Romans 12:19). Therefore, it is those circumstances that we turn to God in all things and ask Him for help. Specifically, we ask that He help us move from an emotional position that the one who wronged us is our enemy to them being our neighbor. We also ask that we move from a position where we want retribution, to a place where we do not treat them badly. Then from a place where we do not treat them badly to a place where we treat them kindly and as God would have us treat them as our neighbor.

Catechism Material: Questions 181–186 (pp. 165–168), and 226–227 (pp. 194–195)

1. Why does God forgive our sins? (Mark all that apply.)
    a. ____ Because of our good works
    b. ____ Because He is merciful
    c. ____ Because of Christ's atoning sacrifice
    d. ____ Because we deserve forgiveness

2. How is it possible for God not to judge us for our sins?
    a. ____ Because our good works outweigh them
    b. ____ Because we are loved by God
    c. ____ Because we are really good people
    d. ____ Because Christ already paid the price for our sins and made us righteous

3. Where do we find the offer of forgiveness and how do we obtain it? _____

    _____

    _____

4. How can you be sure that your sins are really forgiven? Match the verse to the reason.

Verse	Reason
a. Jeremiah 1:5	____ Because Jesus called me
b. Philippians 1:6	____ Because Jesus died for all
c. 1 Peter 2:24	____ Because God keeps His promises
d. Deuteronomy 7:9	____ Because Jesus died for me
e. Romans 6:10	____ Because God sustains me and takes care of me
f. Romans 8:30	____ Because God baptized me and made me His child
g. Romans 8:12–17	____ Because Jesus gives me His body and blood in Holy Communion for the forgiveness of sins
h. Matthew 26:26–29	____ Because before I was even conceived God knew me and set me apart

5. What are the four reasons the catechism gives to hold onto *Justification* by grace alone and by Faith alone (in Latin *sola gratia, sola fide*).
    a. _____
    b. _____
    c. _____
    d. _____

6. Read Isaiah 64:6. Is sola gratia, sola fide accurate, or can we earn our own salvation through good works? Why or why not? _____

    _____

    _____

7. Who's sin is greater: our sin against God or our neighbor's sin against us? Why?_____

    _____

    _____

8. Who's forgiveness is more impressive then: our forgiveness to our neighbor or God's forgiveness to us? Why? _____

    _____

    _____

9. God earnestly desires that we should forgive one another; can another person's sin against us ever justify us in not forgiving them? Why or why not?_____

_____

_____

10. True / False – Forgiveness means that there are never any consequences.

11. True / False – Sometimes forgiveness involves consequences. Why or why not?_____

_____

_____

12. True / False – If a friend does wrong to you, you should immediately stop being friends with them. Why or why not?_____

_____

_____

13. It is easy to say that we must forgive someone when they wrong us, but sometimes it's very difficult to do it. What makes it so difficult?
    a. ____ God
    b. ____ Our sinful nature
    c. ____ Our parents
    d. ____ Life

14. If we are having trouble forgiving someone, what should we pray to God for? (Mark all that apply.)
    a. ____ Strength to forgive them
    b. ____ That God would forgive them for us
    c. ____ Peace in knowing we do not have to forgive them because God does

15. If you are having trouble being a neighbor to someone who sinned against you, what should you do?

_____

_____

16. If someone sins against you, what would God have you do for them? _____

_____

SECTION 6: REVIEW

1. What is the definition of the following terms:
    a. Original Sin: _____
    b. Actual Sin: _____

2. True / False – Original sin does not make it impossible for us to come to God or do good works.

3. What is a sin of omission?_____
    Give an example:_____

_____

_____

4. What type of sin condemns us?
    a. ____ Original Sin
    b. ____ Actual Sin
    c. ____ Both a and b
    d. ____ Neither

5. True / False – We can rightfully blame Adam and Eve for our sin because they sinned first. Why or why not?
    _____

6. What are the four ways that we commit sin?
    a. _____
    b. _____
    c. _____
    d. _____

7. What is confession? _____

8. What is absolution? _____

9. True / False – Pastors are there to help us and absolve us when a sin particularly troubles us through private confession.

10. True / False – We do not need to confess the sins we commit against our neighbor to them.

11. True / False – Absolution, while it may make us feel better, has no actual power to forgive sins. Why or why not? _____
    _____

12. Is penance a requirement of absolution? Why or why not? _____
    _____
    _____

13. True / False – If a person is unrepentant and a Pastor absolves them, their sins are forgiven.

14. Should we have confidence in the confidentiality of our confession? Why or why not? _____
    _____
    _____

15. Repentance involves turning away from one's sins; what does it mean to "turn away from one's sins"?
    _____
    _____

16. True / False – The power of the keys is only on this earth and has no effect in heaven.

17. Where does the authority and power of the Keys come from?
    a. ____ The office of the pastor
    b. ____ The Word of God and His power
    c. ____ The authority of the congregation
    d. ____ The need for reform

18. What is the ultimate purpose of the due process of the keys?
    a. ____ Kick people out of the church
    b. ____ Keep people in line inside of the church
    c. ____ To encourage an openly sinning and unrepentant person to repent
    d. ____ To show the power and authority of the church

19. The due process of the keys must be carried out in...
    a. _____ Love
    b. _____ Contempt
    c. _____ Anger
    d. _____ Indifference

20. If a person has been excommunicated from the church, what is the effect? (Mark all that apply.)
    a. _____ That person is not forgiven for their sins
    b. _____ That person cannot take communion
    c. _____ That person should be avoided
    d. _____ That person should be treated with contempt

21. If a person has been excommunicated from the church and they repent, what is the responsibility of the church? (Mark all that apply.)
    a. _____ Nothing until they demonstrate they are truly sorry and do penance
    b. _____ Forgive them
    c. _____ Welcome them back as a member of the church
    d. _____ Nothing

22. True / False – The Pastor should encourage his congregation to begin the due process of the keys, or start it himself, if a person is openly sinning and unrepentant.

23. True / False – The pastor has no responsibility to encourage the congregation to receive back a person who was excommunicated if they repent.

24. True / False – True forgiveness always means that we forget what happened and allow the person to keep sinning against us.

25. True / False – There are some sins that are so awful that we do not have to forgive our neighbor for doing them against us.

26. What makes it difficult for us to forgive our neighbor sometimes?
    a. _____ Their sin
    b. _____ Our sinful nature

27. True / False – If we do not forgive someone their sins against us it does not really matter because God can still forgive them. Why or why not? _____
    _____
    _____

28. Define Justification: _____
    _____

29. Define "Sola Gratia, Sola Fide": _____
    _____

30. True / False – There can and never are any earthly consequences for a person who sins on this earth and is forgiven. Why or why not? _____
    _____
    _____

SECTION 7 – PRAYER AND THE LORD'S PRAYER

LESSON 44: PRAYER

> **Memorization:** Matthew 7:7–8 –
> *Ask, and it will be given to you; seek, and you will find; knock, and it will be opened to you. For everyone who asks receives, and he who seeks finds, and to him who knocks it will be opened.*

What is prayer? <u>Prayer is an act of worship</u> wherein we bring our <u>petitions</u> before God with our <u>hearts and lips</u> and offer up <u>praise and thanksgiving</u> to Him.[23] (Ps. 19:14, Matt. 6:7, Ps. 10:17, Is. 65:24, Ps. 103:1, Ps. 118:1, Ps. 95, Ps. 96)

Petition: a request or an earnest request for something

To whom should we pray? We should pray only to the <u>True God</u>, Father, Son and Holy Ghost, since to Him alone such honor is due and He alone is able and willing to hear and grant our prayer.[24] (Matt. 4:10, Ps. 65:2, Is. 63:16)

What should move us to pray? God's <u>command</u> and <u>promise</u>, our <u>own</u> and <u>our neighbor's need</u>, and <u>gratitude</u> for blessings received should move us to pray.[25] (Matt. 7:7–8, Ps. 50:15, Luke 5:12–13, Matt. 8:5–13, Luke 17:15–16)

Jesus taught us how to pray. He also encourages us to pray because He loves us.

What distinction should we make in our prayers? When praying for *spiritual blessings*, things necessary for our salvation, we should ask unconditionally; when praying for <u>other gifts</u>, we should ask that God grant them to us if it be His will.[26] (Luke 11:13, Luke 22:42, Matt. 8:2, 1 John 5:14)

It is an important thing to recognize in prayer that our goal is not to bend God's will to ours, but that our desires and will should be bent to be the same as His. By doing that we are both obedient and showing our faith and trust in Him (Luke 22:42). Furthermore, it is both sinful and disgraceful to pray if we are doing it to show our religiousness, piousness, righteousness or faithfulness to God to OTHER people. God tells us that when we pray to impress others, we may receive recognition from them, but not from God, nor do we receive the gifts from God we ask for (Matthew 6:5–6). Finally, prayer is not how we show our religiousness, piousness, righteousness or faithfulness to God in order to impress Him and through that receive gifts from Him. God is not moved by our "works of righteousness" so that now He owes us good things let alone anything. Rather God gives to us through grace, and we receive EVERYTHING from God through grace (Matthew 6:7–8, Luke 17:10).

Catechism Material: Questions 193–204 (pp. 174–180) and Luther's Daily Prayers (pp. 32–34)

---

23   Question 201 from "A Short Explanation of Dr. Martin Luther's Small Catechism" Concordia Publishing House, 1943
24   Question 202 from "A Short Explanation of Dr. Martin Luther's Small Catechism" Concordia Publishing House, 1943
25   Question 203 from "A Short Explanation of Dr. Martin Luther's Small Catechism" Concordia Publishing House, 1943
26   Question 205 from "A Short Explanation of Dr. Martin Luther's Small Catechism" Concordia Publishing House, 1943

1. Who did God give the privilege to pray?
    a. ____ Pastors
    b. ____ All believers
    c. ____ Adults
    d. ____ Teachers

2. What kind of act is prayer?
    a. ____ Worship
    b. ____ Obedience
    c. ____ Love
    d. ____ Faithfulness

3. What are the ways we can talk to God? (Mark all that apply.)
    a. ____ Voice
    b. ____ Thoughts
    c. ____ Hands
    d. ____ Hearts

4. Who should we pray to?_____

5. Who should we NOT pray to? (Mark all that apply.)
    a. ____ Idols
    b. ____ Angels
    c. ____ Saints
    d. ____ The dead (dead relatives, friends, parents, etc.)

6. Who can hear us when we pray?
    a. ____ The dead
    b. ____ The Saints
    c. ____ God
    d. ____ All of the above

7. What are the three things that make us want to pray?
    a. _____
    b. _____
    c. _____

8. What three types of things do we ask for in prayer?
    a. _____
    b. _____
    c. _____

9. What do we "praise and thank" God for?
    a. _____
    b. _____

10. Who helps us pray?_____
    What is the Bible passage that tells us this? _____

11. When we pray, we pray in the name of _____ with _____ and according to the
    revealed _____ of _____. (Fill in the blanks)

12. When we pray, we pray in such a way to bend _____will to be the same as _____ will.

13.   Read 1 John 5:14–15. When we ask for things, why do we have confidence that we will receive it? _____

     _____

     _____

     _____

14.   Does God owe us anything when we pray? Why do we receive anything from God when we pray? _____

     _____

     _____

15.   How often should we pray?_____

16.   When should we especially pray? _____

17.   Where should we pray?_____

18.   Who should we pray for? (Mark all that apply.)

     a.   ____ Our friends

     b.   ____ The dead

     c.   ____ Our neighbors

     d.   ____ Ourselves

     e.   ____ Our enemies

19.   We should pray for spiritual blessings and bodily blessings and to give thanks to God. Give examples of each:

     a.   _____

     b.   _____

     c.   _____

20.   Read 2 Corinthians 12:7–10. If we pray in confidence and faith for God to heal us, and He does not, has

     God heard our prayer? Yes / No

     Has God answered our prayer? Yes / No / Maybe

     How did God answer Paul's prayer for healing? _____

     _____

     What was Paul's response?_____

     _____

     What can we learn from Paul in regard to prayer and God's response? _____

     _____

     _____

21.   Read John 11:1–3, 20–21. What did Mary and Martha want Jesus to do?_____

     _____

     Read John 11:5–6. Was Jesus' response immediate? _____

     Read John 11:32. What happened to Lazarus?_____

     Read John 11:33–44. How did Jesus answer Mary and Martha's prayer/request?_____

     _____

     _____

     Was it the way that Mary and Martha expected? Why or why not? _____

     _____

     _____

22. Based on what you learned from Lazarus and Paul, does God always answer our prayers the way we expect? Yes / No

23. Does God always give us exactly what we asked for in the way that we asked for it and at the time that we asked for it? Yes / No

24. Why should we not pray for the dead? (Give the Bible passage that supports your answer.) _____
_____
_____
_____

25. Read Matthew 5:43–48. Jesus commands that we should love our enemies. We were also reconciled to Christ while we were enemies to God. Why then should we pray for our enemies? (Mark all that apply.)
    a. ____ Because it impresses God.
    b. ____ Because Christ died for them.
    c. ____ Because we were just like them at one point.
    d. ____ Because Christ commanded it.

    Is it sinful to pray for bad things to happen to people we do not like? Should we expect our prayers for such things to happen to be answered with anything else but a "no"? _____
_____
_____

26. Read Matthew 18:21–35. When we pray for judgment and bad things against people we do not like, who will ultimately receive the punishment if we do not repent? Why? _____
_____
_____
_____

27. What is the name of the prayer that Jesus gave us as an example? _____

SUBSECTION: THE LORD'S PRAYER

Lesson 45: Introduction to the Lord's Prayer

> **Memorization:** The Lord's Prayer (Luther's Small Catechism based on Matthew 6:9–13) –
> *Our Father who art in heaven,*
> *Hallowed be Thy name.*
> *Thy kingdom come,*
> *Thy will be done on earth, as it is in heaven.*
> *Give us this day our daily bread*
> *And forgive us our trespasses,*
> *as we forgive those who trespass against us.*
> *And lead us not into temptation, but deliver us from evil;*
> *For Thine is the kingdom, and the power, and the glory, forever and ever.*
> *Amen.*

Which is the most excellent of all prayers? The most excellent of all prayers is the Lord's Prayer, taught by the Lord Jesus Himself in Matthew 6:9–13.[27]

27   Question 213 from "A Short Explanation of Dr. Martin Luther's Small Catechism" Concordia Publishing House, 1943

How may the Lord's Prayer be divided? The Lord's Prayer may be divided into the <u>Introduction</u>, the <u>Seven Petitions</u>, and the <u>Conclusion</u>.[28]

What do we ask in the seven petitions? In the first three petitions we ask for spiritual blessings, in the Fourth petition for material gifts, and in the last three petitions for deliverance from evil.[29]

Catechism Material: Pp. 18–22

1. Who taught us the Lord's Prayer? _____

2. Where is the Lord's Prayer found in the Bible?

   _____

3. The Lord's prayer can be divided into 3 parts. What are they?
   a. _____
   b. _____
   c. _____

4. What do we ask for in the first three petitions?
   a. ____ Material gifts
   b. ____ Deliverance from evil
   c. ____ Spiritual Blessings

5. What do we ask for in the fourth petition?
   a. ____ Material gifts
   b. ____ Deliverance from evil
   c. ____ Spiritual Blessings

6. What do we ask for in the last three petitions?
   a. ____ Material gifts
   b. ____ Deliverance from evil
   c. ____ Spiritual Blessings

God is our loving Father. We can go to Him in prayer freely, joyfully and trusting that He will hear and answer our prayers.

7. Write out each section:
   a. The introduction: _____
   b. The First Petition: _____
   c. The Second Petition: _____
   d. The Third Petition: _____
   e. The Fourth Petition: _____
   f. The Fifth Petition: _____

      _____
   g. The Sixth Petition: _____
   h. The Seventh Petition: _____
   i. The Conclusion: _____

      _____

---

28   Question 214 from "A Short Explanation of Dr. Martin Luther's Small Catechism" Concordia Publishing House, 1943
29   Question 218 from "A Short Explanation of Dr. Martin Luther's Small Catechism" Concordia Publishing House, 1943

Lesson 46: The Lord's Prayer – Introduction ("Our Father")

> **Memorization:** Luther's explanation to the Introduction –
> *Our Father who art in heaven*
> *What does this mean?*
> *With these words God tenderly invites us to believe that He is our true Father and that we are His true children, so that with all boldness and confidence we may ask Him as dear children ask their dear father.*

The word "art" could be substituted in this instance for the word "is." So the introduction could read "Our Father who is in heaven."

Catechism Material: Questions 205–207 (pp. 180–181)

1. If God is our Father, what does that make us?

   _____

2. How did we become children of God?
   a. ____ Because Christ died for us (*Vicarious Atonement*)
   b. ____ Because of our faith in Christ as our Savior
   c. ____ Because we have the Holy Spirit
   d. ____ Because of our Baptism
   e. ____ All of the above

3. How do children come to their parents? (Mark all that apply.)
   a. ____ In safety
   b. ____ Confidently
   c. ____ Without fear
   d. ____ Frequently

God is our loving Father. We can go to Him in prayer freely, joyfully, and trusting that He will hear and answer our prayers

4. So then how does God want us to pray to Him?
   a. _____
   b. _____
   What word(s) tells us that? _____

5. Who should we pray for? _____
   Who should we pray with? _____
   What word tells us that? _____

6. Because our Father is in Heaven, what does that tell us about His power and authority? _____

   _____

   _____

Lesson 47: The First Petition ("Hollowed be Thy name.")

> **Memorization:** Luther's explanation to the First Petition –
> *Hollowed be Thy name.*
> *What does this mean?*
> *God's name is certainly holy in itself, but we pray in this petition that it may be kept holy among us also.*

"*Hallowed*" means holy, blessed or honored. "Thy" can rightly be substituted with the word "Your." Therefore, another way to understand this petition is "Honored be Your name."

Catechism Material: Questions 208–211 (pp. 181–183)

1. Which of the Ten Commandments deals with God's name?
    a. _____ First
    b. _____ Second
    c. _____ Third
    d. _____ Fourth

2. When we say "Hollowed be Thy name" do we make God's name holy? Why or Why not?

    _____

    _____

    _____

    _____

    _____

God's name is holy with or without our help. But because we love Him we should honor and keep His name holy in all that we say and do.

3. By praying this we are asking to keep God's name holy and for God to help us keep His name Holy. What are the two ways we can keep God's name holy?
    a. _____
    b. _____

4. What are the two ways we "*profane*" (i.e., disrespect, treat with irreverence or contempt) God's Holy name?
    a. _____
    b. _____

5. For the following examples write "H" if it is keeping God's name Holy or "P" if it is profaning God's name. (If you are having trouble, refer to the Ten Commandments)

    _____ Going to Bible class   _____ Skipping church

    _____ Cursing anyone   _____ Not thanking God

    _____ Reading the Bible daily   _____ Complaining about what you have

    _____ Not telling others about your Savior   _____ Thanking God for everything

Lesson 48: The Second Petition ("Thy kingdom come.")

> **Memorization:** Luther's explanation to the Second Petition –
> *Thy kingdom come*
> *What does this mean?*
> *The kingdom of God certainly comes by itself without our prayer, but we pray in this petition*
> *that it may come to us also.*
> *How does God's kingdom come?*
> *God's kingdom comes when our heavenly Father gives us His Holy Spirit, so that by His grace*
> *we believe His Holy Word and lead godly lives here in time and there in eternity.*

Part of this petition is asking for the Kingdom of Grace to come to this world. Through asking this, we are asking God to save the people of the world and use us to spread salvation as well. The following is a list of some of the ways that we can accomplish this:

Jesus please come and help everyone, including me, to believe and trust in you!

I.   Live our lives as Christ has taught us to live.
II.   Follow the Ten Commandments.
III. Study the Bible and be ready to answer questions by your friends and family around you about Christ.
IV.   Give money to the church and to missionaries.
V.   Become a pastor.
VI.   Become a missionary pastor.
VII. Pray for your pastor and for missionaries.
VIII. Pray for those around you who do not know Christ to know him, and for those that know Christ that they may continue with Him.
IX.   Go to church and Sunday School or Bible class.
X.   Pray for boldness to do one or many of these or other things so that people might be saved.

Catechism Material: Questions 212–214 (pp. 183–186)

1. There are three kingdoms of God. Match the kingdoms to what they are and the Bible passage talking about them.

God's Kingdom	God is King over...	Bible Passage
a. The Kingdom of Power	____ The church and angels in heaven	____ John 3:5
b. The Kingdom of Grace	____ The whole universe	____ 2 Timothy 4:18
c. The Kingdom of Glory	____ The church on earth	____ Psalm 103:19

2. True / False – In the second petition we pray that the Kingdom of Power will come. Why or why not?

_____

3. What are the two ways we want God's Kingdom of Grace to come to our lives personally?
   a. ____ We go to church
   b. ____ We believe His word
   c. ____ We study the Bible
   d. ____ We live holy lives

4. What are the two ways we want God's Kingdom of Grace to come to the world?
   a. ____ That He would make many believe in Jesus as their Savior
   b. ____ That people would come to church
   c. ____ That God would bless us with lots of earthly things
   d. ____ That we would be used in bringing others to Jesus

5. What do we want the Kingdom of Glory to do?
   a. ____ Keep Holy for us
   b. ____ Prepare a room for us
   c. ____ To come quickly
   d. ____ Make its home here on earth

6. Read 2 Peter 3:1–9. Has God promised to send His Kingdom? Yes / No

   Are God's promises reliable? Yes / No

   When will God's Kingdom of Glory come? _____

   _____

   Why is it taking so long for the Kingdom of Glory to come? (Make reference to the Kingdom of Grace)

   _____

   _____

   _____

7. List two things that you will do right now and one thing you will do in the future to help the Kingdom of Grace come:
   a. _____
   b. _____
   c. _____

Lesson 49: The Third Petition ("Thy will be done.")

> **Memorization:** Luther's explanation to the Third Petition –
> *Thy will be done on earth as it is in heaven.*
> *What does this mean?*
> *The Good and gracious will of God is done even without our prayer, but we pray in this petition that it may be done among us also.*
> *How is God's will done?*
> *God's will is done when He breaks and hinders every evil plan and purpose of the devil, the world, and our sinful nature, which do not want us to hallow God's name or let His kingdom come; and when He strengthens and keeps us firm in His Word and faith until we die. This is His good and gracious will.*

Catechism Material: Questions 215–218 (pp. 186–189)

1. Read 1 Timothy 2:3–4, 1 Thessalonians 4:3–4, and Question 162 (p. 153). What is God's will?

   _____

   _____

   _____

2. Who or what are the three things that oppose the will of God (***three evil powers***)? Match them with the example of how it opposes God's will.

    Thing in opposition   How it is opposed to God's Will

    a. _____ ____ Persecutes Christians and ridicules their beliefs

    b. _____ ____ Encourages us to sin

    c. _____ ____ Lies to us about our salvation and God's Word

3. Do we then, at times, oppose the will of God? Why or why not? _____

    _____

    _____

    _____

    _____

4. When you look at the world and what it praises, what it thinks is good and what it desires, how does the world oppose the will of God?_____

    _____

    _____

    _____

    _____

God do your good and perfect will and not mine! Protect and save me from the evil within and all around me!

5. How did the Devil actively go against the will of God in Genesis 3?_____

    _____

    _____

6. If God's will were not done, what would happen to our faith?

    a. ____ Nothing

    b. ____ It would be strengthened

    c. ____ It would be weakened

    d. ____ It would be lost

7. How does God's will help us?_____

    _____

    _____

8. Sometimes it appears that the enemies of God are winning and will win. When evil comes the way of a believer, what does God say He will do? (Read Romans 8:28) _____

    _____

    _____

    _____

Lesson 50: The Fourth Petition ("Give us this day our daily bread.")

> **Memorization:** Luther's explanation to the Fourth Petition –
> *Give us this day our daily bread.*
> *What does this mean?*
> *God certainly gives daily bread to everyone without our prayers, even to all evil people,*
> *but we pray in this petition that God would lead us to realize this and to receive our daily*
> *bread with thanksgiving.*
> *What is meant by daily bread?*
> *Daily bread includes everything that has to do with the support and needs of the body, such as*
> *food..., home..., money..., a devout husband or wife, devout children..., good government, good*
> *weather..., health, self-control, good reputation, good friends, faithful neighbors and the like.*

Catechism Material: Questions 219–222 (pp. 189–192)

1. True / False – When we pray for daily bread it only refers to food.

2. True / False – Only people who pray for their daily bread receive food for that day.

3. Who depends on God for everything that they have?
    a. _____ Me
    b. _____ My Neighbor
    c. _____ Good Christians
    d. _____ Me and everyone

4. Who deserves these *physical blessings* from God?

   _____

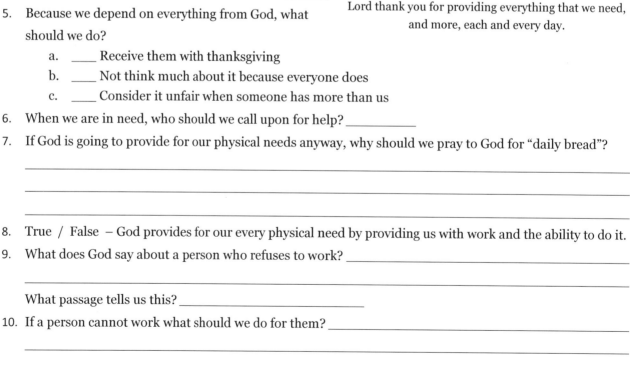

Lord thank you for providing everything that we need, and more, each and every day.

5. Because we depend on everything from God, what should we do?
    a. _____ Receive them with thanksgiving
    b. _____ Not think much about it because everyone does
    c. _____ Consider it unfair when someone has more than us

6. When we are in need, who should we call upon for help? _____

7. If God is going to provide for our physical needs anyway, why should we pray to God for "daily bread"?

   _____

   _____

   _____

8. True / False – God provides for our every physical need by providing us with work and the ability to do it.

9. What does God say about a person who refuses to work? _____

   _____

   What passage tells us this? _____

10. If a person cannot work what should we do for them? _____

   _____

   _____

11. If we can work, but refuse to, what commandment are we breaking by not working for our daily bread (Refer to the summary of the Ten Commandments)? _____

12. What should we do for a person who is out of work?
    a. ____ Nothing, God will provide
    b. ____ Pray for them
    c. ____ Help and encourage them to find work
    d. ____ Share with them until they can find work
    e. ____ b, c, and d

13. God daily provides for us everything we need in the day we need it. How should we live then? _____
    _____
    _____
    _____

14. If God provides for us daily, should we plan for the future? Why or why not? _____
    _____
    _____
    _____

15. Give several examples of "daily bread" that you received today and each day. What/who in your life did God use to provide those things to you?

Daily bread received	Person or thing God used to provide it to me
a. _____	_____
b. _____	_____
c. _____	_____
d. _____	_____

16. Oftentimes we think that being rich is better than being poor. We think that riches would make our lives better. Read Proverbs 30:7–9. What is the danger for the poor and in being rich? _____
    _____
    _____

17. Worrying is the opposite of trusting. Which commandment do we sin against when we worry? (Refer to the summary of the Ten Commandments.) _____

Lesson 51: The Fifth Petition ("Forgive us as we forgive.")

> **Memorization:** Luther's explanation to the Fifth Petition –
> *And forgive us our trespasses as we forgive those who trespass against us.*
> *What does this mean?*
> *We pray in this petition that our Father in heaven would not look at our sins, or deny our prayer because of them. We are neither worthy of the things for which we pray, nor have we deserved them, but we ask that He would give them all to us by grace, for we daily sin much and surely deserve nothing but punishment. So we too will sincerely forgive and gladly do good to those who sin against us.*

Catechism Material: Questions 223–227 (pp. 193–195)

1. What confession do we make in this petition? _____

_____

What then do we need and ask for?_____

2. True / False – It is through the forgiveness of sins that we can confidently and in good conscience ask God for any blessing.

3. How often do we deserve to be forgiven?
   a. ____ Always
   b. ____ Sometimes
   c. ____ Never

4. Read Romans 5:10. When Jesus died for us, was it before or after we asked for forgiveness?
   a. ____ Before
   b. ____ After

5. Read Matthew 18:21–22. How often should we forgive our neighbor their sins?
   a. ____ 490 times
   b. ____ Until we get tired of forgiving them
   c. ____ Until they do not deserve it anymore
   d. ____ Every time we are asked and even when we are not

Lord forgive us, and help us to forgive.

6. What can we expect if we do not forgive our neighbor their sins? _____

_____

7. True / False – When we forgive others their sins (even when they don't deserve it), it shows that we truly believe that we are forgiven and that we truly believe we do not deserve that forgiveness.

8. Is it possible for our neighbor to sin so greatly against us that it outweighs the sins God has forgiven us? Why or why not?_____

_____

_____

Lesson 52: The Sixth Petition (Temptation)

> **Memorization:** Luther's explanation to the Sixth Petition –
> *And lead us not into temptation*
> *What does this mean?*
> *God tempts no one. We pray in this petition that God would guard and keep us so that the devil, the world, and our sinful nature may not deceive us or mislead us into false belief, despair and other great shame and vice. Although we are attacked by these things, we pray that we may finally overcome them and win the victory.*

Temptation is truly all around us and even inside of us. We know that we are encircled by the enemies of Christ because even the world is our enemy and hates believers (John 15:19). Furthermore, our own sinful flesh torments us day and night, tempting us to sin (Mark 7:21–23). Therefore, we cannot escape such a wretched curse until we are dead and enter into His Kingdom of Glory. But if God were to take us completely out of this world and away from such temptation, we would be unable to help those in need. Therefore, Paul said, "for to me to live is Christ, and to die is gain" (Philippians 1:21–26).

God help us to choose the path you would
have us go.

Tempt versus Test:

Today the word tempt in the English language is usually used to talk about someone trying to get us to do something wrong. God, when He "tempts" us, has no desire that we should choose the wrong thing, but rather should choose the right thing. It is like putting a multiple-choice question in front of you and letting you pick the right or good response or the evil response. So, when God "tempts us," the better term is "tests us." He gives us an opportunity to choose the godly and right path.

Catechism Material: Questions 228–230 (pp. 195–198)

1.   Which Bible passage tells us God does not tempt anyone to sin? _____

2. There are two meanings to the words tempt and temptation. How does God "tempt" us? _____
_____

What does it mean that the Devil, the world, and our sinful nature tempt us? _____
_____

3. What is a better word for "tempt" when talking about how God "tempts" us? Why? _____
_____
_____

4. Read 1 Peter 1:6–9. What is the purpose of God testing us and allowing the evil powers to tempt us?
_____
_____
_____

5. What are the three evils that the devil, the world and our sinful nature (the *three evil powers*) are trying to lead us into?

    a. _____

    b. _____

    c. _____

6. Read the following Bible passages and identify if it was God or one of the three evil powers tempting or testing the person, and then explain how they were tempted or tested.

    a. Exodus 16:4–5:_____
      _____

    b. Matthew 4:1–11: _____
      _____

    c. Deuteronomy 8:2: _____
      _____

    d. Job 1:6–12: _____
      _____
      _____
      _____

7. When we pray this petition, why is it impossible for us not to be tempted by the three evil powers?

_____

_____

_____

8. When will we no longer be tempted?
    a. ____ When we go to church
    b. ____ When we Love God with all our heart
    c. ____ When we die and enter into the Kingdom of Glory
    d. ____ When we have enough faith

9. Read 1 Corinthians 10:13. When we are tempted, what does God promise and what do we pray for in this petition?

_____

10. Read Ephesians 6:10–18. What are some of the things God gives us to protect us from temptation?

_____

_____

_____

11. Who is stronger, God or our temptations? _____

12. What is it then that we pray for in this petition?_____

_____

Lesson 53: The Seventh Petition ("Deliver us from evil.")

> **Memorization:** Luther's explanation to the Seventh Petition –
> *But deliver us from evil.*
> *What does this mean?*
> *We pray in this petition, in summary, that our Father in heaven would rescue us from every evil of body and soul, possessions and reputation, and finally, when our last hour comes, give us a blessed end, and graciously take us from this valley of sorrow to Himself in heaven.*

Catechism Material: Questions 231–233 (pp. 198–200)

1. How does God deliver us from evil? (Mark all that apply.)
    a. ____ Allowing us to endure in times of trial
    b. ____ Using times of trial to strengthen our faith
    c. ____ Keeping all forms of evil from us
    d. ____ Correcting us when we sin
    e. ____ Turning pain and suffering into good
    f. ____ Answering every prayer and immediately removing evil from us
    g. ____ Allowing us to die and taking us to heaven to be with Him
    h. ____ Protecting us from evil entering our lives

God works in many ways to help those who are in need, and those who suffer evil in this world.

2. If God does not immediately spare us from evil or allows evil to come into our lives, does this make Him unloving or unkind? Why or why not? _____

    _____

    _____

3. Based on what you have learned, is it God that brings evil into our or anyone else's life? If it is not Him, who or what brings the evil? _____

    _____

    _____

4. Give an example or two of evil that you have seen either in your life or another's. _____

    _____

    _____

    _____

5. Give an example either from the Bible or your life where God delivered someone from evil. _____

    _____

    _____

    _____

6. What is the ultimate deliverance from evil? Why? _____

    _____

    _____

Lesson 54: The Conclusion ("Amen.")

> **Memorization:** Luther's explanation to the conclusion –
> *For Thine is the kingdom and the power and the glory forever and ever. Amen.*
> *What does this mean?*
> *This means that I should be certain that these petitions are pleasing to our Father in heaven, and are heard by Him; for He Himself has commanded us to pray in this way and has promised to hear us. Amen, amen, which means "yes, yes, it shall be so."*

Catechism Material: Questions 234–235 (pp. 200–201)

1. Who has the power to do all things including answering our prayers? _____
2. Who ultimately rules the world and every nation? _____
3. Who rightly deserves every form of glory and honor? _____
4. Who has promised to answer our prayers? _____
5. How long is God able to answer our prayers? _____

    _____

6. When will God's reign end? _____

All power and glory goes to the Lord.

7. How then can we be certain that God will answer and has the power to accomplish what we pray?

_____

_____

_____

8. What does the word "*amen*" mean?_____

9. Why can a Christian add the word "amen" with confidence and assurance to this and every prayer that they pray?_____

_____

_____

SECTION 7: REVIEW

1. Prayer is considered what kind of act?
    a. ____ Obedience
    b. ____ Love
    c. ____ Worship
    d. ____ Kindness

2. Who is provided the privilege to pray?
    a. ____ Everyone
    b. ____ Anyone who goes to church
    c. ____ Pastors
    d. ____ All believers

3. Who should we pray to?
    a. ____ God
    b. ____ All heavenly beings
    c. ____ Angels
    d. ____ Our Ancestors

    When we pray to _____ why do we have confidence that they can hear, answer and carry out the answer to those prayers?_____

    _____

4. What are the three types of things that we ask for in prayer?
    a. _____
    b. _____
    c. _____

5. Who helps us to pray?_____

6. Who should we pray for? (Mark all that apply.)
    a. ____ Our neighbor
    b. ____ The dead
    c. ____ Ourselves
    d. ____ Our pastor
    e. ____ Our enemies
    f. ____ Our country
    g. ____ Our church

7. Do we have to use our voice to pray? Why or why not?_____

_____

8. What is the name of the prayer that Jesus gave to us? _____

9. What are the three sections of the prayer Jesus gave us?

    a. _____

    b. _____

    c. _____

10. How many petitions are there? _____

11. The petitions can be divided into three sections. What do we ask for in each of these sections?

    a. _____

    b. _____

    c. _____

12. Because God is "our Father," what does that mean for how we can come to Him in prayer and what we can ask of Him?_____

_____

_____

13. When we pray that God's name be "hallowed", does that mean that God needs us to make His name holy in order for it to be holy? Why or why not? _____

_____

_____

14. What are the two ways we keep God's name holy among us?

    a. _____

    b. _____

15. When we ask for God's kingdom to come, which kingdoms are we asking to come? (Mark all that apply.)

    a. ____ Kingdom of Power

    b. ____ Kingdom of Grace

    c. ____ Kingdom of Glory

How do each of the kingdoms you marked come? _____

_____

_____

16. Is the promise that God's Kingdom of Glory will come reliable? Why or why not?_____

_____

When will it come?_____

17. What are the three things that resist the will of God?

    a. _____

    b. _____

    c. _____

18. Why is God's will better than ours? _____

_____

19. What exactly is God's will? _____
_____

20. Can God's will win over the things that resist Him? Why or why not? _____
_____

How can you be sure? _____
_____

21. True / False – God only provides the things we need to survive to those who believe and trust in Him. If true, how do unbelievers survive? If false, why should we pray for them if God is going to provide for us either way? _____
_____
_____

22. Who deserves the physical blessings God gives?
    a. ____ No one
    b. ____ Me
    c. ____ Everyone
    d. ____ Believers

23. If God provides for all, do we need to give anything to the poor? _____
_____

24. If a person refuses to work, should we provide for them? Why or why not? _____
_____
_____

25. If a person cannot work due to disability, health, etc., should we provide for them? Why or why not?
_____
_____

26. True / False – Because God promises to care for us, we do not need to plan for our future needs. Why or why not? _____
_____

27. If we do not forgive our neighbor's sins, what will happen to us?
    a. ____ Nothing
    b. ____ God will not forgive our sins
    c. ____ God will forgive our sins
    d. ____ We will just have to do penance

28. Is there anything someone could do that would allow us not to forgive them their sins if they repent?
    a. ____ Yes
    b. ____ No

29. True / False – God tempts us to sin.
    If false, who or what tempts us to sin? _____

30. Ultimately the three evil powers lead us into three evils; what are they?

   a. _____

   b. _____

   c. _____

31. How does God use temptation and evil in this world?

   a. ____ He shields it from believers completely to show His mercy.

   b. ____ He utilizes it to refine believers' character and bring them closer to Him.

   c. ____ God does not utilize them; only Satan does.

32. Is it possible for all temptation to end on this earth? Why or why not? _____

   _____

   When will all temptation end? _____

33. Does it always feel fair for God to allow evil and temptation to come into our lives? Yes / No

   Is it fair for God to allow evil and temptation to come into our lives? Why or why not?_____

   _____

   _____

34. Does it always feel loving when God allows evil and temptation to come into our lives? Yes / No

   Is it loving for God to allow evil and temptation to come into our lives? Why or why not? _____

   _____

   _____

35. What does the word "amen" mean?_____

SECTION 8 – THE SACRAMENTS

LESSON 55: INTRODUCTION TO THE SACRAMENTS

> **Memorization:** Hebrews 4:12 –
> *For the word of God is living and powerful, and sharper than any two-edged sword, piercing even to the division of soul and spirit, and of joints and marrow, and is a discerner of the thoughts and intents of the heart.*

In regard to both sacraments (Baptism and Holy Communion), there is an important distinction to be made between what the Lutheran Catechism teaches and what other religious sects (other churches) teach. That distinction is that the Bible teaches and we believe that Holy Baptism and Holy Communion are things that God does FOR us (i.e., a part of the GOSPEL). The others teach that we do them ONLY because God commands us to do them (i.e., a part of the LAW). They change something that is supposed to give the forgiveness of sins and thus life and salvation into a work of the law.

Catechism Material: Questions 236–238 (pp. 202–203)

1. In order for something to be a *sacrament*, it has to have three things. What are those three things?
   a. ____ Gives forgiveness of sins
   b. ____ Includes a ceremony
   c. ____ It is instituted by God
   d. ____ Is religious
   e. ____ God has combined a visible element with His Word

2. What are the two things that meet these criteria?
   a. _____
   b. _____

3. God has given us many examples of His Word doing powerful and amazing things. By this, we can take comfort that the sacraments really do contain and do the things God says they do. Read the passages and say what the Word of God did.
   a. John 1:1–3:_____
   b. Luke 7:1–10:_____
   c. Matthew 8:16–17:_____

4. Luther's Small Catechism and the Bible teach that the Sacraments are:
   a. ____ Things that GOD DOES for us (Gospel)
   b. ____ Things that WE DO solely because of God's command (Law)

SUBSECTION: HOLY BAPTISM

Lesson 56: What is Holy Baptism?

> **Memorization:** 1 Peter 3:21a –
> *There is also an antitype that now saves us – baptism.*
>
> (And also memorize this in case you need to administer an emergency Baptism:)
>
> *I baptize you in the name of the Father and of the Son and of the Holy Spirit. Amen.*

Baptism – God's work for us:

Holy Baptism is a precious gift that God has given to us and a precious thing that He does for us. It is not something that we do to show our faithfulness to Christ, but Christ's faithfulness to us. It is through Holy Baptism that God adopts and marks us as His children (Titus 3:5–8 and Romans 8:12–17). Through this Baptism, we can have confidence that we are saved because it gives us the Holy Spirit, creates faith and washes away our sins.

The shell with three droplets represents baptism, and the three droplets represent each member of the Trinity (Catechism p. 282).

Therefore we sin greatly and show that the truth is not in us if we turn Holy Baptism into a work of the Law or a ritual insurance plan. Baptism is the beginning of our faith, not the end. That is why Matthew 28:19–20 says "Baptizing them" and "teaching them to observe all that I have commanded you." Those who are baptized must continue in their faith and in learning God's Word. But if a baptized person throws away God's gift of Holy Baptism and does not believe, they have thrown away their salvation and have emancipated themselves from God's adoption. They have condemned themselves through their unbelief (Hebrews 10:26–31). How much worse then do you think it will be for those parents who treat Holy Communion such contempt by believing, and teaching their children, that Baptism is a failsafe and not the beginning of faith and life in Jesus Christ (Mark 9:42)?

Water and God's Word:

The power of baptism does not reside in the water, but rather in the Word of God (Q240 p. 205). Therefore, the requirement is the presence of water (enough to sprinkle). However, the amount of water has been and is a big consideration for some Christian denominations. In some Christian denominations, it is only a baptism when a person is completely immersed in water.

That is why the Catechism emphasizes that the term *"baptism"* in the Bible is used to describe washing in multiple ways including pouring, immersing, etc. (Q239 p. 205). The Catechism cites Mark 7:4 as evidence about this. *Immersion* did occur including immersing one's hands to purify them (however, pouring water over the hands instead of immersing was also acceptable). However, the verse also demonstrates the impracticality and impossibility of completely immersing tables and couches in order to wash them. Therefore, a baptism, or washing, is not synonymous with immersion.

Other evidence exists as well. One example of baptism in the Bible includes the Israelites crossing the Red Sea (1 Corinthians 10:1–2). Consider the imagery of the Israelites crossing the Red Sea. The ground was dry; the water folded back on either side creating walls and open ends on either side of the sea (Exodus 14). This baptism was not done through immersion. Rather those who were immersed were the Egyptians who God destroyed. Another example is the flood which also was a Baptism (1 Peter 3:18–21). This baptism also involved immersion, but not of those who were saved. Instead, the ones who were saved were sprinkled upon by the rain, and those immersed were destroyed.

Opportunity versus Desire:
Another important distinction regarding Holy Baptism needs to be made; it is not the lack of OPPORTUNITY to be baptized that can condemn us, but the lack of DESIRE to be baptized. As a believing Christian, we should earnestly desire to receive all the gifts God gives us and urgently desire to be forgiven of our sins. Baptism is one such gift. Therefore if someone does not have the desire to be baptized, serious concerns should arise. Such concerns include that the person probably is not a believer. However, it could also be that such a person just has not been instructed in the truth about baptism and so does not know its benefits or why they should desire it.

The example in this matter is the thief on the cross (Luke 23:39–43). Presumably, this man is not baptized and yet believes who Jesus is, and Jesus pronounces the most comforting words "Today you will be with me in paradise." His faith was enough to ensure his spot in the Kingdom of Heaven and his lack of opportunity for baptism was not counted against him. The other example is the Ethiopian eunuch (Acts 8:26–38). This eunuch who was not a believer became one when he talked with Phillip. When the Eunuch saw water, his response was to be baptized right then and there. There was no hesitation, no waiting, but rather a sincere desire, hope, and knowledge in the benefit of Baptism.

Who should baptize?
The Catechism teaches that pastors are to administer baptism normally, but anyone can in the case of an emergency. There are several reasons for this. First, you must understand why pastors baptize. God has ordained, set up, and sustains the office of the Pastor. One of the responsibilities of this office is to baptize (Matthew 28:16–20). That is the reason pastors normally baptize. We will focus on the two reasons for God giving this responsibility to pastors from the Bible. The first reason is for order (1 Corinthians 14:33). The second reason is that God establishes this as a way for Him to show His love and care for the church (Jeremiah 23:3–4). In the absence of a pastor and death is imminent, order is not broken by having any Christian baptize. Furthermore, Holy Baptism is from God, and the power is through God's Word. Therefore, God's love carries the weight (1 Timothy 2:3–4), and God's Word carries the power giving ordinary Christians the power and the responsibility to baptize in emergency situations.

Catechism Material: Question 239–254 (pp. 204–213) and a short form for Holy Baptism (p. 216)

1. Who instituted Holy Baptism?_____
2. Holy Baptism has two elements. What are they?
    a. _____
    b. _____
3. Does the water used in Holy Baptism need to be more holy than other water?
    a. ____ Yes
    b. ____ No

4. How much water is needed for Holy Baptism?

    a. ____ Enough to immerse someone

    b. ____ Enough to wash a person's hands

    c. ____ Enough to pour on a person's head

    d. ____ Only enough to sprinkle

5. How much water is described in Acts 22:16 for the use of baptism?_____

6. What gives the water in Holy Baptism power?_____

7. Which of God's Words are used in Holy Baptism?_____

_____

8. Does the amount of water matter? Why or why not?_____

_____

_____

9. Who instituted and commanded Holy Baptism? _____

    What is the Bible passage?_____

10. Read Matthew 28:16. Who was the audience that Christ told to Baptize?

    a. ____ Everyone

    b. ____ The whole church

    c. ____ The 11 disciples (i.e., the Apostles)

    d. ____ Me and you

    Your previous answer and 1 Corinthians 4:1 are the reasons why _____ are the ones who normally carry out Holy Baptism.

11. Who does God want to be baptized?

    a. ____ All nations

    b. ____ Your friends

    c. ____ Your family

    d. ____ Our neighbors

    Therefore Baptism should not be withheld from anyone based on their: (Mark all that apply.)

    a. ____ Race

    b. ____ Age

    c. ____ Religion

    d. ____ Mental status

    e. ____ Gender

12. Who can baptize in an emergency situation?

    a. ____ Anyone

    b. ____ Only a pastor

    c. ____ Any Christian

13. Is an ordinary Christian being disorderly or outside of God's command if they baptize in an emergency situation? Why or why not?_____

_____

_____

_____

14. If a person has not been baptized and is old enough to express their faith and be taught, what should be done before they are baptized?

      a. ____ They should spend a year in instruction

      b. ____ They should be instructed in the chief Christian doctrines

Give an example from the Bible: _____

_____

15. Does Jesus want little children (including toddlers and younger) to come to Him?

      a. ____ Yes

      b. ____ No

16. Specifically in regard to infants and children who are unable to express their faith, what are the four reasons that they are baptized?

      a. _____

      b. _____

      c. _____

      d. _____

Can these reasons also be applied to anyone who is unable to express their faith? Why or why not?

_____

_____

17. After a child is baptized the pastor (Matthew 28:16–20) and the parents (Ephesians 6:4) have a responsibility. What is that responsibility?_____

If a child or person dies shortly after they are baptized and the pastor or parents are not able to carry out that responsibility, have they sinned? (Consider the difference between the lack of <u>opportunity</u> and the lack of <u>desire</u>.) _____

_____

_____

_____

18. When parents bring their children to be baptized, how should the Pastor respond?_____

_____

_____

19. Can someone who has not been baptized be saved? Why or why not?_____

_____

_____

20. According to the catechism, what are the three things that we receive through Holy Baptism?

      a. _____

      b. _____

      c. _____

21. Baptism brings us into His family and marks us as His _____. (Fill in the Blank)

22. Read Titus 3:5. The catechism also states that baptism is a "water-spirit" baptism. What is the spirit that we receive when we are baptized? _____

23. Read Acts 2:38–39. In instances of an infant who dies shortly after they are born and are baptized. Can we have confidence that they are saved? Why or why not? _____

_____

What if a child is stillborn (dead before they are born) to Christian parents? Can we still have confidence that the child is saved? Why or why not? _____

_____

24. Faith in Christ as our Savior saves us. So why do we need Holy Baptism? _____

_____

25. True / False – Baptism is a guarantee of salvation regardless of faith and belief in Jesus Christ.

26. Should everyone be baptized regardless of religious beliefs in order to guarantee their salvation? Why or why not? _____

_____

27. If a person is born into this world once, a person is adopted into a family once, and Baptism is when a person is "born of water and the Spirit" (John 3:1–8) and adopted into God's family, how many times does a person need to be baptized? _____

How many times should they be baptized? _____

28. True / False – God commands sponsors to be used with Baptism.

29. True / False – The Church encourages the use of sponsors.

30. What is the purpose of sponsors? _____

_____

31. Is there another baptism besides the sacrament of Holy Baptism?
    a. ____ Yes
    b. ____ No

32. When a person is baptized through the sacrament of Holy Baptism, do they receive the Holy Spirit?
    a. ____ Yes
    b. ____ No

33. What was the purpose of when the Holy Spirit came with signs to the apostles (Pentecost) and others?
    a. ____ To show that all true Christians speak in tongues
    b. ____ To demonstrate what power a true Christian will have
    c. ____ To show that true faith has power
    d. ____ To demonstrate the truth and power of the Apostles' message

34. What was the difference between John's baptism and the sacrament of Holy Baptism?
    a. ____ John's baptism pointed forward to a Savior and Holy Baptism back to Jesus and His death and resurrection
    b. ____ John's baptism had no power to forgive sins
    c. ____ John's baptism was not as powerful as the Sacrament of Holy Baptism
    d. ____ There was no difference between the two

Lesson 57: Living our Baptism

> **Memorization:** Luther's explanation of what Baptism indicates –
> *What does such baptizing with water indicate?*
> *It indicates that the Old Adam in us should by daily contrition and repentance be drowned and die with all sins and evil desires, and that a new man should daily emerge and arise to live before God in righteousness and purity forever.*
> *Where is this written?*
> *Romans Chapter 6 verse 4: Therefore we were buried with Him through baptism into death, that just as Christ was raised from the dead by the glory of the Father, even so we also should walk in newness of life.*

Catechism Material: Questions 255–260 (pp. 214–216)

1. The *Old Adam* refers to what kind of sin?
   a. _____ Actual sin
   b. _____ *Inherited sin*

2. When it says that the Old Adam should be "drowned by daily contrition and repentance," what does that mean? (*contrition* means "to be sorry" or "sorrow," and repentance has to do with us "turning away from our sins and trusting in God for forgiveness")

   _____
   _____
   _____
   _____
   _____

After we are adopted into God's family through the water of baptism, we must leave our old lives behind.

3. What then is the purpose of daily contrition and repentance?
   a. _____ To show God we really are sorry
   b. _____ To help us resist and overcome evil desires
   c. _____ It is our penitence (apology/punishment) for our sins
   d. _____ Luther says we should do it

4. After drowning the "Old Adam," a "*new man*" should arise. What does this "new man" have?
   a. _____ A new nature
   b. _____ A new spiritual life
   c. _____ A sense of purpose
   d. _____ a and b

5. How do we have to live to have this "new man" "daily emerge and arise"? _____
   _____

6. Use the following words to complete the paragraph:

   Life   Death   Children   Raised   Sins

   When we were baptized we were baptized into Christ's _____. Since we have been baptized into this we are also_____ with Him and we are God's _____. Through this Christ overcame our _____. We too, through our Baptism, can overcome and live a new _____.

7.   What is the *"Trinitarian Invocation"*?_____

_____

How does the "Trinitarian Invocation" remind us of our baptism? _____

_____

SUBSECTION: HOLY COMMUNION

Lesson 58: What is Holy Communion?

> **Memorization:** Matthew 26:26–28 –
> *And as they were eating, Jesus took bread, blessed and broke it, and gave it to the disciples and said, "Take eat; this is my body." Then He took the cup, and gave thanks, and gave it to them, saying, "Drink from it, all of you. For this is My blood of the new covenant, which is shed for many for the remissions of sins."*

Holy Communion consists of four different parts. They can rightly be divided into the visible and invisible parts. The visible parts consist of the Bread and Wine, and the invisible parts consist of the Body and Blood. The catechism and we believe that the body and blood are "in, with, and under" the bread and wine. This is much the same as we view Christ, who was both Man and God at the same time. In that way, the Body is "In" the Bread, and the Blood is "In" the wine, <u>together at the same time</u>. Also like Christ, the people at the time saw Jesus' earthly form only (aside from a few instances and through His Word and Miracles). In the same way, the Body and Blood <u>are hidden</u> "under" the Bread and Wine. Finally, the Godhead of Christ and the Humanity of Christ are bound together inseparably. Likewise, the Body and Blood are "with" the Bread and Wine and are <u>inseparable</u>.

This way of understanding Holy Communion is also understood as *"real presence."* It means that all four elements are really together at the same time. That is contrary to other beliefs. One of those beliefs is transubstantiation. *Transubstantiation* is the practice of the Catholics, and it states that the bread and wine have changed completely into Christ's Body and Blood. The other side of that coin is a Symbolic understanding. The Reformed believe that Christ's Body and Blood are represented by bread and wine (or grape juice) and therefore are not actually present. Moreover, they believe no forgiveness of sins is actually given through Holy Communion; instead it is just a remembrance of His sacrifice.

The reason Luther rejected and the Bible does not teach a transubstantiation doctrine is because of 1 Corinthians 11:26 which refers to the Body and Blood of Christ in Holy Communion as Bread and Wine (this cup). A symbolic doctrinal view is also contrary to the Bible because He says it IS His body and blood. The word "is" is not implied in the Greek, but instead, it is actually used. Moreover, Christ gives us His blood "shed for the remission of sins" (Matthew 26:28). Therefore, we receive the forgiveness of sins in this Sacrament as well.

Catechism Material: Questions 285–293 and 296–298 (pp. 231–240)

1. Holy Communion is only one of the many names for this sacrament. What are the others listed in the Catechism?

    a. _____

    b. _____

    c. _____

    d. _____

    e. _____

2. What does the Greek term used for Eucharist mean? _____

3. Read Luke 22:14–16. What is the name of the Old Testament ceremony that Jesus celebrated with His disciples? _____

4. Read 1 Corinthians 5:7. True / False – Jesus fulfilled the Passover celebration and instituted Holy Communion in its place.

5. True / False – Jesus gives us His Body and Blood in Holy Communion.

6. We know that Holy Communion contains Jesus' body and blood for four reasons. Match the reason with the passage:

Reason	Passage
a. Jesus says it IS His body and blood	____ Luke 22:20
b. Jesus establishes a testament/covenant	____ 1 Corinthians 11:27
c. The Word teaches it is a communion in Christ	____ Matthew 26:26, 28
d. When we take Holy Communion sinfully, we sin against Christ's body and blood	____ 1 Corinthians 10:16

7. How is it possible that Christ could give us His Body and Blood?

    a. ____ Because the pastor says so

    b. ____ Because of His Holy and Precious Word

    c. ____ Because we believe it to be true

8. True / False – When Christ gives us His Body and Blood He is also giving us forgiveness of sins. What things do we receive in Holy Communion? (Mark all that apply.)

    a. ____ Life and salvation

    b. ____ Victory over sin and hell

    c. ____ New life in Christ

    d. ____ Forgiveness of sins

9. What do we proclaim when we take Holy Communion (Mark all that apply.)

    a. ____ Life and salvation in Christ

    b. ____ Unity in Christ

    c. ____ Peace and safety

    d. ____ Unity with those who eat and drink with you

10. What are the four elements in Holy Communion?

Visible Elements	Invisible Elements
(1) _____	(1) _____
(2) _____	(2) _____

11. The Body and Blood of Christ are considered "in, with, and under" the bread and wine. What does each of those terms mean?

    a. In: _____

    b. With: _____

    c. Under: _____

12. Three doctrines about Holy Communion are taught in the world. Match the term with the definition:

Term	Definition
a. Transubstantiation	____ Christ's Body and Blood are in, with, and under the Bread and Wine.
b. Real Presence	____ The Bread and Wine have been transformed into Christ's Body and Blood.
c. Symbolic	____ The Bread and Wine represent Christ's Body and Blood, and we remember Him.

13. Which doctrine of Holy Communion do the Bible and the Catechism teach? _____

14. What is responsible for making the Body and Blood "in, with, and under" the bread and wine?

    a. ____ The pastor's words

    b. ____ God's Holy and Precious Word

    c. ____ We believe it to be true

Therefore, does everyone who takes Holy Communion receive Christ's Body and Blood? Why or why not?

_____

_____

15. True / False –Even though we receive Christ's Body and Blood when we take Holy Communion, Christ is not sacrificed again and again each time we take it.

16. Read Hebrews 10:11–12. How many times was Christ sacrificed for sins? _____

17. Read 1 Corinthians 11:27, 29.

    a. True / False – Everyone who takes Holy Communion receives the forgiveness of sins.

    b. When we do not take Holy Communion properly, what or who do we sin against?

_____

Lesson 59: How Holy Communion is given out and taken properly

> **Memorization:** Luther's explanation of the power of Communion –
> *How can bodily eating and drinking do such great things?*
> *Certainly not just eating and drinking do these things, but the words written here: "Given and shed for you for the forgiveness of sins." These words, along with the bodily eating and drinking are the main thing in the Sacrament. Whoever believes these words has exactly what they say: "Forgiveness of sins".*

Outcomes of Holy Communion:

Holy Communion has two specific outcomes. One outcome is that a person receives the forgiveness of sins. The other outcome is that they sin against the very body and blood of Christ (1 Corinthians 11:27). The difference between these two outcomes comes down to a person's ability to examine themselves and whether they believe the promises given in Holy Communion. If a person cannot examine themselves (e.g., small children or those who have not been instructed), then Holy Communion should not be given to them for their own safety. That is one of the reasons why the Lutheran Church waits until after a person has been confirmed before they take Communion.

Examination:

Question 303 on page 242, of Luther's Small Catechism, deals with individual examination before a person takes Holy Communion. The key to understanding the process of examination begins with understanding Law and Gospel (Section 3, Lesson group 2). The Christian must utilize the Law as a mirror to come to the conclusion that they are indeed sinful, deserving of death and eternal condemnation. From there they then understand that it is impossible for them to save themselves. Following those conclusions, in their sorrow for their sins, they look to Jesus Christ in faith and trust for salvation and forgiveness. They therefore desire and turn from their sins. Moreover, they seek Holy Communion because they know and believe that they receive the forgiveness of sins through Jesus' body and blood in, with and under the bread and wine. To simplify: First, the person recognizes their sins. Second, they repent of and turn away from those sins. Third, they believe in Jesus for forgiveness and salvation. Finally, they seek the forgiveness of sins found in Holy Communion and believe that Jesus' body and blood are in, with, and under the bread and wine.

Pastor's are the butlers of the Lord's Table. They prepare the food, set the table, and ensure we are ready to eat it.

Pastoral and individual responsibility regarding Holy Communion:

Pastors also have a responsibility regarding Holy Communion; they are the gatekeepers, and they are butlers. God is the master of His table and has outlined who can come to His table in Scripture. He has then given this responsibility to the Pastors who act as the gatekeepers of the pasture or butler of the house. Based on what God has said, they are also responsible for letting into the house those that come to the Lord's Table prepared and can examine themselves. As a butler, they not only let the people in but welcome them wholeheartedly with warmth and the comforts of the Lord's house. They are also responsible for keeping out those thieves and swindlers who would destroy the house and themselves. Those are the people who are not prepared and cannot examine themselves. They keep those people out so that they do not hurt themselves spiritually. However, they should still encourage those who do not believe to believe, so that they might eventually come to the Lord's Table worthily.

Likewise, they are the shepherds of the flock. They protect the flock from harm and lead them beside the quiet waters. In this way, they protect the individuals in the congregation from harming themselves if they are unprepared or unable to examine themselves for Holy Communion. They also encourage those who are prepared and able to examine themselves to take Holy Communion. In both ways, this is an act of love by the Pastor.

Some consider the exclusion of people from taking Holy Communion as rude and unloving, but the opposite is true. If a pastor allows anyone and everyone to take Holy Communion, it is like they are the lazy shepherd who allows the sheep to run off the edge of the cliff. He is like the scared shepherd who, for fear of his own life, allows the lion to eat the sheep. In this way, the shepherd has allowed evil to come to the flock, and he did nothing, or nothing effectual, to stop the death of his flock. Indeed, only a fearful expectation of judgment waits for those pastors (Jeremiah 23:1–4). The shepherd who loves his sheep would stop the sheep from running off the cliff or the lion from killing it.

How does a pastor do this? He does this through knowing and caring for his congregation. Therefore, if a previously unknown person comes into his congregation, he should ensure their belief and ability to examine themselves BEFORE he gives them Holy Communion. Moreover, he must preach the need for forgiveness and the purpose of Holy Communion so that the congregation comes to Holy Communion often and ready.

Now does this mean that the individual has no responsibility in the matter? Certainly not! The pastor, while he is responsible, is just a man. He is unable to peer into our hearts. He can only make a decision based on what he has seen and heard. Therefore, if the individual knows that they do not believe, or believes they have no need for forgiveness, then they MUST excuse themselves from Holy Communion. In such a case the pastor, who has looked, but was unable to know, is not at fault.

How often should Holy Communion be given and taken?

Communion as you learned has many benefits. It also strengthens our faith when we are weak. The chief benefit is that it forgives us our sins. So the next question is, how often do you sin? As a believer, you must say that you often sin and sin every day. Thus we should want to take Holy Communion often and every day. One of the things that we do during Holy Communion is that we "proclaim the Lord's death till He comes" (1 Corinthians 11:26). How often should we desire and should we actually proclaim Jesus? It is the same, often, and every day. These two things must, however, be balanced with order and reverence. If it is either disorderly or irreverent, then we are sinning against the Body and Blood of Christ (1 Corinthians 11:17–22). So then, the best answer is, it depends upon the congregation. So long as they do it often, reverently, and orderly, then they are doing it correctly.

We too as individuals must meet those expectations. We must also not despise Holy Communion knowing that we are sinful human beings in desperate need of forgiveness. That is why Luther says that after four times of missing Holy Communion a year it should be feared that the person despises Holy Communion (Luther's preface to the Small Catechism). As individuals, there is another thing to consider as well. When we take Holy Communion, we are taking from the same loaf and showing that we are in agreement in doctrine with those with whom we commune. What this means is, if you take Holy Communion with, for instance, a Baptist church, you are saying you agree with the doctrine of the Baptist church. Therefore, we ought to be careful with whom we commune (1 Corinthians 10:16–17).

Who are unworthy to come to Holy Communion?

It is essential to explain with great diligence who the unworthy guests at [the Lord's] Supper are, namely, those who go to this sacrament without true contrition and sorrow for their sins, without true faith, and without a good intention to improve their life...[30] (Formula of Concord)

To those who are weak or struggling in their faith:

True and worthy communicants, on the other hand, are those timid, perturbed Christians, weak in faith, who are heartily terrified because of their many and great sins, who consider themselves unworthy of this noble treasure and the benefits of Christ because of their great impurity, and who perceive their weakness in faith, deplore it, and heartily wish that they might serve God with a stronger and more cheerful faith and a purer obedience. This most venerable sacrament was instituted and ordained primarily for communicants like this, as Christ says, "Come unto me, all who labor and are heaven laden, and I will give you rest" (Matt. 11:28).[31] (Formula of Concord)

---

[30]   Formula of Concord – Solid Declaration, Article VII. Lord's Supper
[31]   Formula of Concord – Solid Declaration, Article VII. Lord's Supper

Catechism Material: Questions 294–296 (pp. 236–238) and 298–305 (pp. 240–244)

1. When should the church stop celebrating Holy Communion?
   a. ____ When we decide to
   b. ____ When Christ comes to judge the world
   c. ____ When money is tight
   d. ____ When the Pastor decides it is a good idea

2. How many times a year should we take Holy Communion?
   a. ____ Once a week
   b. ____ Every other week
   c. ____ Once a month
   d. ____ Often

3. There are two things that encourage us to take Holy Communion and two things that restrict how often we take it. Categorize them:

Reasons	Encourages	Restricts
a. We need forgiveness of sins	(1) ____	(1) ____
b. We need to keep our reverence to Christ		
c. We need to keep order in the Church	(2) ____	(2) ____
d. We need to keep proclaiming Christ		

   True / False – The pastor has no responsibility in who takes Holy Communion.

4. Pastors are the "gatekeepers" of Holy Communion and the "butlers" of the Lord's house. What is their responsibility regarding Holy Communion? _____
   _____
   _____

5. If you believe you do not need forgiveness for your sins, should you take Holy Communion? Why or why not?
   _____
   _____
   _____

6. If the Pastor is unaware that you believe that you do not need forgiveness, is he responsible if he gives you Holy Communion? Why or why not? _____
   _____
   _____

7. True / False – As long as we know what we believe, it does not matter who we take communion with. Why or why not and what Bible Passage supports your answer? _____
   _____
   _____

8. True / False – Fasting is not required before taking Holy Communion. Which Bible passage supports your answer? _____

9. Is it loving to allow everyone to take Holy Communion? Why or why not?_____

_____

_____

_____

10. As individuals, we need to be able to examine ourselves. When we examine ourselves against the Law, what do we find? (Mark all that apply.)

    a. ____ We are sinful

    b. ____ We cannot save ourselves

    c. ____ We need forgiveness for our sins

    d. ____ We deserve Hell and punishment

11. When we examine Holy Communion, what do we find there? (Mark all that apply.)

    a. ____ Life and salvation

    b. ____ Christ's Body and Blood

    c. ____ Forgiveness of sins

    d. ____ New life in Christ

12. When we have found such a gift in Holy Communion, what should our response be toward God and our sin? (Mark all that apply.)

    a. ____ There should be no change

    b. ____ We should desire to turn away from our sin and do what is right

    c. ____ We should Love God

    d. ____ We should keep living our lives as we see fit

13. Join what you have learned and answered in the last three questions to explain how you should examine yourself for Holy Communion._____

_____

_____

_____

14. If you are weak in your faith should you take Holy Communion? Why or why not?_____

_____

_____

15. There are four types of people that should not take Holy Communion. Explain why each one uniquely should not be allowed to take Holy Communion.

    a. Unrepentant people:_____

_____

    b. Unforgiving people:_____

_____

    c. Those who cannot examine themselves:_____

_____

    d. Unbelievers:_____

_____

16. A person grows up and has a normal person's ability to think and reason. Then they get a disease or disorder, such as Alzheimer's, which progressively deteriorates that person's cognitive (thinking) ability; should they be allowed to take communion with that disease or disorder?

    a. ____ Yes

    b. ____ Yes, until they are unable to examine themselves

    c. ____ Yes, if they were a Christian before the disease

    d. ____ No

17. Some people are born with disabilities that affect the mind and its ability to understand, learn, and articulate information (such as Down's syndrome). Should they be allowed to take communion?

    a. ____ Yes

    b. ____ Yes, if they or their parents are Christians

    c. ____ Yes, if they are a Christian and can verbalize their ability to examine themselves and their understanding of Holy Communion.

    d. ____ No

18. Why should a pastor not allow someone who does not believe the same as those in the congregation to take Holy Communion? _____

_____

_____

SECTION 8: REVIEW

Part 1: What are sacraments?

1. What are the three things that define a sacrament?

    a. _____

    b. _____

    c. _____

2. What are the two sacraments that God has given to His church?

    a. _____

    b. _____

3. True / False – We do the sacraments solely out of obedience to God. (Law)

4. True / False – We do the sacraments because they are God's gift that He does for us. (Gospel)

Part 2: Holy Baptism

5. Who instituted Holy Baptism? _____

6. What is the Bible passage that shows when Baptism was instituted? _____

7. What is the visible element in Holy Baptism? _____

8. How many times should a person be baptized? _____

How many times does a person need to be baptized? _____

9. True / False – Baptism has no real power; it is just a symbol.

10. True / False – In order for a baptism to be real or effective, the person must be immersed in water.

11. True / False – The water used in baptism has no power and is not more holy than other water, except that it is attached to the Word of God which gives it power.

12. When Baptism is performed, the Trinitarian Invocation is used. What is the Trinitarian Invocation?

_____

_____

13. Who normally performs baptisms?
    a. ____ Pastors
    b. ____ Christians
    c. ____ Anyone
    d. ____ Parents

14. In emergency circumstances, who can perform a baptism?
    a. ____ Anyone
    b. ____ Parents
    c. ____ Children
    d. ____ Christians

15. Describe an emergency situation where Baptism would be appropriate:_____

_____

_____

16. God marks us as His children through Baptism. What are the other three things that we receive through Baptism?
    a. ____ Assurance of earthly success
    b. ____ Forgiveness of sins
    c. ____ A guarantee of salvation even if we do not believe
    d. ____ Eternal Salvation
    e. ____ Salvation from death and the devil

17. Which of the following person types should NOT be baptized?
    a. ____ Hispanic persons
    b. ____ Children
    c. ____ Mentally deficient persons
    d. ____ Unbelievers

18. Is it appropriate for parents to have their infants baptized? Why or why not?_____

_____

_____

19. True / False – Once a person is baptized, it is a requirement that they continue in the faith and are taught and learn about God.

20. Is it good and right or even acceptable to use Baptism as an insurance policy for children or unbelievers? Why or why not?_____

_____

21. True / False – Baptism is a requirement for someone to be saved.

Why or why not? _____

_____

22. True / False – There is no difference between someone who lacks the opportunity to be baptized and a person who has no desire to be baptized.

    If false, what is the difference between them? Who will be saved or condemned? _____

    _____

    _____

    _____

23. True / False – It is important that after a person is baptized that they seek to be baptized by the Holy Spirit (Spirit Baptism).

    Why or why not?_____

    _____

24. After a person is baptized, they receive the "new man." What does this new man desire to do?
    a. ____ Lead a new life in Jesus
    b. ____ Please the Old Adam
    c. ____ Rage against God

25. Holy Baptism is the act of God bringing us into His family. This action is in spite of our own sinful nature and hatred towards God. Why then can we look to our Baptism as a reminder, hope, and surety of salvation?

    _____

    _____

    _____

Part 3: Holy Communion

26. Who instituted Holy Communion?_____

27. What Old Testament celebration did it replace?_____

28. True / False – We truly receive Jesus' body and blood in Holy Communion.

    If true, is Jesus, therefore, sacrificed, again and again, each time we take communion? Why or why not?

    _____

    _____

29. True / False – Lutheran's and the Bible teach the doctrine of transubstantiation in regard to Holy Communion.

    What is Transubstantiation? _____

    _____

30. What does the term "real presence" refer to in regard to Holy Communion? _____

    _____

    _____

31. Why is Holy Communion not simply "symbolic" in regard to Jesus' body and blood? _____

    _____

    Why is Holy Communion not simply "symbolic" in regard to us receiving the forgiveness of sins?

    _____

32. How many elements are in Holy Communion?_____

    List each of them and indicate whether they are invisible or visible: _____

    _____

33. Match the term to its definition:

Term	Definition
a. In	____ Inseparable from each other
b. With	____ Hidden from view
c. Under	____ Together at the same time

34. What causes Holy Communion to have the power it does (including forgiving sins)?
    a. ____ The Pastor's words
    b. ____ The individual Christian's belief
    c. ____ The Word of God
    d. ____ The doctrine of the Church

35. Should a person who is weak in faith come to the Lord's Table? Why or why not?_____

    _____

36. True / False – Everyone should come to Communion because it has the forgiveness of sins and it cannot

    harm anyone.

37. Which of the following are reasons that a person should not come to Holy Communion? (Mark all that apply.)
    a. ____ They are struggling with their sins
    b. ____ They do not believe they need forgiveness
    c. ____ They refuse to forgive someone else their sins
    d. ____ They cannot examine themselves

38. Who is given the responsibility of distributing Holy Communion?
    a. ____ The Church
    b. ____ The Pastor
    c. ____ Individual Christians
    d. ____ Parents

39. True / False – The Pastor should watch over his flock and take care that if someone is openly unrepen-

    tant and sinning that they do not take Communion.

40. Why does it matter if we take Holy Communion at another church or with someone who does not believe

    the same as we do?_____

    _____

    _____

41. Unlike Baptism, Communion has a requirement that a person must be able to examine themselves. What

    does it mean for a person to examine themselves?_____

    _____

    _____

    _____

42. If a Christian is unable to take Communion because they cannot examine themselves (for example they have a brain disease that has progressed substantially), and they have not take Communion for years, does this mean they are no longer saved? (Discuss opportunity and ability versus desire) _____

_____

_____

_____

43. If a Christian is bedridden and unable to come to church but still can examine themselves, and they desire Holy Communion, does their Pastor have a responsibility to bring them and serve them Holy Communion? Why or why not? _____

_____

_____

44. If a Christian is willfully sinning and unrepentant, should they be allowed to take Communion?
    a. ____ Yes
    b. ____ No

If they take Communion anyway, and the Pastor is not willfully ignorant, has the pastor sinned? Why or why not? _____

_____

45. God tells us to take Holy Communion "often," how many times a year is that?
    a. ____ Every other month
    b. ____ Every week
    c. ____ Every other week
    d. ____ It depends

46. What are some of the considerations for how often Holy Communion should be taken? _____

_____

_____

Section 9 – The Church

Lesson 60: What is the Church?

> **Memorization:**
>
> Ephesians 5:23b – *Christ is head of the church; and He is the Savior of the body.*
>
> *And*
>
> Romans 12:4–6a – *For as we have many members in one body, but all the members do not have the same function, so we, being many, are one body in Christ, and individually members of one another. Having then gifts differing according to the grace that is given to us, let us use them.*

Invisible Church: all true believers in Christ both dead and alive

The ***Holy Christian Church*** and the ***Communion of Saints*** are different names for the invisible church. They refer to the same thing because "Holy" refers to those who have been sanctified by the blood of Christ and therefore are saints. Moreover, the word "Communion" has to do with the gathering together of people, that is exactly what happens in a church.

Visible Church: Churches (any denomination) that have a group of people gathered around the Word and Sacrament; all people (believers and unbelievers/hypocrites) who claim to be a part of any Christian church or claim to adhere to the Bible and Christian doctrine

The ***catholic*** (universal) ***church*** is also another name for the invisible church. The terms catholic and Catholic are very different. The Catholic Church refers to the religious sect called Catholic. (They have the Pope and Saints, and the Roman Catholic Church was the one that Luther broke away from.)

The parable of the wheat and the tares found in Matthew 13:24–30, 36–43 explains why there are always going to be hypocrites and unbelievers on the earth and in the churches, and we cannot tell the difference. It is because God sows faith and trust in God in the world, creating the invisible church which He gathers into the visible churches. Satan sows unbelievers and hypocrites among them, thus tainting the visible church. Finally, God Himself will make the determination between the visible and invisible church on judgment day. In practical terms, it is not the responsibility of any Christian denomination to tell another Christian denomination that they are all not saved (thus outside of the invisible church), because the Word of God does not return empty (Isaiah 55:11). It is the responsibility of each denomination to stand up for the truth because they are the light of the world (Matthew 5:13–16) and avoid the false doctrines of others (Matthew 7:15–16 & Galatians 1:8). It is not the responsibility of the church to pick and choose among their own congregation those who are believers and who are not, in order to punish and throw them out. It is the responsibility of the church to utilize the office of the keys to excommunicate those who are openly sinning and unrepentant (Section 6).

Catechism Material: Questions 169–179 (pp. 157–165)

1. Who belongs to the "invisible church"?
    a. _____ Everyone
    b. _____ Members of a Christian congregation
    c. _____ True believers, dead and alive
    d. _____ No one

2. Who belongs to the "visible church"?
    a. _____ Everyone
    b. _____ Members of a Christian congregation
    c. _____ True believers dead and alive
    d. _____ No one

3. Who belongs to "The Holy Christian Church"?
    a. _____ Everyone
    b. _____ Members of a Christian congregation
    c. _____ True believers, dead and alive
    d. _____ No one

4. Who belongs to the "catholic church"?
    a. _____ Everyone
    b. _____ Members of a Christian congregation
    c. _____ True believers, dead and alive
    d. _____ No one

5. Who belongs to the "Catholic Church"?
    a. _____ Everyone
    b. _____ Members of a Catholic congregation
    c. _____ True believers dead and alive
    d. _____ No one

6. True / False – There are no one besides true believers in the visible church.
    If it is false, who else is in the visible church?_____

7. Why is the Holy Christian Church also called the Communion of Saints?_____
    _____

8. Who does the Holy Christian Church belong to and who built it?_____

9. What defines a church as being a member of the visible church?
    a. _____ The name Lutheran on it
    b. _____ The name Christian on it
    c. _____ It has a cross
    d. _____ People gathered around Word and Sacrament

10. Are there people who are unbelievers and hypocrites in the visible church and even in your congregation?
    Why or why not?_____
    _____
    _____

11. Are there people who are members of the invisible church in churches outside of your country, denomination, and congregation? Why or why not? _____
    _____

12. Can you tell which is which? Why or why not? _____

_____

13. How many churches are there? Why? _____

_____

_____

14. Read Ephesians 5:23 and Colossians 1:18.

Who is the body of Christ? _____

Who is the head of the church? _____

15. Match the following:

What should we do in regard to...   We should

   a. the invisible church   ____ Avoid them

   b. the visible church   ____ Seek always to be and remain in

   c. false teachers, churches, or religions   ____ Be faithful to it when it teaches the Word purely and
                                                          correctly administers the sacraments

   d. our responsibility to the visible church ____ Support and extend it through our lives, talents, and finances

16. Based on what you learned, what should you look for in a visible church to join it? (Mark all that apply.)

   a. ____ The word Lutheran

   b. ____ The gospel is preached in purity and truth

   c. ____ It is the church your family goes to

   d. ____ The sacraments are administered appropriately

   e. ____ The doctrines of the church are in accordance with Scripture

   f. ____ The people are nice

   g. ____ It is closest to home

   h. ____ The worship style is to our liking

17. What are the four ways we maintain and extend the church?

   a. _____

   b. _____

   c. _____

   d. _____

18. Read 1 Corinthians 9:1–11. Why should we give money to the church and the church as a whole pay a

reasonable and livable wage to the Pastor? _____

_____

Does a Pastor have the right to take time off, and should we complain about it? _____

_____

_____

19. Talk to your pastor, parents, or other members of the church and find out how you can do personal service in the church. What types of personal service did they tell you about?_____

_____

_____

Pick one of them to do and do it. What did you pick and why? _____

_____

_____

LESSON 61: RESURRECTION AND ETERNAL LIFE (LIFE IN THE CHURCH AFTER DEATH)

> **Memorization:** Job 19:25–27 –
> *For I know that my Redeemer lives, and He shall stand at last on the earth; and after my skin is destroyed, this I know, that in my flesh I shall see God, Whom I shall see for myself, and my eyes shall behold, and not another. How my heart yearns within me!*

Some religions and churches believe in a place after death where the soul goes to work off any remaining sins before they can enter into heaven. It has different names, but it is called *purgatory* in the Catholic Church. The Bible teaches against such doctrine through how it describes Jesus' second coming and His judgment. In that judgment, there are only two places a person can go: Heaven or Hell. Hebrews 9:27 also does not allow for such a place because it says a person dies once and then they face the judgment.

Like a caterpillar emerges from its cocoon a new being, we too will be changed in the resurrection (Catechism p. 275).

Catechism Material: Questions 187–191 (pp. 169–173)

1. Does the Bible teach that people will be resurrected?
    a. ____ Yes
    b. ____ No
   What Bible passage supports your answer? _____

2. Does the Bible teach that people are reincarnated?
    a. ____ Yes
    b. ____ No
   What Bible passage supports your answer?_____

3. Who will be resurrected?
    a. ____ No one
    b. ____ Only the good people
    c. ____ Only believers
    d. ____ All human beings

4. What will happen after the resurrection?
   a. ____ Everyone will go to heaven
   b. ____ They will be judged by Christ
   c. ____ Some will go to purgatory before they go to heaven
   d. ____ We do not know

5. What will happen to those who are saved, because they believed in Christ, after they are resurrected?
   a. ____ Their bodies will be forever destroyed so their spirit can be unchained
   b. ____ They will live in eternity with the body they had on earth
   c. ____ Nothing
   d. ____ Their original body will be transformed into a body like Christ has, and they will live in Heaven forever

What Bible passage supports your answer? _____

6. What happens to those who are condemned, because they did not believe in Christ, after they are resurrected?
   a. ____ Their bodies will be forever destroyed so their spirit can be unchained
   b. ____ Both their body and soul will be tormented forever in Hell
   c. ____ They will go to purgatory until they learn to obey God
   d. ____ They will be destroyed and become nothing

What Bible passage supports your answer? _____

7. Read Matthew 25:31–46. When the Son of Man (Jesus) decides where to send people on the Day of Judgment, how many options does He choose from?
   a. ____ 1
   b. ____ 2
   c. ____ 3
   d. ____ 4

Who was Hell originally intended for?
   a. ____ Believers
   b. ____ The devil and his angels
   c. ____ Unbelievers
   d. ____ All creation

8. Why does the concept of purgatory (or anything like it) not fit within Scripture? (Give a Bible passage to support your answer.) _____

_____

_____

9. Read 1 Thessalonians 4:15–17 and Revelation 1:7. Is there anyone who will not be resurrected? Why or why not?

_____

_____

10. What will happen to those who are not dead and so are not resurrected?
    a. ____ The same as those who died before the last day
    b. ____ They will all be destroyed
    c. ____ They will all be saved
    d. ____ We do not know

11. How long does a Christian live?
   a. ____ Forever
   b. ____ Until they die
   c. ____ Depends

12. When does eternal life begin for a Christian?
   a. ____ When they die
   b. ____ When they are born
   c. ____ When they believe

13. Read Matthew 22:31–32. Why does that passage indicate that the souls of believers are with God in Heaven after they die? _____

_____

14. Why does that passage indicate that the resurrection is real and that even though a Christian may die physically, they are still alive? _____

_____

_____

15. Which Bible passage gives you the most comfort and assurance that as a Christian you will live after death with God? Why? _____

_____

_____

LESSON 62: WHAT IS WORSHIP?

> **Memorization:** John 4:21–24 –
> *Jesus said to her, "Woman, believe Me, the hour is coming when you will neither on this mountain, nor in Jerusalem, worship the Father. You worship what you do not know; we know what we worship, for salvation is of the Jews. But the hour is coming, and now is, when the true worshipers will worship the Father in spirit and truth; for the Father is seeking such to worship Him. God is Spirit, and those who worship Him must worship in spirit and truth.*

Worship: to give divine honor, glory, or homage to something; or perform a religious, formal, or ceremonious rendering to something.

The definition of worship cannot include God because worship does not necessarily involve God. However, anything but true worship (i.e., worship of God) is sinful. True worship can only be achieved by Christians (Hebrews 11:6), because without faith a person only worships themselves or creatures of this world. With that in mind, there are several ways to worship. You can worship with your life, with your lips and body, with ceremonies, and with your heart and spirit. We'll first talk about worshiping with your life.

Worshiping with your life:

The definition of worship includes giving honor, glory, or homage. These are the important aspects of worship. We give honor, glory, or homage to someone by obeying them or doing what they ask (which requires using and giving our time, talents, and treasures to them). So, in effect, when we obey God's commandments, we are indeed honoring Him with our lives. For instance, by keeping the Sabbath and resting, we are worshiping God with our lives by doing what He asks (i.e., time). What about when you listen to your parents or boss? When you do what they tell you to do, are you, therefore, worshiping them and breaking the First Commandment? As a Christian, not if we do it for the right reason.

As a Christian, why should we listen to our parents, boss, or another person in authority? It is because God has told us to do so in the Fourth Commandment. Romans chapter 13 verses 1 and 2 tell us that God has established all authorities and to resist them is to resist God. If we do not have faith in God and yet obey those in authority, who are we worshiping with our lives? If we are doing what the boss says to obtain that promotion, then our motivation can be worship of ourselves. If we are doing what the boss says because we like them, then we are worshiping them. If we are doing it because another being we believe is a god told us to do so, then we are worshiping that god. Without faith, we may worship many different things with our lives, but it is never God.

Worshiping with your voice and body:

We worship God with what we say and how we behave towards Him with our bodies. We worship God when we praise Him (2 Samuel 22:4), bow down to Him (Genesis 24:26), sing to Him (Judges 5:3), dance to Him (2 Samuel 6:14), and raise our hands to Him to bless Him (Psalm 134:2). There are indeed many ways that we can worship God with our lips and body. There are many ways that people do, and they worship God differently—some standing, some sitting, some kneeling, some dancing, some singing, etc. How we worship with our bodies or the order of words that we say does not make one "right" or "wrong" (unless we go against God's commandments and blaspheme Him with our words or bodies). An example of blaspheme with our bodies is by standing in defiance of God instead of bowing in humility or standing in respect of Him. The important thing here is that we do everything to the glory of God and understand the meaning and reasons behind what it is we say and do.

Worshiping through ceremonies (formal worship):

There is a difference between a ceremony and a ritual, although ceremonies often become ritualistic. A church service is a *ceremony*; it is a formal activity with a set of defined behaviors. Depending on what church you go to, those defined behaviors may vary a lot. A funeral service or wedding are ceremonies, and they too can vary a lot in what occurs there. They also can vary if they are a ceremony involving or dedicated to God. The difference between a ceremony and a ritual is that in a ceremony the people, or you, are engaged and active. You are doing it to worship God. In a ritual, the people are disengaged and just going through the motions. The reason a person attends a ceremony may be a ritualistic one. For example, they may attend church on Sunday because they are "supposed to." When you or anyone does this, this is not worshiping, and it is not pleasing to God (Mark 7:6 and Zachariah 7:5), even though you may call it "worship."

Formal worship has changed substantially through history. How it has changed and what some of the elements are in a Lutheran Church Missouri Synod (LCMS) traditional service will be discussed in Lesson 67. While the history is discussed and the elements of an LCMS traditional service are described, it should not be taken to mean "this is how a formal worship service must be done." Formal worship contains many elements and traditions that are passed down in congregations, synods, and religious denominations alike. A person and congregation must weigh two things to determine what a formal worship service should be. The first: Is what the people are doing <u>Biblical</u>?

If it is not Biblical, it must be thrown out. The second (which is under or subject to the first): is what the people are doing <u>helpful</u> for the people in the service? The people involved in the worship must get value out of the formal worship structure and not be distracted by it. Jesus fulfilled the ceremonial law, and therefore formal worship can largely be influenced by preference as long as it does not go against the Bible and what is orderly (1 Corinthians 14:26–33). Many things are considered *adiaphora* (i.e., neither commanded nor forbidden). Therefore, it is perfectly acceptable that some worship in one way at one congregation and others completely differently at a different congregation. It is also acceptable that the formal worship change. The traditions of formal worship are not binding always or everywhere.

Worshiping in heart and spirit:
Worship anymore has little to do with where you are physically. In the past, it did because certain ceremonies and sacrifices must have been done at the temple. Now, however, there is no longer a physical temple. Rather God's temple is in our hearts and bodies (1 Corinthians 6:19–20). Regardless of whether or not a person had to go to a place to worship, true worship could not occur if it was not done with the heart (Mark 7:6 and Zechariah 7:5–6). Today there is no temple, but we have built churches to house our formal worship. This building is not a requirement to worship; rather it has to do with where you are in your heart and spirit (which includes your mind) (John 4:23–24). Today we worship in our homes, on the streets, at school, at work, and wherever we are. As long as what we are doing is done to the glory of God, indeed we are worshiping. We do not need to go to a church to pray, praise, or give thanks. Rather we need only go to our heart and spirit and worship there to God who is inside of each Christian. We can sing songs in our hearts, pray to God there, or give thanks for all that He has done as well.

1. Does worship always include God? Why or why not?_____
   _____
   _____

2. What are the four different ways that a person can worship?
   a. _____
   b. _____
   c. _____
   d. _____

3. True / False – A person who does not have faith in God can still worship Him.
   Why or why not? _____
   _____
   _____

4. How does a person worship with their life?_____
   _____
   _____

5. Give three examples of how you can worship with your body or voice.
   a. _____
   b. _____
   c. _____

6. How can a person blaspheme God with their body or voice?_____
   _____

7. True / False – We must go to a church in order to worship God.

8. True / False – Even when we worship in a church, it could be a ritual instead of worship.

9. What does it mean when worship becomes a ritual? Why is a ritual not worship?_____

_____

_____

What Bible passage tells you this?_____

10. True / False – The Bible outlines every detail on how we should worship formally together.

11. True / False – The traditions of worship cannot change and must be the same in every church.

12. What are the two things that determine how a formal worship service should be conducted?

a. _____

b. _____

Which is more important and why?_____

_____

13. If one of the traditions of the church you are attending is not followed one Sunday, is the worship service ruined? Why or why not?_____

_____

_____

14. Why can we worship in our hearts and spirits?

a. ____ We cannot

b. ____ The Holy Spirit is with us, and His temple is our hearts and bodies

c. ____ Our good deeds merit God's attention always

15. What are the three ways we can worship God in our hearts?

a. _____

b. _____

c. _____

SUBSECTION: HISTORICAL AND PRESENT FORMAL WORSHIP

Lesson 63: Worship before the Levitical Priesthood and Nation of Israel

In the creation account, God created the world in six days. On the seventh day, He rested and forever set up the Sabbath as a day of rest for His people. It is on this day that the Ten Commandments tell us that we should rest and worship God. While it was formalized in the Ten Commandments, because it was done in the beginning, this is a necessary part of worship that would have been done in the Garden of Eden (if they were there for more than six days).

After creation, Adam and Eve worshiped perfectly and continually because they were perfect. They did this by walking with God, talking with God, and having firsthand knowledge of God and who He was (Genesis 2). They obeyed God at first and honored His commandment not to eat of the tree of knowledge of good and evil. After the fall (Genesis 3), Adam and Eve no longer continually worshiped God with their lives because of sin. The only way they and their descendants after them could worship is by having faith in God (Hebrews 11:6). God promised that He would send a Savior to save Adam, Eve, and their descendants after them (Genesis 3:14–15). That is the promise that early believers believed in and God built upon several times. This direct contact between God and individuals continued with Cain, Enoch (Genesis 5:24), Noah (Genesis 7:1), Abraham (Genesis 18:13), Jacob (Genesis 31:3), and others.

After the garden, Adam and Eve taught their children to sacrifice to God. Acceptable sacrifices were those that demonstrated that God was first and above those giving the sacrifice and done with the heart. That is what is taught in the account of Cain and Abel (Genesis 4:1–8). Furthermore, the sacrifices we see before the Levitical Priesthood were sacrifices of thanksgiving and trust in God (Cain and Abel, Noah [Genesis 8:20], Abram [Genesis 12:7], Jacob [Genesis 31:54], as well as others) and not for sin.

God did not regiment the sacrifices given before the Levitical Priesthood. Rather each person gave as their heart desired. Abel gave a lamb, Abraham at first his son (whom God spared), and then a ram (Genesis 22:1–19), and Jacob drink and oil (Genesis 35:14). Also, God did not command, regiment, or explain the various offerings or clean versus unclean animals in detail until the Levitical Priesthood (Leviticus 11). However, there was an understanding of the difference between clean and unclean animals because Noah (Genesis 8:20), and perhaps others, knew. How they knew and where it was explained is unknown.

All of these things indicate that worship prior to the Levitical Priesthood was rather fluid. People worshiped whenever and wherever they wanted to and more often than not without a direct command from God about how. They were open to sacrificing what they thought was appropriate so long as it put God first. They also worshiped without sacrificing. We see this while Israel's descendants endured the captivity in Egypt (Exodus 4:30–31). This form of worship without sacrifices continued until God freed Israel's descendants from Egypt and established the Nation of Israel and its Ceremonial laws.

1. In the beginning, why was Adam and Eve's worship continual and perfect?
   a. ____ Because God was with them
   b. ____ Because they knew exactly what God wanted
   c. ____ Because they were perfect and sinless
   d. ____ Because God forced them to
2. What caused Adam and Eve's worship to no longer be continual and perfect?_____
   _____
3. Where in the Bible did God first promise a Savior? _____
4. Before the Nation of Israel and the Levitical Priesthood, what made a sacrifice appropriate?
   a. ____ It had to show God was first above the giver and was done with the heart
   b. ____ It had to be an animal
   c. ____ It had to be done the way God explained it
   d. ____ It had to be done in a certain place and in a certain way
5. True / False – The sacrifices before the Levitical Priesthood were for sins.
6. True / False – People (at least Noah) understood the differences between clean and unclean animals.

7. Why would you say that worship before the Nation of Israel was not very regimented? _____
_____
_____
_____

8. Did anyone have direct contact with God during this time? If so, give an example. _____
_____
_____

Lesson 64: Worship in the Nation of Israel

God began to regiment how people should worship beginning with the Passover, which was a part of the Feast of Unleavened Bread (Exodus 12:1–20). The Passover was a part of the last plague that finally freed the nation of Israel from the land of Egypt. The beginning of the Passover is the removal of all leaven (yeast) from the house. They were required to eat a male lamb or goat without blemish, unleavened bread, and bitter herbs. They must roast it on the fire and paint the blood on the doorpost so that the Angel of death would pass over their houses and not kill their firstborn. After the Angel of Death killed all the firstborns in the land of Egypt, Pharaoh finally lets the people go. With that, the Jews did as God had instructed and asked for gold, silver, and clothing. They continued in their worship and completed the Feast of Unleavened Bread which lasted for seven days, including the Passover. During this feast, they ate only unleavened bread. The entire nation of Israel did this.

To understand the size of the worship performed here, we must look to Number 1:1 which is the first census of Israel. They counted all of the men aged 20 and over able to go to war. This number would not have included the too old to fight, crippled, women, and anyone under the age of 20. It also does not include the Levites. The total that was able to fight was 603,550. Doubling that number for women and adding those who would have been unable to fight or be counted means there were probably more than 1.5 million people in the nation of Israel at the time. To put this in perspective, it would have been about the population of Phoenix, Arizona (1.5 million as of the 2010 census[32]), all worshiping and moving at once.

God continued to regiment worship by including many more feasts and sacrifices. Some of those feasts were the annual Feast of Harvest and the Feast of Ingathering (Exodus 23:14–16), the Feast of Weeks, Feast of Trumpets (Leviticus 23:15–25), and the Feast of Tabernacles (Leviticus 23:33–36). There were sacrifices to consecrate Aaron and his sons to be priests (Exodus 29:1–37), to consecrate the tabernacle (Exodus 29:38–46), for various sins (Leviticus 4), and for the firstborn males (Exodus 13:11–16). There were instructions and rules about how people became unclean and about the trespass offerings (Leviticus 5), unclean animals (Leviticus 11), birth (Leviticus 12), garments for priest (Exodus 28), the Tabernacle (Exodus 26), the Ark of the Testimony (Covenant), and other things in the tabernacle (Exodus 25).

The requirements of the ceremonial law regarding worship were extensive, and it continued through the time of David and Solomon. Solomon built the Temple because God did not allow David (David was a man of war) to build it (1 Chronicles 17:1–14). Over time, the first Temple was damaged and repaired twice (repaired by Jehoash – 2 Kings 12:4–5 and Josiah – 2 Kings 22:3–5) and then destroyed (Jeremiah 52:12–23). A second Temple was built by Jeshua and the priests (Ezra 3). This Temple was damaged several times and repaired several times. Around 20 BC, Herod the Great (a Jew) directed the training of a thousand priests to repair the Temple. He did this to ensure Jewish worship was not interrupted. This is the Temple that Jesus visited during His lifetime. This was the last Temple. In 70 AD the Jews revolted, and during this revolt, the Temple was destroyed. It happened when Titus, the Roman emperor, put down

32   United States Census Bureau, Quick Facts Phoenix Arizona 2010 http://www.census.gov/quickfacts/table/PST045215/0455000

the revolt. The only thing that remains is the West Wall[33]. This wall is commonly referred to as the *Wailing Wall* and still exists today. A new temple has never been built for many reasons including that the Muslims have built their holy shrine known as the "Dome of the Rock" on the site of the Temple. One of the requirements of the Temple is that it must be built on that particular spot, so unless the Dome of the Rock is destroyed, they cannot build the temple. Therefore, since the last Temple was destroyed, the Jews have performed no sacrifices.

Worship in the Nation of Israel was not just about sacrifices and offerings. During this time Solomon, David, and others wrote poems and songs with which to praise, thank, and worship God (Song of Solomon and Psalms). They prayed, danced (2 Samuel 6:14), and sang (Exodus 15). They also built the synagogues. Synagogues were built when there were 10 or more Jews present. Synagogues were used for the Jews to pray and read and study the Scriptures.

God also still maintained a direct contact with His people through the use of Prophets (which are classified as major and minor ones), spoke to Moses face to face (Exodus 33:11), and the Angel of the Lord spoke to all the people (Judges 2:1–4). Through all of these means of worship and God's direct contact with the people, God directed, corrected, and showed the people how He would ultimately save them from their sins.

1. True / False – During the time of the nation of Israel, God made worship very regimented. Why or why not?

_____

_____

2. How did the Jews celebrate the first Passover? _____

_____

_____

_____

3. What were the Jews able to take from the Egyptians because of the Passover?_____

_____

4. Approximately what was the size of the nation of Israel at the time of the Exodus?_____

5. True / False – During the Levitical Priesthood God instituted many sacrifices and feasts, but left the details on how to do those things up to the Jewish people.

6. Name two of the feasts given:

   a. _____

   b. _____

7. What Bible passage contains the instructions for the Tabernacle?_____

---

33   For an eye witness account to the destruction of the temple: The Romans Destroy the Temple at Jerusalem, 70 AD – http://www.eyewitnesstohistory.com/jewishtemple.htm

8. How many times was the Temple of the Lord built?
   a. ____ 1
   b. ____ 2
   c. ____ 3
   d. ____ 4

9. Who built the first temple?
   a. ____ David
   b. ____ Solomon
   c. ____ Moses
   d. ____ Jeshua

10. Who built the second Temple?
    a. ____ David
    b. ____ Solomon
    c. ____ Moses
    d. ____ Jeshua

11. Who repaired the Temple that Jesus visited while He was alive? _____

12. Is the Temple of the Lord still standing today?
    a. ____ Yes
    b. ____ No

    If not, what is one of the reasons it has not been rebuilt?_____
    _____

13. Do the Jews still sacrifice today? If not, why? _____
    _____
    _____

14. Did the people of Israel only sacrifice and give offerings?
    a. ____ Yes
    b. ____ No

    If not, how else did they worship? _____
    _____

15. True / False – God talked with Moses face to face.

16. What were the Synagogues used for? (Mark all that apply.)
    a. ____ Sacrificing
    b. ____ Praying
    c. ____ Reading scripture
    d. ____ Studying scripture

Lesson 65: Worship at the Time of Jesus Through the Apostles and Early Church

John the Baptist was the last prophet according to the Law of Moses, and he was sent to prepare the way for Jesus. His purpose was to proclaim the coming Savior and to call the Jewish people to repentance. He is the first person in the Bible that we know was baptizing people as part of worship, and he also baptized Jesus (Matthew 3). The idea of baptism (or washing) was not new to the Jewish people as they baptized or washed their hands, sofas, pitchers, etc. (Mark 7:4). Jesus continued baptism, but changed its nature from a baptism of the law (Matthew 3:15), into a baptism of grace through His death and resurrection (Romans 6:4). In other words, Baptism is now a part of the Gospel (God's work for us), instead of a part of the Law (solely our work of obedience). Likewise, He took the Passover and turned it from a work of the law into grace when He changed it into the Lord's Supper (Matthew 26:26–29). Jesus also continues the worship traditions of the Jews by preaching and teaching in both the Synagogues (Matthew 13:54), the Temple (John 8:2), and the surrounding open spaces (Luke 5:3). Jesus then fulfilled the ceremonial law of the Jews through His death and resurrection as to make the need for such sacrifices and feasts as taught by Moses obsolete (Hebrews 10:1–14). This also made it known that God no longer needed to be worshiped in a Temple that was built. Rather every believer's body was a temple to God where they could worship (John 4:21–24). This way of worship is what He taught His disciples and had them continue in after He ascended into Heaven.

After Christ's death and resurrection, early Christians did still attend the Jewish synagogues for a time while the Jews permitted it. Ultimately the churches established by the Apostles worshiped in their homes. This worship included preaching (Acts 20:7), reading Scripture (James 1:22), prayer (1 Corinthians 14:14–16), singing (Ephesians 5:19), the sacraments (Acts 2:41 & 1 Corinthians 11:18–34), and almsgiving (the offering for the church and its work) (1 Corinthians 16:1–2). Sometimes the services were long (lasting all night as in Acts 20:7–12). The apostles also performed missionary work, going from city to city (to many nations, not just to the Jews) preaching in the synagogues and before the leaders of the world (Acts 27:21–26). They also wrote many letters to the churches, both exhorting them and rebuking any false teachings or practices (The Epistles). Ultimately all of them, but John, were martyred.

Sometime during the early church, the Christians changed the day of worship to Sunday (Saturday had been the Sabbath day of the Jews). The reason why they did this was to celebrate on the day that Jesus rose from the dead. Also during the early church contentions arose and the Christian church was greatly persecuted during this time. Then Constantine the Great took control of the Roman Empire and converted to Christianity. He decriminalized Christianity. He desired that the Christian churches unify and held the council at Nicaea in 325 AD. This was an important council because out of this the Nicene Creed was born and outlined the primary beliefs of all Christians. It was at this time that those religious leaders in Rome began to wield political and religious authority and continued to gain influence and power after Constantine. Eventually, this would form and formalize what is now the Roman Catholic Church.

To be clear though, the Roman Catholic Church claims its heritage back to the Apostle Peter. That, to them, gives them an air of authority and a claim to the truth. However, it is the same as the Pharisees and Sadducees tracing their lineage to Abraham; it means nothing in regard to them having and knowing the truth (John 8:33–47). Moreover, there were no people with the title "pope" (Peter held no such title) in the beginning and for hundreds of years after him. The word "pope" officially related to the bishops of Rome and began in the 3rd century. Some time later (the 5th century), it was used to refer to a single person holding a specific office. It was used exclusively for the Pope in the 11th century[34]. The Roman Catholic Church is important because they systematically changed the concept of formal worship and the Gospel to something different from the one established by Jesus and the Apostles.

34   Online Etymology "Pope" http://www.etymonline.com/index.php?term=pope 08/18/2016

1. Who was the last prophet according to the Law of Moses? _____

2. True / False – The Jews baptized things before John began baptizing people.

    If true, what did they baptize?_____

3. How did Jesus change John's baptism?

    a. ____ He did not

    b. ____ Jesus made it a requirement to be saved

    c. ____ Jesus no longer required immersion

    d. ____ Jesus changed it from being a part of the law to being a part of the Gospel

4. Jesus fulfilled the _____ Law so that we no longer have to sacrifice animals for our sins.

    (Fill in the blank)

5. True / False – Jesus taught that only true worship happened in a temple or a church.

6. What are three of the places Jesus preached and taught as He went from place to place?

    a. _____

    b. _____

    c. _____

7. Where did the early Christians worship?

    a. ____ In new Christian temples

    b. ____ In their homes

    c. ____ In the streets

    d. ____ They stopped formal worship altogether

8. True / False – The Apostles only went to the Jews to make converts to Christianity.

9. Why did early Christians make Sunday the day of worship or Sabbath?_____

    _____

    _____

    What was the original Sabbath day?_____

10. What is the name of the Roman Emperor who decriminalized Christianity?_____

11. What year was the council at Nicaea?

    a. ____ 225 AD

    b. ____ 300 AD

    c. ____ 325 AD

    d. ____ 375 AD

12. What was the purpose of the Council at Nicaea?

    a. ____ To unify the Christian Church

    b. ____ To establish the Roman Catholic Church

    c. ____ To establish the Roman Emperor at the time as leader of the Christian Church

    d. ____ To excommunicate the heretics in the church

13. The Roman Catholic Church claims a lineage to the Apostle Peter. Does this make them the authority on

    Christian doctrine? Why or why not?_____

    _____

    _____

Lesson 66: Worship in Recent History

The Roman Catholic Church systematically changed formal worship from being in houses to building elaborate churches. They also brought in and dedicated many "relics" of early Christendom which people paid to see. Relics included the bones of saints, and other memorabilia they claimed came from the saints and Christ. They added saints who govern and showcase various aspects of "Christian" living, different jobs, and different locations around the globe.[35] (There are more than 10,000 canonized saints in the Roman Catholic Church.) They glorified Mary (also a saint), the mother of Jesus and pray to her so that she will pray and intercede for them, making her an intermediary to Jesus. Every saint is used in this way, and it is one of the purposes for every saint in the Catholic Church. They denied pastors (whom they call priests, bishops, cardinals, and popes) and other workers in the church (monks, friars, and

nuns) the right to marry. They established indulgences, purgatory, and many religious rites that must be observed by those who are Catholic. Indulgences included paying to see those relics that they had established. The purpose of indulgences was to pay for the sins that a person alive or dead had done or even will commit. These many cases of abuse and regimenting of formal worship led to many rebellions against the Catholic Church including that of Martin Luther.

Martin Luther fundamentally changed formal worship from the Catholic Church. He removed the false idea of looking to saints for guidance, protection, and having them intercede for us to God. He removed the idea of purgatory, indulgences, and *works righteousness*. He restored the use of the Bible in the church in the common language of the people and wrote many hymns and the liturgy in the common language. However, he did not completely abolish symbols inside of the church (e.g., the crucifix, the altar, paintings, stained glass, etc.). That is why there are still many uses of those things inside of the Lutheran Church today. Luther, in his reformation, did not want to abolish all things that were "Catholic," but rather all things that were heresies. That bothered other reformers like the Anabaptists who saw all symbols (or rather the vast majority) as idolatry. This is why in the Baptist churches there are very few (maybe a Cross), if any, Christian symbols in the worship area.

1. True / False – The Roman Catholic Church did not build elaborate churches.
2. How many saints are there?_____
3. True / False – Catholics teach that you can and should ask saints (i.e., pray to them) to pray for you when you need something.
4. True / False – According to the Catholic Church, pastors (i.e., priests) cannot marry.
5. What are indulgences? _____

   _____

6. True / False – Martin Luther thought indulgences and purgatory were Biblically true.
7. True / False – Martin Luther abhorred all symbols used in worship because they are idolatry.

---

35   If you would like to learn more about the saints visit www.catholic.org/saints

8.   How did Martin Luther change worship?
    a.   ____ He removed all things that were Catholic
    b.   ____ He kept all the practices of the Catholic Church
    c.   ____ He removed only the heresies of Catholic worship
    d.   ____ He changed worship to be completely different than the Catholics

Lesson 67: Worship Today

Formal worship today can be thought of as a continuum:

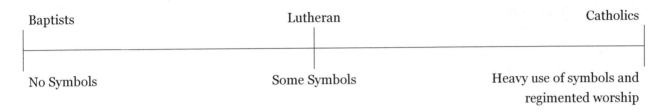

That being said, not all Lutherans are in the middle. Some sway more towards the use of symbols and a more regimented worship and some sway the other way. It is the same for Catholics and Baptists. This just gives you a general idea. There are benefits and downsides to both sides of the continuum. On the left, by removing all or almost all of the symbols in worship, it can reduce distraction and reduce the ability for people to make idols out of objects. However, it can also make the worship area indistinguishable from any other auditorium or area where people go to be entertained. This in and of itself can detract because their surroundings do not enrich their worship. On the other extreme, too many symbols and the use of regimented worship can lead to automation, a focus on an act of doing instead of an act of worship, and can lead to idol worship. Plus with the plethora of symbols, it easily can distract the worshipper. Therefore, one is not necessarily better than the other. Furthermore, just because a worship service lacks a lot of regimented worship does not mean that it lacks worship habits. The services of a Baptist church, Sunday after Sunday are the same (or very similar), just as Catholic worship services are similar. Habitual worship can lead to ritual worship that is not of the heart as well. So to say that one is better or safer is not true. However, just as there are different types of people, different types of formal worship work better for different types of people.

In the Lutheran church, specifically the Lutheran Church Missouri Synod (LCMS), worship does vary. Some churches have a more "contemporary" worship which lacks the formal liturgy (order of service) and uses modern songs. Others are more symbolic and regimented and even include burning incense. Neither is necessarily wrong as long as they include the Word and Sacraments. In other words, they must include the preaching of Law and Gospel and give out the forgiveness of sins freely. They also must rightly utilize and do Holy Baptism and Holy Communion. This is where both the Baptists and the Catholics worship incorrectly. The Baptists (for all their distrust and dislike of symbols) have turned the Lord's Supper and Holy Baptism into only symbols, and say that they do not distribute the forgiveness of sins. While the Catholics still teach of purgatory, penance, and the sale of indulgences and thus withhold true forgiveness.

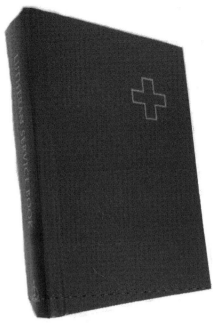

LCMS Lutheran Service Book (hymnal)

Understanding the Basic Elements of an LCMS Traditional Worship Service:

(Not all of the elements will be discussed here. Other elements include the Sacraments and various songs of worship.)

Prelude: The worship service begins with what is known as the "prelude." The prelude is the music that is played before the worship service formally begins with the first Hymn or the invocation from the Pastor. This music signifies the time of preparation for each Christian as they come into the sanctuary to worship. It is during this time that they should pray and prepare mentally for worship. This time is meant to be a quiet time of self-reflection and respect for those in the sanctuary also doing the same.

Invocation: The invocation is the first thing that happens and often includes the first Hymn and specifically includes the making of the cross with the hand and calling upon the name of the Father, Son, and Holy Spirit (Trinitarian Invocation). It is through these words that we remember our baptism, Whose children we are, and Whom we serve. Through our remembrance of our Baptism we are also reminded of the cost of our adoption, our need of forgiveness, and the lengths Jesus went to forgive us (through His death and resurrection). That is why it is appropriate for those baptized Christians to make the sign of the cross themselves during this time.

Confession and Absolution: The confession and absolution is the point in the worship service where the congregation confesses their sins and then asks for forgiveness from God. The Pastor then pronounces (i.e., actually forgives) the congregation their sins through the power of the Keys given to him by God. This comes second because, just as we are reminded of our baptism and who made us adopted children of God, we are reminded of our need for forgiveness. Furthermore, we are also reminded that we cannot properly worship God without first believing in Him and confessing our sins to Him. Through believing and confessing, the congregation receives the forgiveness of sins from God through the pastor. Once we have received forgiveness, we are now prepared to honor and glorify God (Lesson 62). Note: The *absolution* is not an "announcement" of God's available grace or what He has done, but rather the "pronouncement" that we are actually forgiven, which is possible because of God's distribution of the Keys. (Section 6)

Kyrie: The Kyrie (pronounced kirē, ā) is when the church prays as a whole for God to have mercy on the world for its sinfulness and for specific things. We also recognize that without God the world would digress even further into sinfulness and evil, and therefore He does have mercy on the world daily. The Kyrie is specifically when the congregation says or sings "Lord have mercy" (which is the literal translation of Kyrie). While in the traditional order of service this is after the confession and absolution, it can be moved around and can be included with the specific prayers of the church.

Texts of the day: There are four Biblical readings that are used in the traditional worship service. First is the Psalm, the second is usually from the Old Testament, the third is in the New Testament (aside from the Gospels), and the fourth is found in the Gospels. However, only the Old Testament, New Testament and Gospel readings are referred to as the "Texts of the day." The Psalm is either sung or read responsively. The others are usually read (but sometimes they are responsive). Unlike the others, the Gospel is announced by the Pastor, the congregation stands, and an Alleluia is sung. The reason for this is to show respect for the Gospel and our Lord as our Savior. How the texts of the day are, or should be, chosen has been debated and has changed over time. Originally in the first hymnals, the texts were selected to show continuity in subject between all of the texts and the whole service. In more recent years this has changed to create more variety to try and give pastors more of a selection to preach on. (Pastors typically preach on one of the texts.) The texts of the day are outlined within the Hymnal as a one-year schedule, a three-year rotating schedule, and a list of texts for each of the feasts and festivals. The Psalms are merely listed out and selected at the choice and reasoning of the Pastor.

Sermon: The pastor then preaches a sermon which is rightly based on Law and Gospel. The Law is used to convict and convince us of our sins and a need for a Savior (Galatians 3:24) (Law as a Mirror). The Gospel is used to show us how we are saved and who that Savior is (Romans 10:13–14). The last element is direction, or how we should live our lives as a new creation based on scriptural principles (Romans 6:1–4) (Law as a Guide). It is, however, not a law and Gospel sermon when it lacks one of these elements, or if one of these elements is over-emphasized. To lack one of those elements, or to over-emphasize one, is to send a congregation down a dangerous path. That path can be total insecurity (the Law making us wonder if we will actually be saved), total security (the Gospel making us think there is nothing we can do that will condemn us), or total depravity (turning the Gospel or the Law into a message of works righteousness). The balance of these three elements largely depends on the makeup of the individual congregation (Isaiah 42:3) and the pastor knowing his congregation; it is not merely each element having an equal part with the others. For example, the Pastor must distinguish if the congregation is proud (needs more Law), distressed (needs more Gospel), or wandering/wondering what they should do as a Christian (needs more direction).

The *Offering*: The offering is when the church gives the opportunity for the congregation to give of their finances voluntarily. In this way, the congregation worships God with their finances and recognizes that all things come from God. "We give thee but thine alone, whate'er that gift may be. All we have is thine alone, a trust O Lord from thee."[36]

The *Creed*: The Creed can either be the Apostle's Creed, the Nicene Creed, or the Athanasian Creed. It is stated within the service to clearly and concisely allow every Christian to state their basic faith as they believe it themselves ("I believe"). This not only reminds them of what their faith is in but also is a testament as the whole church says it together of what the congregation's belief is.

The Lord's Prayer: It is included because it is the proper way to pray; it is how Jesus taught us to pray and contains anything that might have been missed in the other prayers given by the church.

The *Benediction*: It is the end of the worship service that is meant to send the chosen people of God (that is the congregation) off with the blessings and the peace that comes with being God's people. There are two typical ones that include the *Aaronic* (Numbers 6:24–26) and the *Apostolic* (2 Corinthians 13:14) Benedictions.

1. Match the group to where it is on the use of symbols in worship:

    Group   Use of Symbols
    a. Baptists   ____ Uses many symbols
    b. Lutherans   ____ Uses few symbols
    c. Catholics   ____ In the middle

---

36   "We Give Thee but Thine Own" by William W How 1823–1897. The Lutheran Hymnal

2. What is the benefit and downside of using few or no symbols?_____

    _____

    _____

    _____

3. What is the benefit and downside of using many symbols and a regimented worship service?

    _____

    _____

    _____

4. The Prelude is:
    a. ____ Before the worship service
    b. ____ During the worship service
    c. ____ When the Pastor gives his speech
    d. ____ At the end of the worship service

5. What is the purpose of the Prelude?
    a. ____ To prepare for worship
    b. ____ To praise God during the worship service
    c. ____ To keep you attentive to the Pastor's speech
    d. ____ To thank God for worship at the end of the service

6. The invocation is done to...
    a. ____ Tell God worship is starting
    b. ____ Remind us of our Baptism
    c. ____ Bring God into the church
    d. ____ Allow us to speak in tongues

7. The confession is made at the beginning of the church service because...
    a. ____ It is the most important part of the service
    b. ____ Without it we would be condemned to Hell
    c. ____ It is not done at the beginning it is done at the end
    d. ____ To worship properly, we need to believe in Jesus and be forgiven

8. True / False – The Absolution is an announcement of forgiveness.
    Why or why not?_____

    _____

9. "Kyrie" means:
    a. ____ Lord bless the church
    b. ____ Forgive us our sins
    c. ____ Lord have mercy
    d. ____ Thanks be to God

10. What is the Church doing when it says Kyrie?
    a. ____ Singing thanks be to God
    b. ____ Praying to God for mercy on the whole world
    c. ____ Blessing the Lord for all He has done

11. What are the three "texts of the day" that are used in the church service?

    a. _____

    b. _____

    c. _____

12. Where is the fourth reading from in the Bible?_____

13. Why do we stand for the Gospel?_____

    _____

14. True / False – The selection of the texts of the day is done by focusing either on continuity between the texts or variety for the Pastor.

15. List the three elements of a sermon and tell what happens if that element is over-emphasized:

    a. _____ , _____

    _____

    b. _____ , _____

    _____

    c. _____ , _____

    _____

16. True / False – In order for a sermon to be done properly, each of the three elements must have equal time and focus.

17. True / False – The church has an offering to exploit money from people.

18. Why is there an offering?_____

    _____

19. Why is the Lord's Prayer included in the Church service? _____

    _____

    _____

20. What are the words of the Aaronic Benediction?_____

    _____

    _____

21. What are the words of the Apostolic Benediction?_____

    _____

    _____

LESSON 68: THE CHURCH YEAR AND COLORS

Important celebrations and events in the church year and what they are:

- *Advent*: Focuses on the coming of the Lord (both His first coming and His eventual second coming)
- *Christmas*: The celebration of the Birth of Jesus
- *Transfiguration*: When Jesus was transfigured on the Mount of Olives (Matthew 17:1–9)
- *Ash Wednesday*: The first day of Lent and begins the 40 days of temptation and fasting of Jesus in the wilderness
- *Palm Sunday*: When Jesus rode into Jerusalem on a donkey (Matthew 21:1–17)
- *Maundy Thursday* (Holy Thursday): Jesus Celebrates the Passover with His disciples
- *Good Friday*: Jesus was crucified

- *Easter*: Jesus' resurrection
- *Ascension*: When Jesus ascended to Heaven after the resurrection
- *Pentecost*: When the Holy Spirit came upon the disciples like tongues of fire (Acts 2)
- Holy Trinity (*Trinity Sunday*): Celebrates the triune nature of God and the Trinity that is God

Catechism Material: The Church Year Appendix (pp. 259–268)

1. How many seasons are there in the church year?
   - a. ____ 5
   - b. ____ 6
   - c. ____ 7
   - d. ____ 8

2. What is the first season of the Church year?
   - a. ____ Lent
   - b. ____ Easter
   - c. ____ Christmas
   - d. ____ Advent

3. What does the first half of the church year focus on?_____
   _____

4. What does the second half of the church year focus on?_____
   _____

5. Match the color to its meaning.

Color	Meaning
a. Blue	____ It is a reminder of the need to repent and prepare for Easter
b. White	____ Symbolizes purity, holiness, glory, and joy
c. Green	____ It is the color of fire, and it symbolizes the coming of the Holy Spirit and the blood of the martyrs
d. Purple	____ It is a reminder of the eternal hope we have in Christ
e. Red	____ Represents the Christian life and growth in faith

6. Match the event to its name.

Name	Event
a. Easter	____ The Beginning of Lent and 40 days of Jesus' temptation and fasting
b. Advent	____ When the Holy Spirit descended on the disciples like a tongue of fire
c. Pentecost	____ Jesus' resurrection
d. Ash Wednesday	____ Celebration of the Trinity and the Triune nature of God
e. Trinity Sunday	____ Focus on Jesus' first and eventual second coming

7. Considering what you have learned about worship in lesson 37 and 38, are these events and colors required to have a formal worship service? Why or why not? _____
   _____
   _____

   If these things are not required, why have the colors and the events at all?_____
   _____
   _____

SECTION 9: REVIEW

Part 1: The church and life in it

1. Who belongs to the invisible church? (Mark all that apply.)
   a. _____ All believers
   b. _____ All those who go to a Christian church
   c. _____ Those saints in heaven
   d. _____ Anyone who attends a church

2. Who belongs to the visible church? (Mark all that apply.)
   a. _____ All believers
   b. _____ All those who go to a Christian church
   c. _____ Those saints in heaven
   d. _____ Hypocrites and unbelievers

3. True / False – Only those people who believe and attend Lutheran churches will be saved.

4. Who is the head of the Christian church? _____

5. What is the difference between the "catholic church" and the "Catholic Church"? _____
   _____
   _____

6. What are the three things that you should look for in a visible church to join?
   a. _____
   b. _____
   c. _____

7. The church is maintained and extended through four ways. What are they?
   a. _____
   b. _____
   c. _____
   d. _____

8. True / False – We do not need to pay the pastor a reasonable wage for their service.

9. True / False – The pastor can and should be encouraged to take time off.

10. True / False – After a person dies they are no longer a part of the Christian church.
    Why or why not? _____
    _____

11. Does God view those who have died with faith as dead or alive? _____
    What verse supports your answer? _____

12. Who is going to be resurrected when Jesus comes the second time?
    a. _____ All people
    b. _____ All believers
    c. _____ All living creatures
    d. _____ No one

13. True / False – Even if a person is a Christian they may still have to go to Purgatory to work off their punishment for sins.

14. If a person is an unbeliever, what will happen after they die?
    a. ____ They will go to hell
    b. ____ Their soul will be destroyed
    c. ____ They will go to Purgatory
    d. ____ They will be reincarnated

15. Should we as believers in the church attempt to determine who is a believer and who is a hypocrite and remove the hypocrites from the church? Why or why not? _____

    _____

    _____

    Read 2 Corinthians 6:14–18. Does that mean that we should allow those who are openly unbelieving, teaching, living, and practicing contrary to God's Word to belong and be members of our visible church? Why or why not?_____

    _____

    _____

Part 2: Worship

16. A person is capable and does worship God in four ways. What are those four ways? Give an example of each.
    a. _____ , _____

    _____

    b. _____ , _____

    _____

    c. _____ , _____

    _____

    d. _____ , _____

    _____

17. True / False – Worship always involves God.

    If false, who or what else can a person worship? _____

18. Is it possible for a person who does not have faith in God to worship Him? Why or why not?_____

    _____

    _____

19. Who or what allows a person to worship God?
    a. ____ A church building
    b. ____ A formal service
    c. ____ The Holy Spirit
    d. ____ Hands and a voice

20. What does the term "adiaphora" mean?_____

21. True / False – There are things in a worship service that are "adiaphora."

22. What are the two things that determine if a practice during a worship service is acceptable or right?
    a. _____
    b. _____

23. Has a person who sings all the songs, prays all the prayers, and listens quietly to the sermon worshiped? Why or Why not? (Keep in mind the difference between carrying out a ritual and actual worship).

_____

_____

_____

Part 3: Historical Worship

24. True / False – God has regimented formal worship the same throughout the ages.

25. True / False – Formal worship is different today from when God first created the world.

26. True / False – Adam and Eve's worship was continual and perfect.

27. Who did God first promise the Savior to?
    a. ____ Moses
    b. ____ Noah
    c. ____ Daniel
    d. ____ Adam and Eve

28. When a person made a sacrifice before God brought His people out of Egypt, what made the sacrifice acceptable? _____

29. True / False – Only after God explained to the nation of Israel did people know the difference between clean and unclean animals.

30. True / False – The nation of Israel was very small when they came out of Egypt (only about 40,000 people) If false, about how many people celebrated the Passover? _____

31. Match the following:

    During...   Formal worship was or is...
    a. The time of Adam and Eve   ____ Regimented.
    b. The time of Moses and David   ____ Different for individual churches.
    c. The present time   ____ Unregulated.

32. David was a man after God's own heart; why was he not allowed to build the temple?
    a. ____ He was a man of war
    b. ____ He committed adultery with Bathsheba
    c. ____ He did not kill Saul
    d. ____ He ate the showbread at the Tabernacle

33. How many times was the Temple built? _____

34. Is the temple still around today?
    a. ____ Yes
    b. ____ No

    If not, in what year was it destroyed? _____ Also why has a new temple not been built?

    _____

    _____

35. If sacrifices were done at the temple, what were the synagogues used for? _____

    _____

36. Who was the last prophet according to the Law of Moses?
    a. _____ Moses
    b. _____ John the Baptist
    c. _____ Isaiah
    d. _____ Malachi

37. Why do Christians not practice the ceremonial laws and sacrifices of the Jews before Jesus?
    a. _____ The temple is destroyed
    b. _____ We should, but we do not
    c. _____ Jesus fulfilled all the ceremonial law with His death and resurrection
    d. _____ God left the decision on how we should worship to us now

38. True / False – The Roman Catholic church has the truth because Peter was the first pope.

39. Does lineage determine the accuracy of the interpretation of scripture and authority? Why or why not? (Give a Bible passage to support your answer.) _____ ____ _____

   _____ _____

   _____

40. True / False – The Council of Nicaea was when Luther was excommunicated from the Roman Catholic Church.

41. The Council of Nicaea was held in what year? _____

42. What was the original Sabbath day? _____

43. Why do Christians celebrate the Sabbath on Sunday? _____

   _____

44. True / False – The Anabaptists believe that all (or the vast majority) of symbols are a form of idolatry.

45. True / False – Martin Luther only sought to correct the many heresies of the Catholic Church.

46. True / False – There are many elaborate cathedrals and churches that were built by the Catholic Church.

Part 4: Present Formal Worship

47. True / False – Worship in a Catholic Church is not very regimented with very few symbols and rites.

48. True / False – All Lutherans worship the same way during a formal worship service.

49. Do Lutherans, Baptists, and Catholics worship the same?
    a. _____ Yes
    b. _____ No

   If not, describe the differences. _____

   _____

   _____

   _____

   _____

   _____

50. Is the Lutheran worship service of the LCMS the best? Should all other denominations emulate it? Why or why not? _____

   _____

   _____

51. Which type of formal worship is best?
    a. ____ Regimented worship with lots of symbols
    b. ____ Worship with very few symbols
    c. ____ Neither
    d. ____ It depends on the individual people and their needs

52. Match the term to its definition:

Term:	Definition:
a. Prelude	____ The Pastor sending God's people off with God's blessing
b. Text of the day	____ "Lord have mercy."
c. Sermon	____ When the congregation confesses their sins, and the pastor forgives them
d. Kyrie	____ The time before worship accompanied by music to help people prepare for worship
e. The Benediction	____ When the pastor calls on the Holy Trinity and reminds us of our Baptism
f. The Invocation	____ Refers to the passages taken from the Bible
g. Confession and Absolution	____ When the Pastor preaches

53. Describe the three elements of a good sermon:

    a. Law (as a Mirror): _____

    _____

    b. Gospel: _____

    _____

    c. Law (as a Guide): _____

    _____

    Does a sermon always need to have equal parts of those three elements? Why or why not?

    _____

    _____

    _____

SECTION 10 – THE APOSTLES' CREED

I believe in God the Father Almighty, Maker of heaven and earth.

And in Jesus Christ, His only Son, our Lord, who was conceived by the Holy Spirit, born of the Virgin Mary, suffered under Pontius Pilate, was crucified, died and was buried. He descended into hell. The third day He rose again from the dead. He ascended into heaven and sits on the right hand of God, the Father Almighty. From thence He shall come to judge the living and the dead.

I believe in the Holy Spirit, the holy Christian church, the communion of saints, the forgiveness of sins, the resurrection of the body and the life everlasting. Amen.

This entire section is a summary of much of what you have learned. If you are struggling with any of the questions, refer to the lesson(s) that talk about that particular topic.

LESSON 69: INTRODUCTION TO CREEDS AND FAITH

> **Memorization:**
>
> *I believe.*
>
> And
>
> *Ephesians 2:8–9 – For by grace you have been saved through faith, and that not of yourselves; it is the gift of God, not of works, lest anyone should boast.*

What do you mean when you confess, "I believe in God"? I mean that <u>I know, and accept as true</u>, what the Bible says of God and <u>trust in Him and rely on Him</u> with firm confidence.[37] (Rom. 10:14, Rom. 10:17, Heb. 11:1, Ps. 31:14, Ps. 37:5, James 2:19, Luke 7:1–10, John 4:47–53, Matt. 15:21–28)

When we have belief or faith in something, it requires three things. It requires <u>knowledge</u> of what we have faith in. How can we accept or trust in something we do not know? Faith also requires that we have <u>acceptance</u> that it is the truth. If we do not accept something, how can we trust in it even if we know what it is? If we have heard about something, but we do not believe it (i.e., accept it), it does us no good. Finally, it requires that we <u>trust</u> it. What does it matter if we know and accept something if we do not trust it? That is the triangle of faith.

The example of faith we can use is faith in Jesus Christ as our Savior. If we have never heard of Jesus, how can we accept that He is God and saved us; let alone trust in His salvation? If we only know about Jesus, but do not accept Him as being God and a Savior, it does us no good because we will not trust in Him. Finally, if we do not trust in Jesus as our Savior, but rather in ourselves to save us, then knowing about Jesus and accepting what He has done also give us no benefit.

All three of the creeds (Apostles', Nicene, and Athanasian) are summaries of the Christian doctrine and what a Christian believes. Therefore, if a person confesses the creed and believes it, they are in fact confessing the Christian doctrine and therefore are Christians.

Catechism Material: Questions 86–91 (pp. 102–103) and 113 (p. 119)
Additional Material: The entire Apostles' Creed (beginning of Section 10)

[37]   Question 103 from "A Short Explanation of Dr. Martin Luther's Small Catechism" Concordia Publishing House, 1943

1. A *creed* has three characteristics. What are they a statement of?

    a. _____

    b. _____

    c. _____

2. Every creed begins with the words "I believe." Why is the word "I" emphasized? _____
    _____

3. The triangle of faith has three sides because it has three parts. Write one part on each side of the triangle:

Faith

4. For each side of the triangle, explain why if you take it away you cannot have faith:

    a. _____
    _____

    b. _____
    _____

    c. _____
    _____

5. When I say "I believe" it means that I _____
    _____

6. Read the explanation of the Third Article (P. 147).

    True / False – I chose to come to Christ and believe in Him.

    True / False – My faith is the work that I do to be saved.

    Who creates and keeps me in the true faith? _____

7. How many creeds are there?

    a. ____ 1

    b. ____ 2

    c. ____ 3

    d. ____ 4

    What are their names?_____

8. Which of the creeds are taught in Luther's small catechism?_____

9. True / False – The Apostles' Creed was written by the Apostles.

    Why is it called the Apostles' Creed? _____
    _____

10. The Apostles' Creed (as it is written out above) is separated into three parts. Each part refers to a specific part of the God head. Name them in the order they talked about, then match them with the special work they do:

    Godhead   Special work
    a. _____   ____ Redemption
    b. _____   ____ Creation
    c. _____   ____ Sanctification

11. Each explanation of each article by Luther ends with "This is most certainly true." Luther ends his explanation with this because... (Mark all that apply.)
    a. ____ Luther is reliable
    b. ____ The church tells you it is reliable
    c. ____ I have learned that the article and explanation are based solely on the Bible and what it plainly teaches. Therefore I am convinced through the Holy Scriptures that what is said is reliable and true.

12. Is anyone who confesses and believes these creeds a Christian? Why or why not? _____
    _____
    _____

SUBSECTION: THE APOSTLES' CREED

Lesson 70: The First Article: God the Father

> **Memorization:** Luther's explanation of the First Article –
> *I believe in God the Father Almighty, Maker of heaven and earth.*
> *What does this mean?*
> *I believe that God has made me and all creatures; that He has given me my body and soul, eyes, ears, and all my members, my reason and all my senses, and still takes care of them.*
> *He also gives me clothing and shoes, food and drink, house and home, wife and children, land, animals, and all I have. He richly and daily provides me with all that I need to support this body and life. He defends me against all dangers and guards and protects me from all evil.*
> *All this He does only out of fatherly, divine goodness and mercy, without any merit or worthiness in me. For all this it is my duty to thank and praise, serve and obey Him.*
> *This is most certainly true.*

A simple summary of Luther's explanation of the First Article: God has created everything. Moreover, He created, sustains, and defends me because of His mercy, and I should thank and praise Him for it.

Catechism Material: The First Article (p. 108)

1. What has God created? (Give specific examples.) _____
   _____

2. What does God give you to sustain you? (Give specific examples.) _____
   _____
   _____

3. What are the means by which God sustains you? (Give specific examples.) _____

    _____

4. What does God guard you against? (Give specific examples.) _____

    _____

5. Why does God do this and what have you done to earn it? _____

    _____

    _____

6. What should you do in response to all God has created and done for you? _____

    _____

7. Why do you believe everything that is stated in The First Article? _____

    _____

    _____

Lesson 71: The Second Article: God the Son

> **Memorization:** Luther's explanation of the Second Article –
>
> *And in Jesus Christ, His only Son, our Lord, who was conceived by the Holy Spirit, born of the Virgin Mary, suffered under Pontius Pilate, was crucified, died and was buried. He descended into hell. The third day He rose again from the dead. He ascended into heaven and sits on the right hand of God, the Father Almighty. From thence He shall come to judge the living and the dead.*
>
> ### What does this mean?
>
> *I believe that Jesus Christ, true God, begotten of the Father from eternity, and also true man, born of the Virgin Mary, is my Lord, who has redeemed me, a lost and condemned person, purchased and won me from all sins, from death, and from the power of the devil; not with gold or silver, but with His holy, precious blood and with His innocent suffering and death, that I may be His own and live under Him in His kingdom and serve Him in everlasting righteousness, innocence, and blessedness, just as He is risen from the dead, lives and reigns to all eternity.*
>
> *This is most certainly true.*

A simple summary of Luther's explanation of the Second Article: God was born of a virgin to become True God and True man. He suffered during His life and was crucified at the hands of Pontius Pilate for my sins. Through this, He conquered sin, death, and the devil, and rose again on the third day. He did this of His own will to save me, a lost and condemned sinner. He now sits on the right hand of God, protecting and interceding for me daily, and will come again to bring me to Heaven to be with Him.

Catechism Material: The Second Article (p. 119) and questions 114 (p. 120), 117 (p. 121), 124 (p. 127), 128 (p. 131), 142 (p. 138), and 151 (pp. 146–147)

1. Who does the second article talk about? _____

2. True / False – In the second article you profess that Jesus is only True God.

    Why or why not? _____

    _____

3. What makes Jesus True God?
    a. ____ God created Him a God
    b. ____ God the Father begot Him
    c. ____ Jesus is not True God

4. What makes Jesus True Man?
    a. ____ His father was Joseph
    b. ____ The Holy Spirit conceived Him
    c. ____ The virgin Mary was His mother

5. What did Jesus save us from?
    a. _____
    b. _____
    c. _____

6. What does Jesus give those who believe in Him as their only Savior?
    a. ____ Nothing
    b. ____ Eternal life
    c. ____ Good things during this life

7. What do you mean when you say "I believe in Jesus Christ" (Mark all that apply.)
    a. ____ I know and trust in Him
    b. ____ He is my Lord
    c. ____ He is only True Man
    d. ____ He is my Redeemer
    e. ____ He is my only Savior from sin, death, and the devil
    f. ____ His life gave me the ability to save myself
    g. ____ He gave me eternal life

8. In the Second article, it contains information about Jesus' State of Humiliation and Exaltation. Write "H" for Humiliation and "E" for Exaltation next to the description:

    ____ From thence He shall come to judge the living   ____ Sits on the right hand of God the Father
    and the dead

    ____ Born of the Virgin Mary   ____ Died and was buried

    ____ On the third day, He rose again from the dead   ____ Was crucified

    ____ Suffered under Pontius Pilate   ____ Ascended into Heaven

    ____ Conceived by the Holy Spirit   ____ Descended into Hell

9. Why did Jesus do this for you and the whole world? _____

    _____

    What did you or anyone else do to deserve all of this?_____

    _____

10. What did Jesus use to pay for our sins?_____

    _____

11. Why do you believe everything that is written in The Second Article?_____

    _____

    _____

Lesson 72: The Third Article: God the Holy Spirit, the Church, Forgiveness, and Eternal Life

---

Memorization: Luther's explanation of the Third Article –
I believe in the Holy Spirit, the holy Christian church, the communion of saints, the forgiveness of sins, the resurrection of the body and the life everlasting. Amen.
What does this mean?
I believe that I cannot by my own reason or strength believe in Jesus Christ, my Lord, or come to Him; but the Holy Spirit has called me by the Gospel, enlightened me with His gifts, sanctified and kept me in the true faith. In the same way He calls, gathers, enlightens, and sanctifies the whole Christian church on earth, and keeps it with Jesus Christ in the one true faith.
In this Christian church He daily and richly forgives all my sins and the sins of all believers. On the Last Day He will raise me and all the dead, and give eternal life to me and all believers in Christ.
This is most certainly true.

Catechism Material: The Third Article (p. 147) and questions 153 (p. 148), 170–171 (pp. 158–159), and 180 (p. 165)

1. What are the five points of the Third Article?

    a. _____

    b. _____

    c. _____

    d. _____

    e. _____

2. What is the work of the Holy Spirit? (Mark all that apply.)

    a. ____ Enlightens the whole Christian church

    b. ____ Create faith through the Gospel

    c. ____ Sustain Christians in their faith

    d. ____ Make people speak in tongues

3. Can a person believe in Jesus of their own will without the Holy Spirit? Why or why not?

    _____

    _____

    _____

4. Is the Holy Spirit distinct from God the Father and God the Son?

    a. ____ Yes

    b. ____ No

5. True / False – The visible church and the invisible church are the same.

6. True / False – There is one church that is invisible and has visible attributes.

7. Even though a person may be a part of a visible church, they are not necessarily a part of the invisible church. Why? _____

    _____

    _____

8. True / False – The communion of saints only refers to those Christians who have already died.

9. Why should we forgive anyone and everyone when they sin against us?_____
_____
_____

10. Why did God forgive us?
   a. ____ Because He desired to
   b. ____ Because of our goodness
   c. ____ Because God the Father forced the Son to die for us
   d. ____ He has not because He did not need to

11. Why do you believe in the forgiveness of sins?
   a. ____ Because without it, we are all condemned
   b. ____ Because God the Father has died for our sins
   c. ____ Because the Holy Spirit intercedes for us
   d. ____ Because God the Son died for my sins and the sins of all Humanity

12. True / False – After a Christian dies, they are dead forever.

13. Will God actually raise people from the dead?
   a. ____ Yes
   b. ____ No

14. How does God view those who have died as a true believer?
   a. ____ Dead
   b. ____ In limbo before the judgment
   c. ____ Alive, and their soul is with Him
   d. ____ We do not know

15. What will happen to Christians and those who do not believe on the last day? _____
_____
_____

16. Why must a person believe in the invisible church? _____
_____
_____

17. Do you believe in life everlasting and the resurrection? Why or why not? _____
_____
_____
_____

18. Why do you believe everything that is written in The Third Article? _____
_____
_____

Section 10: Review

1. Write out the First Article of the Apostles' Creed from memory:

    _____

2. Write out the Second Article of the Apostles' Creed from memory:

    _____

    _____

    _____

    _____

    _____

    _____

3. Write out the Third Article of the Apostles' Creed from memory:

    _____

    _____

    _____

4. Label each side of the triangle of faith on the triangle below:

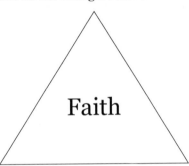

5. Explain how each of the three sides of faith is required in order for someone to have faith: _____

    _____

    _____

    _____

6. When do you mean when you say "I believe"?_____

    _____

SECTION 11 – TABLE OF DUTIES (BIBLICAL LIVING IN PRACTICAL WAYS)

> **Memorization:** Luther's Small Catechism –
> *Let each his lesson learn with care,*
> *And all the household well will fare.*

The table of duties is a collection of important Bible passages as they relate to different positions and occupations people find themselves in life. This section is by no means exhaustive in the scope or responsibilities of each status or occupation. It is merely to give a person the basic understanding of the responsibilities, the responsibility to care for, and, in some cases, the authority of that position based on a few of the Bible passages that talk about such things.

The memorization means that everyone should learn what they are supposed to do and how they are to interact with each other. If everyone knows what they are supposed to do, then everyone can and should interact properly according to Scriptures. If everyone interacts properly, then the home and work will function well, and contentions will decrease.

This section is designed to be completed after Section 1–10. By completing those sections, you have been practicing reading and interpreting Scripture for yourself. The focus of this section is to reinforce the experiences you have gained by giving you individual Bible passages to read and come to conclusions yourself. If you are having trouble with this section, refer to the prior lessons that talk about that particular topic.

LESSON 73: PASTORS AND THOSE UNDER THEIR CARE

> **Memorization:** Jeremiah 3:14–15 –
> *"Return, O backsliding children," says the Lord; "for I am married to you. I will take you, one from a city and two from a family, and I will bring you to Zion. And I will give you shepherds according to My heart, who will feed you with knowledge and understanding.*

Pastors are our earthly shepherds given to us by Jesus to watch over and care for all those who are a part of their flock.

Read 1 Timothy 3:1–7. In the qualifications of a pastor, the Bible lists that they must be a "husband of one wife." That is not to suggest that a Pastor has to be married. (Paul was not married [1 Corinthians 7:7].) The qualification has to do with sexual immorality and gender. (Pastors are only supposed to be men.) Sexual immorality that would disqualify someone includes homosexuals, those who are married to multiple wives (polygamists), adulterers, and those who would live with their girlfriends outside of marriage or have sex with them outside of marriage. ("A bishop must be blameless" [Titus 1:7].)

Pastors are referred to as "bishops" (Titus 1:7), "elders" (Titus 1:5), "shepherds" (Jeremiah 3:15), and "teachers" (James 3:1) in the Bible. If you would like to learn more about pastors, then search for those key words in the Bible.

Catechism Material: To Bishops, Pastors, and Preachers (pp. 35–36), What the Hearers Owe Their Pastors (p. 36), and question 278 (p. 228)
Additional Bible passages (Pastors): Matthew 15:9, 1 Corinthians 14:26–33, Galatians 2:11–13, and 2 Timothy 4:1–2
Additional Bible passages (Hearers): Acts 17:11, Galatians 5:13, 1 Thessalonians 5:11, 25, and Revelation 2:2–3

1. What Bible passage gives us some of the qualifications of a pastor?_____

2. Which are some of the qualifications of a pastor? (Mark all that apply.)
    a. ____ Married
    b. ____ Contentious
    c. ____ Able to teach
    d. ____ Gentle
    e. ____ Wealthy
    f. ____ Male
    g. ____ Heterosexual
    h. ____ Selfish
    i. ____ Sexually immoral

3. True / False – A pastor can be someone who has recently converted to Christianity.
    Why or why not? _____
    _____

4. True / False – It is the responsibility of the pastor to refute those who teach incorrectly.

5. True / False – A pastor should encourage people in sound doctrine.

6. True / False – We should pay our pastors a reasonable and livable wage.

7. True / False – Pastors do not have any responsibility when it comes to how we act and what we believe.

8. True / False – Only Pastors can preach and administer the sacraments.
    Why or why not? _____
    _____
    _____

9. Which commandment tells us how we should treat our Pastor?
    a. ____ First Commandment
    b. ____ Third Commandment
    c. ____ Fourth Commandment
    d. ____ Sixth Commandment

10. Why should we honor our pastors?_____
    _____
    _____

11. Do the members of the congregation need to honor, cherish, and support the pastor regardless of whether or not he "deserves it"? Why or why not? _____
    _____
    _____

12. True / False – As hearers of the pastor, the members of his congregation should diligently check to see if what he is saying is true.

13. How can a member of a congregation encourage and care for their pastor? (Mark all that apply.)

    a. ____ Pray for them

    b. ____ Argue with them when they are wrong

    c. ____ Speak well of them

    d. ____ Serve them willingly without complaint

LESSON 74: THE GOVERNMENT AND CITIZENS

> **Memorization:** Romans 13:1–2, 6–7 –
> *Let every soul be subject to the governing authorities. For there is no authority except from God, and the authorities that exist are appointed by God. Therefore whoever resists the authority resists the ordinance of God, and those who resist will bring judgment on themselves. For because of this you also pay taxes, for they are God's ministers attending continually to this very thing. Render therefore to all their due: taxes to whom taxes are due, customs to whom customs, fear to whom fear, honor to whom honor.*

Catechism Material: Of Civil Government and Of Citizens (pp. 36–38)

Additional Bible passages (Government): Deuteronomy 1:17 and Exodus 21:23–25

1. Who established the governments? _____

2. What is one of the purposes of the government?

    a. ____ To steal its citizens' money

    b. ____ To control

    c. ____ To punish the evildoer

    d. ____ To destroy

3. How does that allow the government to protect its citizens? _____

_____

_____

_____

_____

We must obey the government, and the government should be there to help and protect us. The government should also punish those who do wrong.

4. True / False – The government and those in authority should judge matters without partiality.

5. When a citizen or person does something wrong, how should the government handle it?

    a. ____ Punish them with extreme consequences.

    b. ____ Avoid punishing anyone as much possible.

    c. ____ Only punish the evildoer if it is convenient.

    d. ____ Punish the evildoer with a reasonable punishment fitting the crime.

6. Do the citizens of a government have the right to riot, destroy, and "punish" the government or those in authority if it or they do something they do not like? Why or why not? _____

_____

_____

7. True / False – Citizens should not encourage each other to obey and respect the government and those in authority.

8. What do citizens owe the governments? (Mark all that apply.)
    a. ____ Honor
    b. ____ Respect
    c. ____ Taxes
    d. ____ Our lives

9. If we visit a foreign country, what do we owe their government? (Mark all that apply.)
    a. ____ Honor
    b. ____ Respect
    c. ____ Taxes
    d. ____ Our lives

10. True / False – We should pray for our governments.

11. Give a Bible passage that tells us we should pay taxes. _____

12. Which commandment does God give us regarding the government?
    a. ____ First Commandment
    b. ____ Fourth Commandment
    c. ____ Sixth Commandment
    d. ____ Eighth Commandment

Lesson 75: Husband and Wives

> **Memorization:** Ephesians 5:22–25, 28 –
> *Wives, submit to your own husbands, as to the Lord. For the husband is head of the wife, as also Christ is head of the church; and He is the Savior of the body. Therefore, just as the church is subject to Christ, so let the wives be to their own husbands in everything.*
> *Husbands, love your wives, just as Christ also loved the church and gave Himself for her... So husbands ought to love their own wives as their own bodies; he who loves his wife loves himself.*

Marriage is held together by Christ
(Catechism p. 281).

Read Ephesians 5:22–33. That Bible passage is one of the best descriptions of what a marriage should be according to the Bible and how the husband and wife should interact. The husband should act like Christ who loves the church so much that He went so far as to die for her. He listens to her pleas and desires, considers them, does them, and helps her. Just like a husband ought to love his wife and consider her needs and desires above his own. He should listen to her, cherish her and build her up in words and deeds. Likewise, a wife ought to respect her husband as the leader of the house, loving and cherishing him.

Consider this prayer about marriage (based on Matthew 5:43–48): God help me always to love my wife (or husband). Though I pray this may never come to pass, but if the day comes that due to grief, sorrow, pain, or anger that I can no longer love her as my wife, help me to love her as my neighbor. Even still Lord if my home lacks unity and divisions come, please help me to love her as my enemy. In all things help me to know that I am without excuse to love her both unconditionally and unfathomably as You have loved me. Then restore and resolve me to always love her as my wife. Amen.

Read Proverbs 31:10–31. It is an excellent example of what a wife or a woman should do in their life and how they should live in a marriage. It talks about a woman working both inside and outside the home, giving to the poor, taking care of the house and the children. It talks about a wise wife (and wisdom comes from God) who instructs her children and takes care of her house well. Contrast that with Proverbs 27:15–16 which talks about a wife who is contentious (nagging, angry, and constantly arguing). It describes that type of wife as a terrible thing.

Catechism Material: To Husbands and To Wives (p. 38)
Additional Bible passages (Both): Mark 10:5–12, 1 Corinthians 7:10–11, Colossians 3:12–13, and Hebrews 13:4
Additional Bible passages (Wives): Proverbs 14:1, Proverbs 21:19, and Proverbs 27:15–19

1. Who brings a husband and a wife together? _____

2. Who is the head of the household?
    a. ____ Husband
    b. ____ Wife

3. True / False – God is above both the wife and the husband.

4. What is the example of how a husband is to love his wife?
    a. ____ Jacob and Rachel
    b. ____ Jesus and the Church
    c. ____ Abraham and Sarah
    d. ____ David and Bathsheba

5. What is the example of how a wife is to respect her husband?
    a. ____ Jacob and Rachel
    b. ____ Jesus and the Church
    c. ____ Abraham and Sarah
    d. ____ David and Bathsheba

6. What commandment teaches how a husband and wife should interact?
    a. ____ Third Commandment
    b. ____ Fourth Commandment
    c. ____ Sixth Commandment
    d. ____ Tenth Commandment

7. True / False – Because the husband is the head of the house, the wife has no say in anything and must just go along with the husband.
    Why or why not? _____
    _____
    _____

8. True / False – The husband is in control so they should yell, demand their way as such, and be mean to their wife if she disobeys.
    Why or why not? _____
    _____
    _____

9. Is it sinful for a husband to act as a tyrant over his wife? Why or why not? _____

_____

_____

10. True / False – The husband should build up his wife with his words, deeds, and actions.

Why or why not? _____

_____

_____

11. True / False – The wife should nag her husband until she gets what she wants.

Why or why not? _____

_____

_____

12. Is it sinful for a wife to nag and continually argue with her husband? Why or why not? _____

_____

_____

13. True / False – The wife should build up her husband with her words, deeds, and actions.

Why or why not? _____

_____

_____

14. True / False – The Bible teaches that a woman's place is only in the home.

Why or why not?_____

_____

15. Read Proverbs 14:23 and Matthew 12:36. Based on those verses and the other things you have learned,

how does God feel about laziness and idle chatter (gossiping) on the part of either the husband or the wife?

_____

16. True / False – Both the husband and wife need to work, labor together, and support each other in order

to have a successful and God-pleasing marriage.

17. True / False – The work of the wife is always the same as the work of the husband.

Why or why not?_____

_____

_____

18. How often should a husband or wife forgive their spouse?
    a. ____ Only when their spouse is really sorry
    b. ____ When their spouse makes it up to them
    c. ____ When what they did was not a big deal
    d. ____ Every time their spouse sins against them

19. When can a husband or wife stop loving their spouse?
    a. ____ God requires that they love each other in every situation
    b. ____ When the spouse hurts the other's feelings
    c. ____ When the spouse sins against the other
    d. ____ When that feeling just is not there anymore

LESSON 76: PARENTS AND CHILDREN

> **Memorization:** Ephesians 6:1–4 –
> *Children, obey your parents in the Lord, for this is right. "Honor your father and mother," which is the first commandment with promise: "that it may be well with you and you may live long on the earth." And you, fathers, do not provoke your children to wrath, but bring them up in the training and admonition of the Lord.*

Read Deuteronomy 6:1–9. Parents are responsible for teaching and training their children about God. That is not something that can be abdicated (given away) to anyone, to the government, or even to the church. Parents have been given that responsibility with no exception or ability to substitute. While parents may be helped by the Pastor and the Church (which is part of the church's and pastor's responsibility), the parents must diligently train their children in the Word of God.

Ephesians 6:4 states that parents (referring specifically to fathers) that they should not "provoke [their] children to wrath." The NIV uses the word "exacerbate." What this means is that parents should not be "overbearing" and focused exclusively on their rule of law and only their agenda. Rather they should train their children in godliness and encourage them in God's Word. They should also encourage their children in their children's interests that do not go against God's Word. Also, they should not dismiss the concerns and struggles of their children because they were once children, and their concerns and struggles at the time were big then too. However, this does not mean that parents should not discipline or that they should not push their children to succeed. Rather, discipline should be done to accomplish the goal of training the children. If one method does not effectively train the child, then another method must and should be used. Also, not a single method is appropriate for all situations. Finally, as parents, they should encourage their children to succeed even in their children goals and desires as long as those goals are not sinful.

Some methods of discipline open to parents:
- Physical discipline (e.g., spanking) – Physical discipline (i.e., corporal punishment) is allowed and protected in all 50 states in the United States by parents towards their children at the time of this writing. However, it should never be confused with physical abuse. Physical discipline hurts, but physical abuse injures, breaks, disfigures, and bruises a child. Physical discipline is instructive, but physical abuse is destructive. Physical discipline is for training, but physical abuse is for vengeance and revenge.
- Grounding (e.g., taking away privileges including time with friends, a favorite toy or activity, going to bed without dinner, etc.)
- Location discipline (i.e., timeout) – removing privileges by forcing the child to stay in a specific spot for a specific period of time (e.g., corner, bathroom, room, etc.)
- Not protecting them from the consequences of their actions (e.g., if they get a speeding ticket, forcing them to pay the ticket)
- Immersion (e.g., if they are eating candy before dinner, making them eat enough of it to get sick)

- The talk (i.e., explaining why what the child did was wrong, the effect it had, and what the right thing to do would have been.) (More than likely this should be included in every form of discipline.)
- Forgiveness

Catechism Material: To Parents and To Children (p. 38)
Additional Bible passages (Parents): Exodus 21:23–25, Proverbs 13:24, Proverbs 22:6, and Hebrew 5:12
Additional Bible passages (Children): Proverbs 1:8–9 and Proverbs 6:20–26
Additional Bible passages (Both): Proverbs 4, Matthew 5:13–16, Romans 3:23, Hebrews 12:11, and Colossians 3:12–13

1. Parents are required to train their children in...
   a. ____ Entrepreneurship
   b. ____ Engineering
   c. ____ The Word of God
   d. ____ Baseball

2. True / False – The parents will not be held responsible for teaching their children about God as long as they have the church do it.
   Why or why not? _____

   _____

3. What commandment governs how we respect and learn the Word of God?
   a. ____ Third Commandment
   b. ____ Fifth Commandment
   c. ____ Seventh Commandment
   d. ____ Ninth Commandment

4. Below are the three ways parents train their children. Identify how a parent can train their child in each of those three ways.
   a. Instruction (by teaching):_____

   _____

   b. Discipline: _____

   _____

   c. Godly living (by example):_____

   _____

5. True / False – Parents should not push their children to succeed.

6. True / False – Parents should only focus on their goals and not their children's.
   Why or why not? _____

   _____

   _____

7. Is it ever permissible or right for a parent to stop loving their child because of something they did? Why or why not? _____

   _____

   _____

8. True / False – Parents have no right to discipline their children because they have sinned and done things wrong too.

Why or why not? _____

_____

_____

9. True / False – It is hateful, hurtful, and unloving for a parent not to discipline their children when they do wrong.

Why or why not? _____

_____

_____

10. What is the purpose of discipline?
    a. ____ To allow a parent to release their anger
    b. ____ To train children for how they should live
    c. ____ To give parents an opportunity to spank their child
    d. ____ To give parents an opportunity to yell at their child

11. What is effective discipline? (Mark only ONE answer)
    a. ____ Spanking/physical discipline
    b. ____ Grounding/time out
    c. ____ A conversation about right and wrong
    d. ____ Whatever discipline method produces the effect of changing the child's behavior

12. True / False – Discipline is used for training, but if the child does not know why they were disciplined or what the correct actions they should have taken were, it is not effective.

13. If a parent always or almost always forgives the child for their actions and rarely if ever disciplines them, what does that teach the child about consequences for their actions? _____

_____

_____

_____

14. If a parent refuses to forgive their child for something they did, what does that show about their faith and belief about the forgiveness they received from God? _____

_____

_____

15. True / False – In the United States it is legal in all 50 states for a parent to physically discipline their child.

16. What are the ultimate goals of the parents when they discipline and train their children? (Mark all that apply.)
    a. ____ Teach them about their need for a Savior and Jesus
    b. ____ Teach them how to succeed in life by living a godly and right way
    c. ____ Teach them that their actions have consequences whether young or old
    d. ____ Teach them that discipline is unfair and should be avoided through lying

17. True / False – Willful negligence, abandonment, and refusal to discipline a child is a sin.

18. Should a parent expect that they will be able to raise their child perfectly without mistakes? Why or why not?

_____

_____

19. True / False – God knows that even Christian parents are sinful and will make mistakes (i.e., sin), but He still promises grace to them and to their children.

20. What commandment governs how children should interact with their parents?
    a. ____ Second Commandment
    b. ____ Fourth Commandment
    c. ____ Seventh Commandment
    d. ____ Ninth Commandment

21. Children owe their parents love and respect...
    a. ____ When their parents give them love and respect.
    b. ____ If their parents earn it.
    c. ____ Because God gave them their parents.
    d. ____ Only when their parents give and do what they want.

22. Children ought to obey their parents...
    a. ____ When they want to.
    b. ____ Only when they believe what the parents are asking them to do is "right."
    c. ____ Because then they can avoid being punished.
    d. ____ Always and in everything unless it clearly goes against God's Word (e.g., stealing).

If parents do ask their child to do something against God's Word, like stealing, how should they respond?

_____

_____

_____

_____

23. True / False – If the parents do something wrong, it is up to the child to discipline the parent.

24. Why should a child listen, learn, and accept discipline from their parents? (Mark all that apply.)
    a. ____ It teaches them how to live godly lives
    b. ____ It instructs them in the truth
    c. ____ It is done out of love for them that children would succeed in life
    d. ____ God promises to bless them through obeying their parents

25. Should a child expect that their parents will be perfect in raising them? Why or why not?_____

_____

_____

26. Does God expect a child to forgive their parents if the parents do something wrong to them? Why or why not? _____

_____

_____

LESSON 77: WORKERS AND THEIR EMPLOYERS

> **Memorization:** Ephesians 6:5–9 –
> *Bondservants, be obedient to those who are your masters according to the flesh, with fear and trembling, in sincerity of heart, as to Christ; not with eyeservice, as men-pleasers, but as bondservants of Christ, doing the will of God from the heart, with goodwill doing service, as to the Lord, and not to men, knowing that whatever good anyone does, he will receive the same from the Lord, whether he is a slave or free.*
> *And you, masters, do the same things to them, giving up threatening, knowing that your own Master also is in heaven, and there is no partiality with Him.*

Catechism Material: To Workers of All Kinds and To Employers and Supervisors (pp. 38–39)
Additional Bible passage (Workers): 1 Peter 2:18–25

1. True / False – You should only work hard when the boss is looking.

2. True / False – You should serve your employer like you would serve Christ.

3. Why do you work hard for your employer?

    a. _____ To make lots of money

    b. _____ For the reward from Christ

    c. _____ To build prestige for yourself

    d. _____ For the next promotion

4. True / False – As an employer, you should threaten your employees to get the most out of them.

5. Why should you not show favoritism as an employer?

    a. _____ Because God does not show favoritism toward us

    b. _____ It is bad for moral

    c. _____ You will make some people happy but others very mad

    d. _____ You should show favoritism

6. What should you do if your employer asks or demands that you do something that goes against God's commandments? _____

    _____

    _____

7. True / False – God says that if my employer is not a Christian, I do not have to do what he says.

8. If your employer is rude, does not pay you well, and treats you poorly, does God expect you to still do a good job for them? Why or why not? _____

    _____

    _____

9. Considering your boss is your neighbor, and your neighbor owns the company you work for, how do the Seventh and Eighth Commandments apply to you regarding your actions and attitudes towards them?

_____

_____

_____

10. Considering your employee is also your neighbor, how do the Seventh and Eighth Commandments apply to you in regard to your actions and attitudes towards them? _____

_____

_____

_____

LESSON 78: YOUTH, WIDOWS, AND EVERYONE

> **Memorization:** 1 Peter 5:5–11 –
> *Likewise you younger people, submit yourselves to your elders. Yes, all of you be submissive to one another, and be clothed with humility, for "God resists the proud, But gives grace to the humble." Therefore humble yourselves under the mighty hand of God, that He may exalt you in due time, casting all your care upon Him, for He cares for you.*
> *Be sober, be vigilant; because your adversary the devil walks about like a roaring lion, seeking whom he may devour. Resist him, steadfast in the faith, knowing that the same sufferings are experienced by your brotherhood in the world. But may the God of all grace, who called us to His eternal glory by Christ Jesus, after you have suffered a while, perfect, establish, strengthen, and settle you. To Him be the glory and the dominion forever and ever. Amen.*

When the passage in the Bible refers to widows, it is referring to a woman who has lost her husband. In these questions, the word widow also includes a widower (a man who has lost his wife). When talking about widows, the real context here is about people who have lost a spouse and need help taking care of themselves or their family. In Biblical times, the woman's livelihood was vastly supported by her husband. So when her husband died, often they were unable to make enough money to care for themselves or their family. That is why the extended family was supposed to step in to help until she remarried. This concept might seem dated in today's world because most women work and women can have their own career. However, there are still times when someone might lose their spouse and be unable to work or find work. There may be a case when even as a single person you lose your job and are unable to care for yourself for a time. These passages apply to those situations.

We must all help one another.

A family should first help their own family before the church does. Likewise, a person should not become poor (whether their own doing or not) and claim helplessness or take advantage of the church or their family.

Catechism Material: To Youth, To Widows, and To Everyone (p. 39)
Additional Bible passage (Widows): 1 Timothy 5:3–16
Additional Bible passages (Everyone): Romans 13:8–10, Galatians 5:13–16, 1 Corinthians 13:1–8, 1 Timothy 5:1–2, 1 Peter 2:11–12, and 1 Peter 3:14–17

1. As a youth, you should be humble because...
   a. ____ You do not know anything
   b. ____ Older people will not listen to you anyways
   c. ____ Actually you should not be humble because no one will listen to you if you are
   d. ____ God rewards the humble and opposes the proud
2. True / False – The young should be submissive to the older.
3. True / False – Everyone should be humble towards each other.
4. True / False – The youth should not chastise the older, but should urge them to do right when they do wrong.
5. True / False – The older should treat the younger as family and equals in Christ.
6. True / False – When the Bible talks about widows and taking care of them, it no longer applies to us today.
7. True / False – As a widower, because you are a man, you should not receive any help from your family or church.
8. True / False – These passages can also apply to single adults in financial need.
9. As a widow, you should:
   a. ____ Seek as much pleasure as you can
   b. ____ Look to God for hope and security
   c. ____ Immediately find another spouse
   d. ____ Stop working and wallow in hopelessness
10. The widow who dedicates themselves to pleasure...
    a. ____ Has a right to because of their misery
    b. ____ Should be held in high regard
    c. ____ Has done nothing wrong
    d. ____ Is dead in their sins
11. Who should help take care of a widow who has family?
    a. ____ The Church
    b. ____ Their family
    c. ____ Their friends
    d. ____ Strangers
12. Who should help take care of a widow who has no family?
    a. ____ The Church
    b. ____ Their family
    c. ____ Their friends
    d. ____ Strangers
13. True / False – A widow must be careful not to get caught up in this world and its pleasures.

14. True / False – A younger widow is recommended to remarry.

    Why or why not? _____

    _____

15. What commandment sums up the last seven commandments? _____

    _____

    How does that apply to how everyone should live and treat each other? _____

    _____

    _____

16. Give three examples of how love acts and then write out an example of how to do that in real life:

    a. _____: _____

    _____

    b. _____: _____

    _____

    c. _____: _____

    _____

17. True / False – Everyone should study and learn the Scriptures so that they are prepared to answer those who have questions about their faith.

18. How is a Christian suffering even though what they did was righteous (they suffer because of their faith) considered "blessed"? _____

    _____

    _____

    How is this different than suffering for one's own sin? _____

    _____

    How can God use our suffering for righteousness to help others? _____

    _____

19. What should we do for everyone? (Mark all that apply.)

    a. ____ Make prayers and requests for them

    b. ____ Intercede for them

    c. ____ Live your life for them

    d. ____ Give thanks for them

SECTION 11: REVIEW

1. Give an overall summary of how a pastor should behave in their role:_____
    _____
    _____
    _____

    What are some specific actions you (or they) can take to fulfill this role in a godly way?_____
    _____
    _____
    _____

    How can you encourage someone else to carry out this role in a godly way?_____
    _____
    _____
    _____

2. Give an overall summary of how a member of a church should behave in their role: _____
    _____
    _____
    _____

    What are some specific actions you (or they) can take to fulfill this role in a godly way?_____
    _____
    _____
    _____

    How can you encourage someone else to carry out this role in a godly way? _____
    _____
    _____
    _____

3. Give an overall summary of how the government should behave in their role: _____
    _____
    _____
    _____

    What are some specific actions you (or they) can take to fulfill this role in a godly way? _____
    _____
    _____
    _____

    How can you encourage someone else to carry out this role in a godly way? _____
    _____
    _____
    _____

4. Give an overall summary of how a citizen should behave in their role: _____

_____

_____

_____

What are some specific actions you (or they) can take to fulfill this role in a godly way?_____

_____

_____

_____

How can you encourage someone else to carry out this role in a godly way?_____

_____

_____

_____

5. Give an overall summary of how a husband should behave in their role:_____

_____

_____

_____

What are some specific actions you (or they) can take to fulfill this role in a godly way? _____

_____

_____

_____

How can you encourage someone else to carry out this role in a godly way?_____

_____

_____

_____

6. Give an overall summary of how a wife should behave in their role:_____

_____

_____

_____

What are some specific actions you (or they) can take to fulfill this role in a godly way?_____

_____

_____

_____

How can you encourage someone else to carry out this role in a godly way?_____

_____

_____

_____

7. Give an overall summary of how a parent should behave in their role:_____

_____

_____

_____

What are some specific actions you (or they) can take to fulfill this role in a godly way?_____

_____

_____

_____

How can you encourage someone else to carry out this role in a godly way?_____

_____

_____

_____

8. Give an overall summary of how a child should behave in their role:_____

_____

_____

_____

What are some specific actions you (or they) can take to fulfill this role in a godly way? _____

_____

_____

_____

How can you encourage someone else to carry out this role in a godly way? _____

_____

_____

_____

9. Give an overall summary of how an employer or boss should behave in their role: _____

_____

_____

_____

What are some specific actions you (or they) can take to fulfill this role in a godly way? _____

_____

_____

_____

How can you encourage someone else to carry out this role in a godly way? _____

_____

_____

_____

10. Give an overall summary of how an employee should behave in their role:_____
_____
_____
_____

What are some specific actions you (or they) can take to fulfill this role in a godly way?_____
_____
_____
_____

How can you encourage someone else to carry out this role in a godly way?_____
_____
_____
_____

11. Give an overall summary of how a youth should behave in their role: _____
_____
_____
_____

What are some specific actions you (or they) can take to fulfill this role in a godly way? _____
_____
_____
_____

How can you encourage someone else to carry out this role in a godly way? _____
_____
_____
_____

12. Give an overall summary of how a widow should behave in their role:_____
_____
_____
_____

What are some specific actions you (or they) can take to fulfill this role in a godly way?_____
_____
_____
_____

How can you encourage someone else to carry out this role in a godly way?_____
_____
_____
_____

13. Give an overall summary of how everyone should behave towards everyone else:_____

_____

_____

_____

What are some specific actions you (or they) can take to fulfill this role in a godly way?_____

_____

_____

_____

How can you encourage someone else to carry out this role in a godly way?_____

_____

_____

_____

SECTION 12 – BEYOND THE BASICS

This section deals with particular topics and doctrines of the Lutheran church that are more intricate and not outlined in the catechism. These particular lessons are intended for people who want to further their understanding of Lutheran doctrine beyond the small catechism. However, due to the intricacy of these topics, these lessons will only cover the basic elements.

LESSON 79: TITHING (STEWARDSHIP)

> **Memorization:** 2 Corinthians 9:6–9 –
> *But this I say: He who sows sparingly will also reap sparingly, and he who sows bountifully will also reap bountifully. So let each one give as he purposes in his heart, not grudgingly or of necessity; for God loves a cheerful giver. And God is able to make all grace abound toward you, that you, always having all sufficiency in all things, may have an abundance for every good work. As it is written:*
> *"He has dispersed abroad,*
> *He has given to the poor;*
> *His righteousness endures forever."*

10 percent is not included in the Moral Law:

The word *tithe* and the concept of tithing are often and most associated with giving 10 percent of a person's income, profit, or belongings. The word and practice trace itself back to Abraham when he gave God 10 percent of all that he had (Genesis 14:18–20). When Abraham gave this 10 percent, it was not out of obligation or request, but it was a free gift given to God to honor Him. This continued into the time of the Israelite nation where God commanded that they give 10 percent to Him (Leviticus 27:30). The concept of a tithe then turned into a part of the civil/political and ceremonial law of the Israelites. The concept of 10 percent giving in the civil/political and ceremonial law is separate from the moral law. The moral law in the First and Third Commandments require a person to give to God from their heart to honor God and support the church and its work. (We honor and trust God above all things, and we honor the Sabbath day by supporting the church.) This separation is clearly shown when Jesus compared the poor widow and the rich who gave to the church (Mark 12:41–44). Jesus, and therefore God, were and are concerned with the condition of the heart and desire to honor God, not the amount.

What does this mean for those in the church? It means that the poor, or those struggling financially, are not required to give 10 percent. Rather, if they give what they can out of their trust and love for God, then they keep the First and Third Commandments better than those who only give out of their wealth.

Giving from the heart:

The other part Jesus emphasized was that "do not let your left hand know what your right hand is doing" (Matthew 6:1–4). The idea is that when a person does something charitable, or in this case gives to the church, that they do not do it so they can be praised by the people around them (Matthew 23:1–7). When a person gives from the heart, they give regardless of praise and instead give out of thankfulness and love to God. In fact, a person should shun praise for the giving that they do. Rather they should give because God saved them, and they recognize that all things come from God (think of the fourth petition of the Lord's Prayer). Moreover, when a person gives to the church, they are actually giving to God (Hebrews 7:8–10). Therefore, if a person makes a promise to give something to the church, then they should do it. They should also not pretend to give more than they have actually given just to get praise from the church or God (Acts 5:1–11).

What does this mean for those in the church? It means that when a person gives to the church, they should do it out of a thankful heart, praising and glorifying God with their gift; for indeed their gift goes to God and not to His human representatives. It also means that people should not use secrecy to withhold or minimize the glory and praise that is done through giving (Malachi 3:8–10). A person does that, by withholding what they can, should, or promised to give to the church, for themselves.

10 percent is a guide:

As Christians, we are no longer under the firm heel of the law. Rather we exist and operate under the Gospel using the Law as a guide (Section 3 and Galatians 5). Therefore, if we believe that we must give 10 percent and anything else is an affront or sin to God, we put ourselves under the Law. If we place ourselves under the law, then we are required to keep the whole of the law, which is impossible. Rather, the concept of 10 percent is the law being used as a guide. If we are giving less than 10 percent, we should seek to give more if we can, even if it means making personal sacrifices. If we give more than 10 percent, good, but that does not make us more righteous than someone else. It also means that if we can give more than 10 percent, we should consider doing so. To give only 10 percent because that is our "obligation" instead of what we have purposed in our heart, is also wrong. What we have is in our own hand to give to the Lord as we desire and purpose. Therefore, giving more because we have more and someone expects it out of us or to gain glory for ourselves is also wrong (Acts 5:1–4).

What does this mean for those in the church? We ought to view the idea of 10 percent as a guide. We should strive to give 10 percent when we can. However, if we cannot due to sickness, poverty, or disability, we should give from the heart what we can. Moreover, we dare not use this as an excuse to give less because then we are putting ourselves ahead of God. Finally, 10 percent is a standard, but if we have the ability to give more, we should if it comes from our own desire and not out of a sense of obligation or coercion.

The concept of tithing does not only refer to money:

Giving money to the church in the form of tithes is important. Without money to pay for the pastor and all of the needs of the church building, it would not be sustainable. However, simply throwing money at the church is not going to spread the Word of God. People have to give their time, talents, and energies to make a church run and be successful. That too is a part of tithing. It is a part of giving glory and honor to God. Those things include serving on boards, being ushers or Sunday school teachers, etc. They also include regular people on Sunday morning being friendly, greeting one another, and making new people and visitors feel at home. It also includes serving in the community to help those who are poor, visiting and encouraging the sick and disabled, and reading and studying the Word of God (so we can answer questions and have an idea of what to say to others about our faith). Consider this, on the last day, Jesus is going to say to the righteous (Matthew 25:34–36, 40):

> "Come, you blessed of My Father, inherit the kingdom prepared for you from the foundation of the world: for I was hungry and you gave Me food; I was thirsty and you gave Me drink; I was a stranger and you took Me in; I was naked and you clothed Me; I was sick and you visited Me; I was in prison and you came to Me. … Assuredly, I say to you, inasmuch as you did it to one of the least of these My brethren, you did it to Me."

But if we refuse to acknowledge those who visit the church, if we refuse to help those who are sick even among the members of our own church, or if we do not help those who are struggling, we have refused the Son of God who died on the cross for our sins. Indeed actions, just like money, are a part of tithing.

What does this mean for those in the church? We ought to understand that not only financial giving is required, but also our time, talents, and abilities. By doing so, we support the functions of the church. We must also recognize, help, and encourage not only the members of our congregation but those outside the church and especially the strangers (visitors) that come into our midst as well. Through all these things, we actually serve and help God because those poor, those sick, those needy, and those strangers are just the earthly face of God.

Everything we give and do for God, we should do cheerfully to His glory. It is through these simple acts, that we support God's will that heaven should be filled.

Cheerful giving:

We should not think that because the amounts of our gifts are given in secret, that the act of giving should be done without joy. Rather each gift that we give, whether great or small, should be done with joy. For by giving to the church through our time, talents, and money, we support the will of God through His church. And what is that will? It is that "all men should come to the knowledge of the truth" (1 Timothy 2:4) (Lesson 49). Therefore, we through our gifts, great and small, are bringing the truth of the gospel to the world. In doing so, God can save all the more. How wondrous and amazing a thing that we lowly sinners should help those who are being saved!? The very city of heaven is being filled up through our gifts! Therefore singing, dancing, and great joy to God are most certainly appropriate with every gift (2 Corinthians 9:1–15).

What does this mean for those in the church? A person in the church should give of their time, talents, abilities, and money with great joy. Through these simple acts, we give to God and support His will that the whole of heaven should be filled.

How then should the doctrine of tithing be used?

It should be used to encourage a person in the following ways:
- Encourage a person to give of their time, talents, abilities, and money to the church, poor, and charities based on love and thankfulness to God (which ultimately shows that they are putting God first).
- Encourage a person to give what they promised to give because they promised it to God.
- Encourage a person who is struggling financially that God loves and appreciates them for even the small contributions that they give.

It should be used to discourage a person for giving with the following reasons:
- When a person gives because they feel obligated to do so (e.g., I'm giving because I should or to satisfy someone else).
- When a person gives one thing (for example money) to exonerate them from giving anything else (for example time) (e.g., I gave 10 percent this month, so I do not have to help with any other church needs).
- When a person gives a small amount because no one is looking or they would rather use what they should give towards themselves (e.g., I put in my 20 dollars this week, so God and I are good, and I can buy my brand new, big, beautiful television).
- When a person gives a large amount to get glory or recognition for themselves (e.g., I am going to give a bunch of money to the church, so people know I am a good person).

How should the concept of 10 percent be used?

It should be used as a reference to help people make their own determination on how much they should give.

1. True / False – In order to tithe properly, a person must give 10 percent of their income.

2. If a person is struggling financially and cannot or does not give a full 10 percent of their income, are they sinning? Why or why not?_____

   _____

   _____

3. With whom did the concept of tithing begin?
   a. _____ Adam and Eve
   b. _____ Noah
   c. _____ Abraham
   d. _____ Moses

4. When we give, should other people know how much we give? Why or why not? _____

   _____

   _____

5. True / False – Tithing refers to a person giving more than just money.

6. What is the reason a person gives?
   a. _____ Out of obligation
   b. _____ Out of thankfulness and love to God
   c. _____ Out of compulsion
   d. _____ To be praised

7. True / False – Whatever we give to the church or others, we are really giving to God.

8. True / False – When a person says they will give something, they should give it because they promised it to God.

9. True / False – When we give out of obligation or compulsion, it is just as God-pleasing as giving out of thankfulness and love to God.

   Why or why not?_____

   _____

   _____

10. As a Christian, if we can give more than 10 percent of our income...
    a. _____ We absolutely should because we have more than other people.
    b. _____ We have no need because 10 percent is the requirement.
    c. _____ We should consider doing so, but we are not obligated to.
    d. _____ We should give more if we get recognized for doing so.

11. As a Christian, if we are giving less than 10 percent of our income...
    a. _____ We should examine why and determine if we can give more.
    b. _____ We do not have to give any more because tithing is not obligatory.
    c. _____ We should think less of ourselves because we are sinning.
    d. _____ The pastor should sit down and have a talk with us about our sin.

12. What are the things a person tithes? (Mark all that apply.)
    a. ____ Time
    b. ____ Abilities
    c. ____ Money
    d. ____ Talents

13. True / False – If we give a full 10 percent, we do not have to do anything around the church.

14. Why do we help those who are sick or in need, and do things around the church?
    a. ____ Because God commands us to do them
    b. ____ Because it makes us look good to those around us
    c. ____ Because it makes us good members of a congregation
    d. ____ Because in doing so we do those things to God

15. Should we be open, warm, and inviting to those visitors that come to our church?
    a. ____ Yes
    b. ____ No
What Bible passage supports your answer?_____

16. When we give or do things for the church, how should we feel about it?
    a. ____ We should do it somberly, so people do not praise us.
    b. ____ We should do it with a smile on our faces, so people think we are happy about it.
    c. ____ We should feel obligated to do it.
    d. ____ We should do it with true joy, knowing that it is for God and through it, heaven will be filled

LESSON 80: DESERTION

> **Memorization:** 1 Corinthians 7:10–11, 15–16 –
> *Now to the married I command, yet not I but the Lord: A wife is not to depart from her husband. But even if she does depart, let her remain unmarried or be reconciled to her husband. And a husband is not to divorce his wife. ... But if the unbeliever departs, let him depart; a brother or a sister is not under bondage in such cases. But God has called us to peace. For how do you know, O wife, whether you will save your husband? Or how do you know, O husband, whether you will save your wife?*

The Catechism lists desertion as one of the reasons for a marriage ending (Question 56 p. 82). A good way of understanding the topic is that it is a one-sided divorce without the paperwork. Essentially, one person dissolves the marriage through their willful and continuous (or willful, frequent, and regular sinning). It is a complex issue. What makes it complex is that there are no hard and fast rules for when desertion occurs. No one overt action defines desertion. Rather human understanding and decision must be used to determine when desertion has occurred. That is why desertion falls under the purview of the pastor's care for the flock. He is the one who is supposed to counsel the members of his congregation on sin.

Desertion is all about sin. When the sins that lead to desertion have occurred, forgiveness and reconciliation are sometimes possible and warranted. Therefore, in such a case, there is no dissolution of the marriage. At other times forgiveness may be needed, but the earthly consequences of sins (in this case, formal divorce or even criminal charges) may be necessary. Therefore, the final decision on whether or not desertion has occurred needs to be made between a pastor and the party who has been victimized.

This lesson is designed to give an overall understanding of desertion. It does not cover every aspect of desertion. Each individual circumstance must be evaluated based on its own conditions and circumstances. If you suspect you are a victim of desertion, contact your individual pastor. In instances of physical abuse, your local authorities should be involved. A marital counselor, aside from your pastor, may also be appropriate.

Desertion: Willful and continuous (or willful, frequent, and regular) sinning by one spouse that dissolves the marriage due to abandonment, sexual neglect, physical neglect, or abuse.

Physical desertion:

Where desertion is most easily understood is when one person in the marriage, without the consent or agreement of the other, physically and permanently leaves the marriage. An example would be a husband walking out on his family, never to return. One of the factors here is it is a one-sided agreement. In other words, the wife in that particular example is not telling the husband to "get out" or "never come back." The second key factor is the husband has no intent to return and reconcile. So, after a period of time, he does not return to the house, or he does not continue to provide for the house. Also, he does not give any indication or make any attempts to reconcile. (Leaving and sending money once a month or year with no other correspondence is still desertion.)

Physical desertion does not include when one party has to temporarily leave because of work, military duty, or other forced obligation. In other words, if two people are married and one person goes off on a business trip for a month but intends to return and continue the marriage, it is not desertion. It is not desertion for a soldier to go to war for extended periods (years) at a time. In these instances, there is no permanent desire to leave by the soldier or the employee. Likewise, it does not include a temporary separation to work on issues.

Sexual desertion:

One of the ways that the Sixth Commandment is kept is through "being fruitful and multiplying." What that inevitably requires is sex. Marriage involves sex, and one partner cannot maliciously withhold it from the other. Does that mean that if your spouse only gives you sex once a week and you want it every day, they have deserted you? NO! Rather this is a prolonged and one-sided decision to withhold. Discussion, counseling, and intervention must be done before the marriage is dissolved. Moreover, the decision to withhold sex must be an active decision made by one party, and not a passive, forced-upon decision. That means that if a person becomes sick, disabled, or otherwise incapable of having sex, it is not desertion on their part.

Desertion through neglect:

This type of desertion has to do with one party actively refusing to care for the needs of the other spouse. For example, the husband refuses to work or help around the house to provide for the family or his wife. Another example is if the husband gets sick (for example Alzheimer's), and the wife refuses to care for him. It is NOT when one spouse gets sick, disabled, or otherwise is incapable of caring for the other spouse's physical or emotional needs.

Desertion through abuse:

This is the last and possibly the most complicated element of desertion. This type of desertion occurs when one party maliciously and persistently abuses the other party in the marriage physically or emotionally. It is NOT a simple case of "they're just not nice to me." Rather it is a persistent abuse that puts the life and wellbeing of the other spouse in jeopardy. For example, a wife beats her husband, uses weapons against him, and threatens to kill him. It can also be consistent verbal threats and intimidation from one party to the other. For example, the wife could demand that the husband comes home at the same time every night and threaten harm or death to him if he does not do it. Plus, she refuses to allow him to leave the house by himself at any other time by threatening to leave him. If yours or another's life is in danger, the police and not the pastor, friend, etc., may need to be your first call.

Desertion resolution:

In all the instances of desertion, remediation and reconciliation should be attempted. It should be attempted through counseling and seeking to learn how two married people should interact according to God's will. It also involves forgiveness, repentance, and an actual effort to be better. To be clear, remediation has not occurred when the offending party says "I'm sorry," and for a few days, weeks, or months, is nice to the victim to manipulate the victim into staying, and then afterward is just as hostile and abusive. That *cycle of domestic violence* is not appropriate and should not be tolerated.[38] Even so, there will be a time of struggle because it is generally impossible for a person to change permanently overnight (Section 6). The resolution may require an undetermined, but temporary, time of physical separation. Moreover, a resolution may not be possible if the sinning party does not correct their behavior. Finally, and

However, a husband and wife need to vehemently attempt to reconcile and overcome it with God's help.

especially in cases of desertion through abuse, the victim must be protected from the abuser. A resolution should not be forced because that will put the victim back in danger. In instances of physical abuse (or even neglect), it is not better to "save" a marriage at the expense of one spouse or their children's wellbeing. All sin is equally condemning and the "sanctity of marriage" does not justify, negate, or excuse the sins of the abuser. Also, keep in mind there is no set time for how long remediation should be attempted.

Divorce in cases of desertion:

If desertion has occurred and remediation is unable to take place, or could not be accomplished, divorce is the legal proceeding that makes the desertion official. In that case, divorce is the by-product of the sin of desertion by one party. Divorce because of desertion is not the sin of adultery (1 Corinthians 7:10–16).

How should the concept of desertion be used?

The church, and specifically the pastor, should use the concept of desertion to protect those who are being victimized in a marriage. One (or more) sin(s) does not justify another sin (in this case divorce). Therefore, the sanctity of marriage does not justify the enabling of one spouse to victimize (i.e., sin against) the other. However, it should not be used to encourage divorce because someone is simply in an unhappy marriage or just dissatisfied with their marriage or spouse (see lesson 44). Therefore, reconciliation and forgiveness should be vehemently attempted, but the victim should equally be vehemently protected.

1.   Define the term "desertion": _____

_____

_____

---

38   Domestic violence is a serious situation. Know the signs and symptoms of it so you do not become a victim or victimizer. If you need help, call the national domestic hotline at 1–800–799–7233 (TTY 1–800–787–3224) or 911. For more information visit: www.thehotline.org or www.domesticviolenceroundtable.org

2. Name the four different ways desertion can occur:

    a. _____

    b. _____

    c. _____

    d. _____

3. What are the two factors involved in physical desertion? (Mark two)

    a. ____ The spouse that leaves must be chased out by the other

    b. ____ One spouse leaves willingly with no intent to return or reconcile

    c. ____ The spouse that stays is not encouraging the other to leave

    d. ____ The spouse that stays must refuse to reconcile

4. True / False – If a husband and wife get into an argument and the husband leaves for a time, it is desertion. Why or why not? _____

_____

_____

5. Is temporary separation to work on issues considered desertion? Why or why not? _____

_____

_____

6. True / False – If one spouse refuses to have sex every day with the other and instead only wants sex every other day, it is sexual desertion.

7. Sexual desertion is when...

    a. ____ One person in the marriage withholds sex for a few days

    b. ____ One person in the marriage cannot have sex anymore

    c. ____ One person in the marriage has sex with someone else

    d. ____ One person in the marriage maliciously refuses to have sex with the other

8. Desertion through neglect means... (Mark all that apply.)

    a. ____ One spouse refuses to work and help around the house

    b. ____ One spouse refuses to care for the physical or emotional needs of the other

    c. ____ One spouse does not do enough around the house

    d. ____ One spouse is out of work and cannot find another job

9. True / False – Desertion through neglect occurs when the spouse who becomes sick or disabled can no longer care for the other.

Why or why not? _____

_____

10. True / False – Desertion through abuse requires one spouse to physically leave marks on the other.

11. Desertion through abuse includes: (Mark all that apply.)

    a. ____ When a spouse persistently hits the other

    b. ____ When a couple gets into a physical argument

    c. ____ When a spouse says something mean to the other

    d. ____ When a spouse persistently berates, threatens, or belittles the other

12. True / False – In all situations of abuse a pastor should be called before the police.

13. True / False – In instances where sins that lead to desertion are occurring, remediation and reconciliation should be attempted.

14. Who can help with remediation/reconciliation? (Mark all that apply.)
    a. ____ Pastor
    b. ____ Counselor
    c. ____ Marital counselor
    d. ____ The police

15. True / False – Temporary separation is an acceptable tool to be used during a time for remediation and reconciliation.

16. True / False – After a person says they are sorry and asks for forgiveness, reconciliation and remediation has always occurred.
    Why or why not?_____
    _____

17. When a person is an abuser or is doing sins that lead to desertion in a marriage, is it always possible for them to stop their sin all at once and not relapse? Why or why not?_____
    _____
    _____

18. What is the cycle of domestic violence?_____
    _____

19. When a person is deserted and a divorce happens, has adultery occurred on the part of the victim?
    a. ____ Yes
    b. ____ No

20. True / False – The sanctity of marriage is more important than the victim's wellbeing in instances of desertion.

21. True / False – The pastor of a couple or person, who believes they are being victimized by sins that lead to desertion, should be contacted and consulted.

22. True / False – All instances of desertion are the same, and so it is easy to determine when it has occurred and the time to get a divorce.

LESSON 81: ELECTION (THE DOCTRINE OF PREDESTINATION)

> **Memorization:** Ephesians 1:3–6 –
> *Blessed be the God and Father of our Lord Jesus Christ, who has blessed us with every spiritual blessing in the heavenly places in Christ, just as He chose us in Him before the foundation of the world, that we should be holy and without blame before Him in love, having predestined us to adoption as sons by Jesus Christ to Himself, according to the good pleasure of His will, to the praise of the glory of His grace, by which He made us accepted in the Beloved.*

The Lutheran doctrine of *election* seeks to balance two seemingly opposed truths. The first of those truths is that God predestined or elected those who were going to be saved before the world was even formed (Romans 8:29–30 and Ephesians 1:3–6). Therefore, because He predestined us, we are secure in our salvation despite all the attempts of the Devil, the World, and our Sinful Nature (John 10:28–29). Then comes the second truth which states that we can reject God and fall away from our faith (2 Peter 2:18–22).

How can a person be both secure in their faith and able to be lost?

A person is secure in their faith because of many things. First of which is the beginning of their faith. All faith comes from the Word of God and by the Holy Spirit: "No one can say that Jesus is Lord except by the Holy Spirit" (1 Corinthians 12:3). Their faith, our faith, comes from the Holy Spirit and not from us or our "good works," better works, or better personality (2 Timothy 1:8–9). Therefore, if God chose us while we were still His enemies, how can we worry about losing our faith? "[God] who has begun a good work in you will complete it until the day of Jesus Christ" (Philippians 1:6). Therefore, we put our strength and trust in God because He who has saved us will continue in His saving work despite us.

It is through our choosing to abandon His grace, despise His sacrifice, and burn His love to the ground by willful, repeated, and unrepentant sinning that we lose our salvation. This is the Christian who once believed and trusted in Jesus, who now actively chooses not to obey His commands. It is that person who no longer believes they need forgiveness for their sins or that because they have forgiveness they can do whatever sins they please (Romans 6:1–4). For this person, despite the faith they once had, "God will not be mocked" (Galatians 6:7–10), and they will be destroyed (Hebrews 10:26–31). That is wholly different than the Christian who is struggling with their sin (repeated or not), desperate for forgiveness and relief from it, and turning to God with only the hope that God might forgive them (Section 6). That simple act of desiring and turning to God for forgiveness demonstrates God's love, forgiveness, and the fact that the Holy Spirit, and therefore faith, are still inside them. It is so because our sinful nature prevents us from turning to God, and it is only by the Holy Spirit that we can turn to Him (Lesson 27).

Jesus stands at the door begging for us not to leave. However, just like He allowed Adam and Eve to choose sin, He also will allow us to choose to leave.

Lutheranism is not *Calvinism*:

The Lutheran understanding of election is different than the understanding of John Calvin. In fact, because John Calvin was also a theologian during the time of Luther, Luther and he argued over this very topic. This topic is important to understand because Calvin's doctrinal teachings are a cornerstone of Baptist beliefs on this topic.

Calvin, like Luther, believed that God predestined people to heaven. However, and unlike Luther, he also believed that God also predestined people to Hell. A person who is predestined to heaven will be saved and a person predestined to hell will be condemned, regardless of circumstances and events on earth. That leads to the belief "*once saved, always saved*." This means that once a person accepts Jesus as their Savior, it is impossible for them to fall away. If they do appear to fall away, it was because they never really accepted Jesus in the first place, or that God must or will bring them back regardless of their future decisions. Faith, therefore, is immutable (unable to be lost). Moreover, there is nothing that can be done for those who are predestined to hell.

First, the idea that God predestines someone to hell is false. The basic evidence for that comes first from correctly understanding the will of God. ("[God] desires all men to be saved and come to the knowledge of the truth" [1 Timothy 2:4].) Secondly, hell was not prepared (or predestined) for humankind. Rather hell was created for the devil and his evil angels. Humankind was intended to be perfect and go to heaven (Matthew 25:41). Therefore, God's will is that all should be saved, not that some should be saved and others should be lost. Secondly, God's intention was not that any should be lost and rather only the devil and his evil angels should occupy hell. However, because of our sinful nature and because of our rejection of God, He is compelled to put those unbelievers with the devil in hell.

The idea that once a person is saved, they can never be lost, is also false. Galatians 6:7–10 and Hebrews 10:26–31 make it clear that a person who once believed can reject God. Another clear rejection of this idea is the parable of the sower found in Matthew 13:1–9 (which is explained in Matthew 13:18–23). In that parable, the Holy Spirit comes to some, and no life is created. However, the Holy Spirit does come to others, and life springs up. This is the faith and salvation found in believing. However, after a time, those people who have life for one reason or another die. These are those Christians who believe for a time and then fall away. The final category contains those who do have faith, and their faith grows, producing fruit and life all around them. Therefore, if the Holy Spirit can come and create life, and life passes away, people who have faith are capable of losing it.

How should the doctrine of Election be used?
The doctrine of election should be used to strengthen and encourage those people who are struggling with their sins. It is through this doctrine that comfort and assurance can be given to them. For it is because God gave them their faith and God already overcame their sins that they do not need to worry their faith is lost. Moreover, the Holy Spirit (and therefore faith), must be present in them for them to struggle with their sins. Finally, it is God's will that they be saved, and God is faithful to them regardless of their faithlessness. It should also be used against those willful and unrepentant sinners that refuse to struggle against their sins. This is done because God, while He is rich in mercy, grace, and love, is also a God of justice. He will not be mocked, and our liberty found in the Gospel should not be used as an excuse to sin. (Note: This is also why Baptism is an assurance, but it is not insurance.)

Catechism Material: Question 191 (pp. 172–173)

1. True / False – The doctrine of election means that we were elected to be a member of the church through a vote of the congregation.
2. What is another name for the doctrine of predestination? _____
3. What are the two truths that the Lutheran doctrine of election seeks to balance?
    a. _____
    b. _____
4. A person is secure in their faith because... (Mark all that apply.)
    a. ____ Faith is not their work, but God's.
    b. ____ God chose us to be saved before the beginning of the world.
    c. ____ God saved us while we were still enemies of God.
    d. ____ God began the good work of our faith and will see it to completion.

5. A person is capable of losing their faith because... (Mark all that apply.)
    a. ____ We are able to reject God.
    b. ____ Satan, the world or our sinful nature can steal our faith away.
    c. ____ God is also a God of justice.
    d. ____ God will not be mocked.

6. How does a person lose their faith? (Mark all that apply.)
    a. ____ They willfully chose to sin and are unrepentant of it.
    b. ____ They do something really sinful that is impossible to come back from.
    c. ____ They use the grace of God as an excuse to sin.
    d. ____ They sin on a regular basis and struggle with it.

7. True / False – John Calvin and Martin Luther taught the same doctrine regarding the topic of Election.

8. What did John Calvin teach? (Mark two)
    a. ____ Christians can lose their faith.
    b. ____ A person cannot be predestined to hell.
    c. ____ Unbelievers are predestined to hell.
    d. ____ Christians are predestined to heaven.

9. What else did John Calvin teach? (Mark two)
    a. ____ An unbeliever who is predestined to hell cannot be saved.
    b. ____ An unbeliever who is predestined to hell can be saved.
    c. ____ Christians who are predestined to heaven cannot lose their faith.
    d. ____ Christians who are predestined to heaven always act like a Christian.

10. Give two Bible passages that demonstrate a Christian can lose their salvation:
    a. _____
    b. _____

11. Give a Bible passage that states that hell was created for the devil and his evil angels and not human beings:_____

12. What is one of the places in the Bible that gives the parable of the sower? _____

13. How does the parable of the sower demonstrate that faith is created by God and can be lost?

    _____

    _____

    _____

14. When a Christian is struggling with their sin and is worried about their salvation, how should the doctrine of election be used?_____

    _____

    _____

15. When a Christian is willfully sinning and is unrepentant of their sins, how should the doctrine of election be used?_____

    _____

    _____

16. Given what you have learned, is Baptism an assurance or is it insurance?
    a. ____ Assurance
    b. ____ Insurance

GLOSSARY

95 Theses: Lesson 10, p. 16	A set of talking points or complaints against the Catholic church posted by Martin Luther.
Aaronic Benediction: Lesson 67, p. 163	The blessing of Aaron and the priests to the people of Israel – "The LORD bless you and keep you; the LORD make His face shine upon you, and be gracious to you; the LORD lift up His countenance upon you, and give you peace." (Numbers 6:24–26)
Abortion: Lesson 33, p. 77* Catechism Q52, p. 77	Murdering (if the life of the mother is not in danger) an unborn child.
Absolution: Lesson 41, p. 95* Lesson 67, p. 162 Catechism Q272, p. 226	Another word for forgiveness.
Active Obedience: Lesson 23, p. 48* Catechism Q122A, p. 125	When Jesus actively on this earth kept the law perfectly because His divine nature (True God) allowed and caused Him to do so.
Adiaphora: Lesson 62, p. 152	"Neither commanded nor forbidden" – It is the concept that the Bible does not dictate every aspect of one's life or worship. Things that are not dictated by Scripture are up to the discretion of man.
Advent: Lesson 68, p. 165	The first season of the Christian church year. It focuses on when Jesus came the first time and when He will come the second time on judgment day. It includes the four Sundays preceding Christmas.
Amen: Lesson 54, p. 122* Catechism Q234, p. 200	Means "so shall it be."
Apostle: Lesson 12, p. 23*	A person who was sent specifically by Jesus to preach and teach in the New Testament.
Apostolic Benediction: Lesson 67, p. 163	The blessing of Paul to the churches and believers in Corinth and all Achaia – "The grace of the Lord Jesus Christ, and the love of God, and the communion of the Holy Spirit be with you all. Amen." (2 Corinthians 13:14)
Ascension: Lesson 68, p. 166	It celebrates the day that Jesus ascended into Heaven after His resurrection. This occurred 40 days after Easter.

---

* Term is used but not defined in this location.

Ash Wednesday: Lesson 68, p. 165	It celebrates the first day of Lent and it is 46 days before Easter. This also coincides with the fasting done by Jesus during His time in the wilderness. Some Christians use this opportunity to give up something for Lent (fast) as well until Easter. Fasting does not occur on the six Sundays prior to Easter making the total number of days for fasting 40. Ashes are distributed on this day to symbolize fasting in "sackcloth and ashes" and also as a reminder that we were created from dust and will die. So the pastor says, "Remember you are dust, and to dust you shall return," when the ashes are applied to the forehead.
Audible: Lesson 23, p. 48	Referring to something that can be heard with the ear. In particular to the voice of God, when it was heard and understood with the ear.
Baptism: Lesson 56, p. 127 Catechism Q239, p. 205	The word "baptism" means to wash. It can mean washing by dipping, pouring, sprinkling, or immersing in water. It is commonly used interchangeably with the term "Holy Baptism."
Begotten: Lesson 16, p. 34	The offspring or child of (the naturally born child of).
Benediction: Lesson 67, p. 163 Catechism p. 265	It is when the pastor sends the people of the congregation off with a blessing from God and with God's peace. There are two: the Aaronic (Numbers 6:24–26) and the Apostolic (2 Corinthians 13:14) blessings.
Blaspheme: Lesson 30, p. 88* Catechism Q28, p. 63	A term used when someone mocks God. Mocking God can include making fun of (or light of) or speaking evil about His name, Him, or His Word.
Bodily Need: Lesson 33, p. 79	Anything that is necessary to sustain and protect a person's body (e.g., food).
Born Again: Lesson 27, p. 56	The spiritual transformation that occurs when a non-believer becomes a believer in Christ. Typically understood outside of the Lutheran church as the moment in time when a person prays and accepts Jesus as their Savior.
Calvinism: Lesson 81, p. 208	Specifically, refers to the teachings of John Calvin (1509–1564). In this context, it refers to his teachings on election (predestination) and the doctrine of "once saved, always saved."
Catechism: Lesson 9, p. 14* Catechism Q10, p. 52	"A book of instruction usually in the form of questions and answers."
Catholic Church: Lesson 60, p. 145	The term "catholic church," with a small "c," means universal church and refers to all believers in the church both dead and alive. It does not refer to the "Catholic Church" which refers to a Christian denomination (a visible church) on earth.
Ceremonial Law: Lesson 14, p. 27 Catechism Q14, p. 55	In catechism and Biblical contexts, this term refers to the various requirements and rules about how sacrifices, feasts, and religious holidays were to be performed. Those things ultimately were fulfilled through Jesus who was the ultimate sacrifice for us, and so the Christian is no longer subject to those rules and requirements.

---

* Term is used but not defined in this location.

Ceremony: Lesson 62, p. 151	A formal activity with a set of defined behaviors.
Charles Darwin: Lesson 4, p. 6	Charles Darwin (2/12/1809–4/19/1882) was a naturalist that took a voyage on the HMS Beagle and wrote the book The Origin of Species, which detailed his theory of natural selection and evolution. He is considered the "father" of evolution.
Christmas: Lesson 68, p. 165	It is the day Christians celebrate the birth of Jesus. It is celebrated on the 25th of December.
Civil Law: Lesson 14, p. 27 Catechism Q14, p. 55	The term Civil Law (or Political Law) in the catechism and Biblical contexts, refers to the state law of Israel (i.e., the law that relates to the functioning of the government and society, and the punishments for breaking that law). This particular set of laws is no longer in effect because the nation state of Israel no longer exists as it was, and we do not live under it.
Communion of Saints: Lesson 60, p. 145 Catechism Q169, p. 157	Also called the "Holy Christian Church," the "invisible church," and "catholic church." All those believers in Christ, both dead and alive.
Complete Creation: Lesson 18, p. 36	The concept that when God created everything, everything was created completely capable of carrying out its task (fully functional) and having all of its appendages (fully formed).
Confession and Absolution: Lesson 67, p. 162	It is the time of the worship service (usually the second thing that happens) where the congregation states their sin and that they are sinful, deserving only condemnation. Then the Pastor absolves (i.e., forgives) the congregation of their sins. This occurs early in the worship service because it is only through faith and the forgiveness of sins we can come to God.
Confirmed in Bliss: Lesson 21, p. 42	A term used to describe the Holy Angels when God, after the rebellion of Satan, made them unable to turn to evil or disobey His commands.
Contrition: Lesson 57, p. 132 Catechism Q274, p. 226	This is when someone is sorry for their sins.
Conversion: Lesson 27, p. 56 Catechism Q160, p. 152	In the Lutheran Church, it means that a person has turned from their old ways and now believes in Jesus, trusts in Him as their Savior, and seeks to lead a new life.
Covet: Lesson 38, p. 87	Coveting is a sinful desire for something that does not belong to you. The desire for something becomes sinful when you feel it is "not fair" that they have it and you do not. It also becomes sinful when you believe you have the right to take something that does not belong to you. Finally, it becomes sinful when you have the expectation that you can take something regardless of who it really belongs to.
Creation: Lesson 18, p. 36	The special work of God the Father. It includes His whole work of creation in the beginning and His continuing work of creating and sustaining life today.

* Term is used but not defined in this location.

Creationism: Lesson 6, p. 9	The belief that God or some other being created life on this planet. While it can be ascribed to any person's belief in a higher being that created the planet or life on this planet (e.g., a person could believe aliens created this particular earth and life), it is typically ascribed to Christians. Some scientists, biologists, etc. see evidence for this belief in nature and through scientific study.
Creed: Lesson 67, p. 163 Lesson 69, p. 173* Catechism Q86, p. 102	A statement of belief. It includes what a person, organization, or church believes, teaches, and confesses.
Curb: Lesson 14, p. 27* Catechism Q77, pp. 96–97	In the context of the Catechism, it is one of the functions of the Law. It is mostly carried out by the conscience among unbelievers who, even though they do not know, have, or understand the written law, keeps them from murdering, stealing, etc. This function of the law is shown readily in the similarity of laws across nations and cultures, despite religious and philosophical differences.
Cycle of Domestic Violence: Lesson 80, p. 205	Refers to the common timeline that occurs in domestic violence situations. It begins with a time where tensions rise, usually to external factors outside the victim (money, job, children, the abuser's emotional state, etc.). It is then followed by the physical or emotional abuse by the abuser to the victim. Finally, comes the "honeymoon" stage where the abuser is sweet, nice, loving (possibly overly so) in order to make up for the abuse and manipulate the victim to stay. After this honeymoon stage, the cycle continues.
Day-Age Theory: Lesson 19, p. 38	The idea/doctrine that when the Bible uses the term "day" in Genesis to refer to the days of creation, it is not an actual day and can be interpreted as any length of time. It is here that people insert the millions/billions of years to allow for God to utilize evolution for the creation of the earth. They use 2 Peter 3:8 to support this idea/doctrine.
Desertion: Lesson 35, p. 82* Lesson 80, p. 204 Catechism Q56, p. 82	Willful and continuous (or willful, frequent, and regular) sinning by one spouse that dissolves the marriage due to abandonment, sexual neglect, physical neglect, or abuse.
Despise: Lesson 11, p. 19	It is when a person more than hates something or someone and avoids it or them. It also means to treat something or someone as being worthless.
Divine Attributes: Lesson 16, p. 34 Lesson 27, p. 56 Catechism Q155, p. 148	Characteristics that only God can have. Examples include His being omniscient, omnipresent, omnipotent, eternal (without beginning or end), and unchangeable.
Due Process of the Keys: Lesson 42, p. 97	It is the process by which the church retains the sins of an unrepentant member of its congregation as outlined in Matthew 18:15–20.
Due Process: Lesson 42, p. 97	The rights that an individual has when they are accused of a crime. In the United States, it includes the right of representation, trial by a jury of one's peers, a speedy trial, and the concept that a person is innocent until proven guilty.

* Term is used but not defined in this location.

Term	Definition
Easter: Lesson 68, p. 166	It celebrates the day that Jesus rose from the dead and showed Himself to the disciples. The date of Easter varies because it is celebrated on the first Sunday after the full moon for the Spring Equinox. It is done this way to coincide with the Jewish Celebration of Passover, which is based on this calculation.
Election: Lesson 81, p. 207 Catechism Q191, pp. 172–173	The doctrine of the Lutheran Church that states that those who are a part of the invisible church have been selected to be a part of it before they were even conceived. The Lutheran Church does not teach that people are preselected to go to Hell, rather that people choose to go there by refusing to believe (also known as Eternal Election of Grace or Predestination).
Euthanasia: Lesson 33, p. 77* Catechism Q52, p. 78	The act of murdering someone due to a medical, mental, or physical deficiency, or also do to their age.
Evangelist: Lesson 12, p. 23*	Someone who preaches and teaches the Word of God to others in order to convert them to the Christian faith. In particular, a person who works at expanding the number of people in the Christian Religion.
Evolution: Subsection: Evolution, p. 6	The concept that refers to when something changes and becomes more complex or better suited to its environment. This term is commonly interchanged with the "Theory of Evolution."
Flagellum: Lesson 5, p. 7	Refers to the tail structure of bacteria which is used by the bacteria for movement.
Forever Rejected: Lesson 21, p. 43	A term used to describe the Evil Angels (Demons and Satan) when God, after the rebellion of Satan, made it impossible for them to turn from their evil and does/did not offer any form of salvation or forgiveness to them.
Fraud: Lesson 36, p. 84 Catechism Q59, p. 85*	This word refers to the act of obtaining something from someone that does not belong to you through the use of lying. Examples include misrepresentation of who you are to obtain something. Grossly overstating the value or quality of the product you are selling. Intentionally hiding a defect in a product or item you are selling. Selling something you have no actual power to sell. Creating a contract, deed, or other legal paperwork in order to obtain or otherwise claim ownership to something you have no real legal claim to.
Fully Formed: Lesson 18, p. 36	The concept that when God created something in the beginning, it had all of its parts and appendages.
Fully Functional: Lesson 18, p. 36	The concept that when God created something in the beginning, it was completely capable of performing whatever task or function God gave it.
Gap Theory: Glossary, p. 222	The idea that the earth existed before the story of creation and death occurred during that point and time (thus accounting for the millions/billions of years), but then the earth was remade during creation. (See theistic evolution.)
Genocide: Lesson 33, p. 77	A word that means murdering a large group of people due to their race, religion, ethnicity, or political affinity.

* Term is used but not defined in this location.

Good Friday: Lesson 68, p. 165	This is the day that celebrates the day that Jesus died on the cross to pay for our sins. It is celebrated the Friday after Ash Wednesday and before Easter.
Gospel: Lesson 15, p. 30 Catechism Q8, p. 52 Catechism Q85, p. 101	The term literally means "good news." It is the term used by the Catechism and the Bible to refer to the good news of Jesus and our salvation through Him (shows us our Savior).
Gospels: Lesson 12, p. 23	It refers to the first four books of the New Testament. They include Matthew, Mark, Luke, and John.
Guide: Lesson 14, p. 27* Catechism Q77, pp. 96–97	In the context of the Catechism, it is one of the functions of the law. This function is solely for the use of believers to show them how they should live their lives in accordance with God's will. Without belief, there is no desire to follow God's will, and therefore unbelievers are unable or unwilling to utilize this function of the Law.
Hallowed: Lesson 47, p. 112	Holy, blessed, or honored.
Holy Baptism: Lesson 56, p. 127 Catechism p. 204	Also known as Baptism, it is a sacrament by which an individual through the water and God's Word receives the Holy Spirit, is washed of their sins, receives the salvation of their souls, and receives the adoption by God to be His children. It consists of water (any amount so long as it is present) and the pronouncement of God's Word: "I baptize you in the name of the Father and of the Son and of the Holy Spirit" (Matthew 28:19).
Holy Christian Church: Lesson 60, p. 145 Catechism Q169, p. 157	Also called the "invisible church," the "Communion of Saints," and "catholic church." All those believers in Christ, both dead and alive.
Holy Communion: Lesson 58, p. 133 Catechism p. 231	Also known as the Sacrament of the Altar, the Lord's Supper, the Lord's Table, the Breaking of Bread, the Eucharist (Greek word for "giving thanks"), and simply Communion. It is the second sacrament which was instituted by Jesus Christ on the Passover. It acts as the replacement for the Passover celebration of the Jews because Jesus is the true Lamb that takes away the sins of the world, and through it, we receive forgiveness of sins.
Holy Trinity: Lesson 16, p. 34 Catechism Q94, p. 107	Three distinct persons in one divine being, specifically referring to God the Father, God the Son, and God the Holy Spirit.
Human Nature: Lesson 40, p. 93	Each person's natural (what they are born with) or usual desires. In other words, it is how human beings usually act unless an outside force stops or changes their behavior.
Immersion: Lesson 56, p. 127	A baptismal requirement by some Christian denominations that believe that a person cannot or is not truly baptized unless they are fully submersed in water.
Inherited Sin: Lesson 57, p. 132* Catechism Q255, p. 214	Refers to the concepts of "original sin" and "sinful nature."

---

* Term is used but not defined in this location.

Intellectual Property: Lesson 38, p. 87*	Property that cannot be touched (i.e., is not physical). Examples include music, ideas, patents, business plans, etc.
Invisible Church: Lesson 60, p. 145 Catechism Q169, p. 157	Also called the "Holy Christian Church," the "Communion of Saints," and "catholic church." All those believers in Christ, both dead and alive.
Invocation: Lesson 67, p. 162 Catechism p. 266	When the Pastor formally begins worship and specifically when he makes the sign of the cross and calls upon the name of the Father, Son, and Holy Spirit. This is to invoke the memory of our Baptism and remind us Whose children we are and to Whom we belong. (See Trinitarian Invocation.)
Irreducible Complexity: Lesson 5, p. 8	The idea that for something to be functionally beneficial it must also have some form of complexity (i.e., it has more than one part).
Justification: Lesson 43, p. 102* Catechism Q182, p. 166	The Lutheran concept that we can be saved because our sins and the punishment they deserve have been paid for by Christ, because Christ took our punishment for them on the cross.
Kill: Lesson 33, p. 78	A term that means taking the life of another person. It can be done lawfully (sometimes called justifiable homicide) or unlawfully (murder).
Kingdom of Glory: Lesson 23, p. 49* Catechism Q125C, p. 130	One of the three kingdoms that Christ rules over. This particular kingdom refers to all believers who have died and now are in glory in heaven.
Kingdom of Grace: Lesson 23, p. 48* Catechism Q125C, p. 129	One of the three kingdoms that Christ rules over. This particular kingdom refers to the whole Christian church on earth, which He governs and protects.
Kingdom of Power: Lesson 23, p. 48* Catechism Q125C, p. 129	One of the three kingdoms that Christ rules over. This particular kingdom is the whole world in which Jesus governs with His power.
Kyrie: Lesson 67, p. 162 Catechism p. 266	(Pronounced kirē, ā) Literally, means "Lord have mercy." It is the time in the church service when the church prays for the church, the whole world, and any specific things. This recognizes that it is only through God's mercy that good things come and happen.
Law: Lesson 14, p. 26 Catechism Q7, p. 51 Catechism Q85, p. 101	The term has multiple meanings. Specific to the context of the Catechism and Bible it refers to the portions of the Bible that show us what God requires us to do and thus how we fail (it shows us our sin and need for a Savior). It has three functions (Curb, Mirror, and Guide) and three types (Political/Civil, Moral, and Ceremonial).
Legion: Lesson 21, p. 43	A great number of persons or things (A Roman legion had 6000 persons)
Lord's Prayer:	See "*The Lord's Prayer.*"
Martin Luther: Lesson 10, p. 15	Martin Luther (11/10/1483–2/18/1546) was a key figure in the Protestant Reformation, considered the founder of "Lutheranism," wrote many books including Luther's Small Catechism and translated the Bible into German.

* Term is used but not defined in this location.

Maundy Thursday: Lesson 68, p. 165	It is the Thursday before Easter and celebrates the night Jesus celebrated the Passover with His disciples, instituted Holy Communion and was betrayed.
Means of Grace: Lesson 15, p. 31* Lesson 27, p. 55 Catechism Q161, p. 152*	The means by which the Holy Spirit strengthens and brings people to faith. Those means are the Word (Bible) and Sacraments (Holy Baptism and Holy Communion). The Holy Spirit does use preaching, but only if what is being preached is the Word. That means that preaching cannot be separate from the Word for it to be effective.
Messianic Prophecy: Lesson 22, p. 45*	The prophecies in the Old Testament that point towards the Messiah.
Millennialism: Lesson 25, p. 51 Catechism Q149, p. 144	The belief that for 1000 years Christ or His church will reign on earth, and peace and prosperity will occur during that time.
Mirror: Lesson 14, p. 27* Catechism Q77, pp. 96–97	In the context of the Catechism, it is one of the functions of the law. It shows both believers and unbelievers their sins and how they do not measure up to God's requirements, and thus they need a Savior.
Moral Law: Lesson 14, p. 27 Catechism Q14, p. 55	In the context of the Catechism and Bible, this term refers to the requirements God has for every person in order for them to be holy and thus be eligible to live with Him in heaven. The best example of the moral law is the written law of the Ten Commandments.
Murder: Lesson 33, p. 78	Term meaning to take the life of another person without the lawful authority to do so. It can be done negligently (carelessly or unintentionally), premeditated (preplanned and carried out), or intentionally but without planning.
Natural Selection: Lesson 4, p. 6	A concept by Charles Darwin that states that when a mutation occurs, it will be naturally selected and thus survive if it creates a benefit for the organism in which the mutation occurred. That benefit must allow it to survive (i.e., obtain food/water/shelter) better than those with whom it competes.
New Man: Lesson 57, p. 132* Catechism Q257, p. 215	The Bible's description of the new nature that has been seeded into a believer that desires to do good works and the will of God. It fights against the Old Adam (Ephesians 4:17–24).
New Testament: Lesson 12, p. 23 Catechism Q2, p. 48	The term referring to the books of the Bible written about and after the time of Jesus.
Offering: Lesson 67, p. 163	It is when the church takes free will (voluntary) donations to the church for the work of the church and to sustain the church and pastor.
Office of the Keys: Lesson 42, p. 97 Catechism pp. 224–230	It is the term used to describe the authority of the church, its members, and the pastor to both forgive and, after due process of the keys is completed, retain sins.
Old Adam: Lesson 57, p. 132* Catechism Q255, p. 214	The Bible's description of a person's original nature and desires before they have been converted. It is the nature of a believer that still desires to sin and go against God. It fights against the New Man (Ephesians 4:17–24).

* Term is used but not defined in this location.

Old Testament: Lesson 12, p. 23 Catechism Q2, p. 48	The term refers to the books of the Bible written before the time of Jesus and pointing towards Him.
Omnipotent: Catechism Q93, p. 105	One of the divine attributes of God; it means that He is all powerful.
Omnipresent: Catechism Q93, p. 106	One of the divine attributes of God; it means He is present everywhere.
Omniscient: Catechism Q93, p. 105	One of the divine attributes of God; it means He knows everything (all-knowing).
Once Saved, Always Saved: Lesson 81, p. 208	The doctrine of Calvin that states once a person confesses and believes in Jesus as their Savior, their faith can never be lost.
Original Sin: Lesson 40, p. 93 Catechism Q81, p. 98	The concept that people are born with the natural inclination towards sin and are naturally sinful because it is passed down to every descendant of Adam (us). Meaning that from conception people are damnable enemies of God, hate Him, and cause every human being to perform actual sins.
Palm Sunday: Lesson 68, p. 165	The celebration of Jesus' coming into Jerusalem riding on a donkey. It is celebrated the Sunday before Easter.
Passive Obedience: Lesson 22, p. 45* Catechism Q122B, p. 126	The term referring to when Jesus on this earth had the ability to suffer and die because His human nature (True man) allowed Him to be able to.
Penance: Lesson 42, p. 97	An act of punishment or suffering imposed by the church for an individual to receive forgiveness for their sin(s) or for them to demonstrate that they truly are repentant/sorry for their sin(s) and thus deserving of forgiveness.
Penitent: Catechism Q186C, p. 168	A word that refers to the feeling of sorrow or remorse for one's sins.
Pentecost: Lesson 68, p. 166	The special pouring out of the Holy Spirit at a specific place and time in the New Testament which showcased God's power and the truth of the Apostles' preaching and teaching (Acts 2).
Personal Union: Lesson 22, p. 45 Catechism Q121, p. 124	Jesus is wholly and completely God and Man at the same time without divisions or schisms. He is indivisibly True God AND True Man.
Petition: Lesson 44, p. 106	A request or an earnest request for something.
Physical Blessings: Lesson 50, p. 116* Catechism Q219, p. 190*	All of the things that God gives to us for this life to survive, live, and more than survive (food, shelter, money, a spouse, life, health, money, talent, skills, etc.)
Physical Rest: Lesson 31, p. 70	Time off from working; a break from physical labors.

* Term is used but not defined in this location.

Political Law: Lesson 14, p. 27 Catechism Q14, p. 55	The term Political Law (or Civil Law) in the Catechism and Biblical contexts, refers to the state law of Israel (i.e., the law that relates to the functioning of the government and society and the punishments for breaking that law). This particular set of laws is no longer in effect because the nation state of Israel no longer exists as it was, and we do not live under it.
Predestination: Lesson 81, p. 207 Catechism Q191, pp. 172–173	The doctrine of the Lutheran Church that states that those who are a part of the invisible church have been selected to be a part of it before they were even conceived. The Lutheran Church does not teach that people are preselected to go to Hell, rather that people choose to go there by refusing to believe (also known as Eternal Election of Grace or Election).
Prelude: Lesson 67, p. 162	The music that is played before the church service formally starts. It is used as a time for meditation and prayer in preparation for worship.
Proceeds: Lesson 16, p. 34	Originates or comes from.
Profane: Lesson 47, p. 112	To disrespect or treat with irreverence or contempt.
Prophet: Lesson 12, p. 23*	A person who speaks God's Word.
Purgatory: Lesson 61, p. 148	A doctrine of the Catholic Church which states that a person/soul goes to this location to purify themselves, pay for, or receive sufficient temporal punishment for sin before they can go on to heaven.
Radiometric Dating: Lesson 7, p. 10	Commonly known as "Carbon Dating." Radiometric dating is the term that refers to any age calculation based on dating atoms based on a specific rate of decay.
Real Presence: Lesson 58, p. 133 Catechism Q291, pp. 234–235	The Lutheran concept that the Body and Blood of Jesus Christ are actually present in (together at the same time), with (inseparable), and under (hidden from view) the bread and wine.
Redemption: Lesson 26, p. 53*	(Also called Salvation,) It is the special work of God the Son. It includes His whole work from being born of a virgin, living a perfect life, dying on a cross, being buried to rising again.
Regeneration: Lesson 27, p. 56 Catechism Q160, p. 152	In the Lutheran Church, it means to be made new again through the Holy Spirit. When a person is made new, that means they are given a New man and Salvation.
Repentance: Lesson 42, p. 97 Catechism Q274, p. 226	The term used when a person is sorry for their sins, turns from them, and believes in Jesus as their Savior. Evidence of repentance is the act of turning from their sins and no longer doing them or (because of temptation and their sinful nature) they struggle against them albeit imperfectly.
Retain Sins: Lesson 42, p. 98	It is another way of saying "withhold forgiveness." This formally occurs when a congregation completes the due process of the keys, and the person is excommunicated from the church.

* Term is used but not defined in this location.

Robbery: Lesson 36, p. 84 Catechism Q59, p. 85*	The act of taking something that does not belong to you while using force.
Roman Flagrum: Lesson 24, p. 50	An instrument with a short handle and two or three thongs (whips) attached to it. The thongs would have pieces of metal attached to them. The instrument was commonly used by the Romans to flog (whip) criminals. It was probably used against Jesus by the Roman Soldiers when Pontius Pilate had Him beaten and scourged/flogged.
Sabbath: Lesson 31, p. 70*	In the Old Testament, it was a specific day (Saturday) set aside by God as a day of rest and worship to God. In the New Testament, it is not a specific day, but is still a time set aside for rest and worship of God.
Sacrament: Lesson 55, p. 126* Catechism Q236, p. 202	A sacred act that was instituted by God, it gives the forgiveness of sins, and it combines both a visible element and the Word of God.
Sanctification: Lesson 15, p. 31 Lesson 27, p. 57 Catechism Q156, pp. 149–150	The special work of the Holy Spirit. In the wide sense, it means the whole work of the Holy Spirit including bringing people to faith/salvation and sanctification in the narrow sense. In the narrow sense, it only refers to the work of the Holy Spirit allowing us and directing us to lead a godly life (even though we cannot live a perfect godly life until our sanctification is completed in heaven).
Sermon: Lesson 67, p. 163	It is the time during the service when the pastor explains or teaches the congregation the Word of God. A sermon should include Law (to convict us of our sins and need for a Savior), the Gospel (to show us who our Savior is), and then direction (the Law as a guide to show us how to live according to God's Will).
Sin of Commission: Catechism Q83, p. 100	The term used when a person sins by doing something they should NOT do, or rather are required to not do, according to the law.
Sin of Omission: Lesson 40, p. 93	When a person sins by NOT doing something they should or rather are required to do, according to the law.
Sinful Nature: Lesson 40, p. 93	The concept that people are born with the natural inclination towards sin, and it is inherited from their parents all the way from Adam. It makes it impossible for a person to please God or follow His commandments unless they are reborn by the Holy Spirit. (See Original Sin and Human Nature.)
Sola Gratia, Sola Fide: Lesson 43, p. 102	Latin for "By grace alone, by faith alone." This is one of the basic tenants of Christianity that we are saved not by anything we do or have done, but by the grace of God alone through faith alone.
Spiritual Blessings: Lesson 44, p. 106	Those things that are necessary for our salvation, our salvation, and all of those things that God gives us to be believers in Him and follow His will.
Spiritual Rest: Lesson 31, p. 70	Peace that is found in God's Word which gives us comfort during times of distress and stress, the assurance of forgiveness and salvation, and the promise of the True rest to come.

* Term is used but not defined in this location.

State of Exaltation: Lesson 25, p. 51 Catechism Q141, p. 138	The current state of Jesus in which "He now fully and always uses His divine powers."
State of Humiliation: Lesson 24, p. 49 Catechism Q127, p. 130	It refers to when Jesus limited His divine powers. It occurred from the time of conception until He was crucified on the cross.
Suicide: Lesson 33, p. 77* Catechism Q52, p. 78	Murdering oneself or utilizing another person to murder oneself (assisted suicide).
Texts of the Day: Lesson 67, p. 162	Refers to the specific Bible readings chosen by the church to focus the service and sermon around. Typically, there are three passages chosen: one from the Old Testament, one from the Epistles, and one from the Gospels. A psalm is also read or sung during the service, but is not necessarily referred to when this term is used.
The Lord's Prayer: Subsection: The Lord's Prayer, pp. 109–122 Lesson 67, p. 163 Catechism pp. 174–201	The prayer that Jesus taught all of His children and the church to pray. It contains everything for which a Christian should pray. The church prays this prayer because of Jesus' command and to make sure that the church prays for everything it should.
Theft: Lesson 36, p. 84 Catechism Q59, p. 85*	The simple act of taking something that does not belong to you particularly without using force.
Theistic Evolution: Lesson 19, p. 38	The idea or doctrine that states the Bible and Evolution can coexist. Specifically, that Evolution can occur within the confines of the Bible and that God DID use evolution when He created the world. Typically, the day-age theory is used to support this (but other assertions do exist like the *Gap Theory*).
Theory of Evolution: Lesson 4, p. 6	A theory (i.e., something that is not scientifically proven) put forth by some naturalists and scientists which states that all life on earth evolved from simpler organisms into the organisms we see today through a process called "Natural Selection." Some scientists/biologists etc. see evidence for this theory in nature and through scientific study.
Three Evil Powers: Lesson 49, p. 115 Lesson 52, p. 119 Catechism Q229, p. 196	Satan, the world, and our own sinful nature each work to tempt and cause us to sin with the ultimate purpose that we should come into false belief, despair, and greater sins.

* Term is used but not defined in this location.

Threefold Office of Christ: Lesson 23, p. 48* Catechism Q125 pp. 127–130	This refers to Jesus having three particular offices, which are Prophet, Priest, and King. – In His office of Prophet, He carried it out by preaching and teaching to the whole world during His lifetime, sending the apostles and pastors to preach then and now, and sending the Holy Spirit to us through Word and Sacrament. – He fulfills His office as Priest by first fulfilling the law perfectly and then being the ultimate and perfect sacrifice for us, and now by interceding for us to the Father. – In the office of King, He rules over all creation, governs and protects the whole Christian church, and will come again to judge the living and the dead.
Tithe: Lesson 79, p. 199	The money, time, or goods that people give to the church for the glory and honor of God. Tithing is often associated with 10 percent of income, which is why some prefer to refer to this concept as "stewardship."
Torah: Lesson 23, p. 48*	In the narrow sense, it is the word that the Jews use to refer to the first five books of the Bible.
Total Depravity of Man: Lesson 40, p. 93	It is the concept that as human beings we are completely corrupt and completely incapable of following God and His commands or loving Him and coming to Him of our own free will. Rather our will is inherently bound to do evil. This depravity is passed on from generation to generation through conception from Adam.
Transfiguration: Lesson 68, p. 165	It is the celebration of when Jesus was transfigured before the disciples before His crucifixion, on the Mount of Olives. See Matthew 17:1–9.
Transubstantiation: Lesson 58, p. 133	The Catholic belief that the Holy Communion invocation actually transforms the bread and wine wholly into the body and blood of Jesus Christ.
Trespass: Lesson 40, p. 93* Catechism Q78, p. 98	Another word for Sin.
Trinitarian Invocation: Lesson 57, p. 133 Catechism Q260, pp. 215–216	When a person or pastor states "In the name of the Father and of the Son and of the Holy Spirit" and thus calls upon each member of the Godhead in the Holy Trinity. Through this, a person is reminded (recalls), declares (claims), and confesses all of the rights and benefits one receives through their baptism.
Trinity Sunday: Lesson 68, p. 166	It celebrates God as being the Holy Trinity and occurs on the first Sunday following Pentecost.
Triune: Lesson 29, p. 65 Catechism Q19, p. 56	Three distinct persons in one divine being. (See also Holy Trinity.)
True God: Lesson 22, p. 45 Catechism Q119, pp. 121–123	Having the complete divine nature and being of God.

* Term is used but not defined in this location.

True Man: Lesson 22, p. 45 Catechism Q120, pp. 123–124	Having the complete human nature and being of human beings.
True Rest: Lesson 31, p. 70	The ultimate rest that is found when we enter into Heaven and no longer have to strive against sin, the world, or the devil.
Universal Atonement: Lesson 26, p. 53* Catechism Q140, p. 137	Jesus' substitution payment for everyone's sins so that everyone may enter into heaven if they have faith.
Verbal Inspiration: Lesson 12, p. 24* Catechism Q3, pp. 48–49	The concept that God wrote the Bible through the use of various people. He provided them with His own Words by providing them with thoughts that they expressed in the Bible.
Vicarious Atonement: Lesson 46, p. 111 Catechism Q139, p. 136	Jesus' substitution payment for all believer's sins so that we do enter into heaven through faith.
Visible Church: Lesson 60, p. 145 Catechism Q177, p. 161	Churches (any denomination) that have a group of people gathered around the Word and Sacraments; all people (believers and unbelievers/hypocrites) who claim to be a part of any Christian church or claim to adhere to the Bible and Christian doctrine.
Wailing Wall: Lesson 64, p. 156	It is all that remains of the Jewish temple after it was destroyed in the Jewish revolt (in 70 AD). It is the western wall. Jews and people go there to pray.
Water-Spirit Baptism: Catechism Q252B, p. 211	The Lutheran belief that through Baptism it is not merely symbolic with water, nor is it merely a spiritual baptism of the Holy Spirit. Rather that Baptism contains both water and the Holy Spirit, through the Word of God, and thereby a person receives the adoption of God as children, the forgiveness of sins, the Holy Spirit, faith, and salvation of our souls.
Works Righteousness: Lesson 66, p. 160	The idea that in order for a person to go to heaven they must earn or obtain it by taking some form of action or by doing good works no matter how few. In other words, it is the idea that a person must do something, no matter how inconsequential, to obtain God's forgiveness. It also includes the idea that Jesus' sacrifice is not totally complete, and we still must pay for or suffer for our sins in any way in order to get into heaven after we have faith. This concept can take many forms and includes indulgences (making payments for sins), and the concept of purgatory (suffering the consequences of sins after death).
Worship: Lesson 62, p. 150	To give divine honor, glory, or homage to something; or perform a religious, formal, or ceremonious rendering to something. Worship can be done with someone's life, through their body and voice, through ceremonial/formal worship, or through a person's heart and spirit.

* Term is used but not defined in this location.

REFERENCES

Baker, R. A., Craun, C., & Gibson, J. (n.d.). CH101 The Fourth Century. Retrieved August 2016, from http://www.churchhistory101.com/council-nicea-325.php

Bissey, J. (2016, July). *Worship*. Reading presented in AZ, Peoria.

Brain, M. (n.d.). How Carbon-14 Dating Works. Retrieved July 2016, from http://science.howstuffworks.com/environmental/earth/geology/carbon-142.htm

British Broadcasting Company. (n.d.). Martin Luther (1483–1546). Retrieved August 2016, from http://www.bbc.co.uk/history/historic_figures/luther_martin.shtml

Darwin, C. (1859). Retrieved July 2016, from http://literature.org/authors/darwin-charles/the-origin-of-species/

Drachman, B., & Kohler, K. (n.d.). Ablution. Retrieved January 2017, from http://www.jewishencyclopedia.com/articles/338-ablution

Forensic Facial Reconstruction. (n.d.). Retrieved July, 2016, from http://anthropology.si.edu/writteninbone/facial_reconstruction.html

Frequently Asked Questions about Saints. (n.d.). Retrieved August 2016, from http://www.catholic.org/saints/faq.php

Harper, D. (n.d.). Pope (n.). Retrieved August 2016, from http://www.etymonline.com/index.php?term=pope

Legends about Luther: 95 Theses. (n.d.). Retrieved August 2016, from http://www.luther.de/en/legenden/tanschl.html

Linder, D. O. (n.d.). Martin Luther's Hearings Before the Diet at Worms (1521): An Account. Retrieved August, 2016, from http://law2.umkc.edu/faculty/projects/ftrials/luther/lutheraccount.html

Lucy Bones Recreation [Personal photograph taken in Creation Museum, Kentucky]. (2016, November 1). Luther, M. (1943).

A short explanation of Dr. Martin Luther's Small catechism: A handbook of Christian doctrine. St. Louis, MO: Concordia Pub. House.

Luther, M. (1991). *Luther's Small Catechism, with Explanation*. St. Louis, MO: Concordia Pub. House.

The Lutheran Hymnal. (1941). Saint Louis, MO: Concordia Publishing House.

Lutheran Service Book Pew Edition (03–1170). (2006). St. Louis, MO: Concordia Publishing House.

Masland, R. (n.d.). The Neuronal Organization of the Retina. Retrieved July 2016, from http://www.cell.com/neuron/fulltext/S0896-6273(12)00883-5

Martin Luther [Personal photograph taken in Reformation Exhibit, Creation Museum, Kentucky]. (2016, November 1).

National Eye Institute – Diagram of the Eye. (n.d.). Retrieved July 2016, from https://nei.nih.gov/health/eyediagram

Than, K. Oldest Dinosaur Found? (2012, December 6). Retrieved July 2016, from http://news.nationalgeographic.com/news/2012/12/121205-oldest-dinosaur-found-tanzania-science-archaeology/

Parts of the Liturgy. (n.d.). Retrieved August, 2016, from http://www.lcms.org/page.aspx?pid=1116

PBS. (n.d.). The Characters – Frederick the Wise. Retrieved August 2016, from http://www.pbs.org/empires/martinluther/char_frederick.html

Phoenix city Arizona QuickFacts from the US Census Bureau. (n.d.). Retrieved August 2016, from http://www.census.gov/quickfacts/table/PST045215/0455000

Roman Legion. (n.d.). Retrieved July 2016, from http://www.unrv.com/military/legion.php

Saints & Angels – Catholic Online. (n.d.). Retrieved August 2016, from http://www.catholic.org/saints/

Sarfati, J. D., & Matthews, M. (2002). *Refuting evolution 2: What PBS and the scientific community don't want you to know*. Retrieved July 2016, from http://creation.com/refuting-evolution-2-chapter-10-argument-irreducible-complexity

Seyer, H. D. (1983). *Working Through Luther's Small Catechism*. St. Louis, MO: Concordia Publishing House.

Smithsonian's National Museum of Natural History. (n.d.). AL 288–1 | The Smithsonian Institution's Human Origins Program. Retrieved July 2016, from http://humanorigins.si.edu/evidence/human-fossils/fossils/al-288-1

Snelling, A., PhD. (Director). (2009). *Radioactive and Radiocarbon Dating: Turning Foe into Friend* [Motion picture on DVD]. United States of America: Answers in Genesis.

Tappert, T. G. (1959). The Book of Concord: The Confessions of the Evangelical Lutheran Church. Philadelphia, PA: Fortress Press.

Luther's Large Catechism and Treatise on the Power and Primacy of the Pope

Tappert, T. G. (1959). The Book of Concord: The Confessions of the Evangelical Lutheran Church. Philadelphia, PA: Fortress Press.

Formula of Concord – Solid Declaration, Article VII. Lord's Supper

Than, K. Oldest Dinosaur Found? (2012, December 6). Retrieved July 2016, from http://news.nationalgeographic.com/news/2012/12/121205-oldest-dinosaur-found-tanzania-science-archaeology/

The Romans Destroy the Temple at Jerusalem, 70 AD. (2005). Retrieved January 2017, from http://www.eyewitnesstohistory.com/jewishtemple.htm

Todar, K., PhD (n.d.). Structure and Function of Bacterial Cells. Retrieved July, 2016, from http://textbookofbacteriology.net/structure_2.html

Veith, W. J., PhD. (n.d.). Is Carbon-Dating Accurate? Retrieved July 2016, from http://amazingdiscoveries.org/C-deception-carbon_dating_radiometric_decay_rates

What is Domestic Violence? (n.d.). Retrieved March 2017, from http://www.domesticviolenceroundtable.org/domestic-violence.html

APPENDIX I – SUMMARY OF THE DO'S AND DON'TS OF THE TEN COMMANDMENTS

The First Commandment: You shall have no other gods.

Do:

1) Fear God above all.
2) Love God above all.
3) Trust God above all.

Don't:

1) Think something else besides the Holy Trinity is a god and worship it.
2) Believe or trust in something other than the Holy Trinity.
3) Love, trust, or fear anything above the Holy Trinity.
4) Worship anything other than the Holy Trinity regardless if you trust and believe in it.

The Second Commandment: You shall not misuse the name of the Lord your God.

Do:

1) Call upon Him in trouble.
2) Pray to Him.
3) Praise Him.
4) Give thanks to Him.

Don't:

1) Uselessly/carelessly use His name.
2) Curse.
3) Swear.
4) Use satanic arts.
5) Lie or deceive.

The Third Commandment: Honor the Sabbath day by keeping it Holy.

Do:

1) Hold preaching of the Word sacred.
2) Gladly hear the Word of God.
3) Gladly learn the Word of God.
4) Gladly meditate on the Word of God.
5) Honor the teaching and preaching of the Word.
6) Diligently spread the Word of God.

Don't:

1) Do not attend worship.
2) Do not use Word and Sacrament faithfully.
3) Use Word and Sacrament negligently.

The Fourth Commandment: Honor your father and your mother.
Do:
1) Regard those in authority as representatives of God.
2) "Gladly provide what [those in authority] need or require."
3) Obey those who are in authority in everything.
4) Love and cherish those in authority.
5) Show respect to those who are older (aged).
Don't:
6) Disrespect those in authority.
7) Anger those in authority through disobedience and sin.

The Fifth Commandment: You shall not murder.
Do:
1) Help and support your neighbor in every bodily need.
2) Be merciful, kind, and forgiving.
3) Avoid and do not use any drugs or substances that harm the body or mind, and help your neighbor to do the same.
Don't:
1) Commit murder.
2) Commit abortion.
3) Commit euthanasia.
4) Commit suicide.

The Sixth Commandment: You shall not commit adultery.
Do:
1) "Consider sexuality to be a good gift of God."
2) Treat "marriage is God's institution—a lifelong union between one man and one woman."
3) "Reserve sexual intercourse for the marriage partner alone."
4) "Control sexual urges in a God-pleasing way."
Don't:
1) Get divorced.
2) Commit adultery.
3) Desert your spouse.
4) Have sex when you are unmarried.
5) Commit rape (forcible sex).
6) Commit homosexuality.
7) Commit incest.
8) Commit sexual child abuse.
9) Use obscenity.
10) View pornography.
11) Have sexually impure thoughts.
12) Have sexually impure desires.

The Seventh Commandment: You shall not steal.

Do:

1) Improve our neighbor's possessions and income.

2) Protect our neighbor's possessions and income.

3) "Help your neighbor in every need."

Don't

1) Commit theft.

2) Commit fraud.

3) Commit robbery.

The Eighth Commandment: You shall not give false testimony.

Do:

1) Defend our neighbor from false accusations.

2) Praise our neighbor.

3) Put the best construction on our neighbor's words and actions.

Don't:

1) Lie.

2) Gossip.

3) Bear false witness.

The Ninth Commandment: You shall not covet your neighbor's house.

Do:

1) Be content with your non-living possessions.

2) Help your neighbor keep their non-living possessions.

Don't:

1) Covet your neighbor's non-living property.

2) Scheme to take your neighbor's non-living property either openly or secretly.

The Tenth Commandment: You shall not covet your neighbor's wife or servants.

Do:

1) Be content with your living possessions.

2) Help your neighbor keep his living possessions.

Don't:

1) Covet your neighbor's living property.

2) Scheme to take your neighbor's living property either openly or secretly.

Made in the USA
Middletown, DE
19 May 2023

30950743R00130